Re-Telling Our Stories

IMAGINATION AND PRAXIS: CRITICALITY AND CREATIVITY IN EDUCATION AND EDUCATIONAL RESEARCH

VOLUME 9

SCOPE
Current educational reform rhetoric around the globe repeatedly invokes the language of 21st century learning and innovative thinking while contrarily re-enforcing, through government policy, high stakes testing and international competition, standardization of education that is exceedingly reminiscent of 19th century Taylorism and scientific management. Yet, as the steam engines of educational "progress" continue down an increasingly narrow, linear, and unified track, it is becoming increasingly apparent that the students in our classrooms are inheriting real world problems of economic instability, ecological damage, social inequality, and human suffering. If young people are to address these social problems, they will need to activate complex, interconnected, empathetic and multiple ways of thinking about the ways in which peoples of the world are interconnected as a global community in the living ecosystem of the world. Seeing the world as simultaneously local, global, political, economic, ecological, cultural and interconnected is far removed from the Enlightenment's objectivist and mechanistic legacy that presently saturates the status quo of contemporary schooling. If we are to derail this positivist educational train and teach our students to see and be in the world differently, the educational community needs a serious dose of imagination. The goal of this book series is to assist students, practitioners, leaders, and researchers in looking beyond what they take for granted, questioning the normal, and amplifying our multiplicities of knowing, seeing, being and feeling to, ultimately, envision and create possibilities for positive social and educational change. The books featured in this series will explore ways of seeing, knowing, being, and learning that are frequently excluded in this global climate of standardized practices in the field of education. In particular, they will illuminate the ways in which imagination permeates every aspect of life and helps develop personal and political awareness. Featured works will be written in forms that range from academic to artistic, including original research in traditional scholarly format that addresses unconventional topics (e.g., play, gaming, ecopedagogy, aesthetics), as well as works that approach traditional and unconventional topics in unconventional formats (e.g., graphic novels, fiction, narrative forms, and multi-genre texts). Inspired by the work of Maxine Greene, this series will showcase works that "break through the limits of the conventional" and provoke readers to continue arousing themselves and their students to "begin again" (Greene, *Releasing the Imagination*, 1995, p. 109).

Re-Telling Our Stories

Critical Autoethnographic Narratives

Foreword by Carolyn Ellis

Edited by

Gresilda A. Tilley-Lubbs
Virginia Tech, USA

and

Silvia Bénard Calva
Universidad Autónoma de Aguascalientes, Mexico

SENSE PUBLISHERS
ROTTERDAM/BOSTON/TAIPEI

A C.I.P. record for this book is available from the Library of Congress.

ISBN: 978-94-6300-565-4 (paperback)
ISBN: 978-94-6300-566-1 (hardback)
ISBN: 978-94-6300-567-8 (e-book)

Published by: Sense Publishers,
P.O. Box 21858,
3001 AW Rotterdam,
The Netherlands
https://www.sensepublishers.com/

All chapters in this book have undergone peer review.

The following chapters are reprinted here with permission from the publishers:

Chapter 4: Tilley-Lubbs, G. A. (2009). Good intentions pave the way to hierarchy: A retrospective autoethnographic approach. *Michigan Journal of Community Service Learning, 16*(1), 59–68.

Chapter 6: Tilley-Lubbs, G. A. (2014). The inquisition/torture of the tenure track. *Creative Approaches to Research, 7*(2).

Chapter 8: Bénard, S. M. (2013). From impressionism to realism: Painting a conservative Mexican city. *Cultural Studies ⇔ Critical Methodologies*.

Cover image by Yessenia Bautista

Printed on acid-free paper

TABLE OF CONTENTS

FOREWORD

Autumn arrived today at our North Carolina mountain cabin, where my partner Art Bochner and I are on a writing retreat. Bundled up in a southwestern throw in front of the burning gas fireplace, I am warmed by the orange blaze emanating from authentic looking ceramic logs and smouldering lava rocks. The wind blows the trees to and fro outside our windows; the fall yellows and reds are just starting to colour the tips of some leaves. Reading *Re-Telling Our Stories*, I am warmed further by the heartfelt emotion and invitations into the lives of these evocative storytellers. What a gift to me, and to all of us. These texts make me feel excited and optimistic about what critical autoethnographic scholarship—a blend of autobiography, ethnography and critical pedagogy—can be. The writers, many young and first-time authors, take me on a journey to new places, helping me understand better cross-cultural experiences; conflicts in work, family, and relational life; and fears, disappointments, and successes in educational experiences.

Many of the narratives describe living within and between cultures, where newcomers and others have to twist themselves into pretzels to fit in one and then the other. For example, there are stories about being in Nicaragua with the Peace Corps, immigrating to the US from China, identifying as Native American and First Nations women, and working as an au pair in a foreign country. Some of the stories tell about interactions between various groups within a culture, such as service workers and adults in foster homes, and social scientists/visitors and residents in an area destroyed by a tornado. Critical pedagogy is wrapped within stories written by teachers—some of whom also are students—who critically examine the reciprocal roles of teacher and student. These authors try to provide an experience for and teach to the whole student in our schools and colleges; they seek ways to connect with and help students, in particular those from other cultures; they call on their own experiences to understand their students and call on their students' experiences to understand their own. They deal head on yet sensitively with their own and their students' trauma, such as the terror of mass shootings and the pain of being bullied. Other stories focus on the self as vulnerable other, who must cope with divorce or other family traumas. A common plot in all these stories involves movement toward healing, empowerment, and belief in self while continuing to try to understand and respond to issues of oppression; gender, class, and other forms of relational domination; and race, color, and language discrimination.

As I read, vivid thoughts of my first encounters with Kris Tilley-Lubbs and Silvia Bénard Calva play through my mind, stimulated by their descriptions of meeting me and working with each other. I recall Kris waiting patiently to speak to me after attending a workshop Art Bochner and I gave on narrative and autoethnography at the International Congress of Qualitative Inquiry (ICQI) in

Illinois in 2008. In our conversation, she was enthusiastic and animated. "Who is this woman who speaks about and embodies her passion for autoethnography so openly and passionately?" I wondered. After that interaction, I was not surprised when she attended a two-day workshop I gave on the same topic for Research Talk's Qualitative Research Intensive, held in New York in 2009. Silvia also participated with this small group of women. From the moment I met Silvia, it was apparent she had a story to tell and, similar to Kris, she had a passion for writing it, even if she had to accomplish it in her second language. Though all the women attending that workshop shared amazing stories, Silvia and Kris stood out as they modelled for the other women how to tell about their own lives and how to support others who tell deep and emotional stories. I could feel the closeness developing between these two women, and I felt sure that I would hear again from them. And indeed I have. I have enjoyed the work they have been doing in autoethnography since 2009, visiting with them annually at the ICQI, and being introduced to students they have sent my way.

Now Silvia and Kris have joined their voices in this collection, and the result is synergistic—the whole is greater than the sum of what the two writers could have produced alone. As editors, they bring together strengths that come from the intersection of their differences and similarities. They come from diverse cultures and speak different native languages; one is educated in sociology and the other in education; one has deep roots in social science and the other has more of a humanities and literary focus; one is more interested in theory and the other in critical and applied pedagogy. Yet both are bilingual and communicate with each other in Spanish and English; both focus on storytelling, examining the role of the researcher in research, and narrating one's story; both are passionate about exploring the connections between Mexican and US culture; both are caring and giving, humane scholars and mentors who want to make a difference and are willing to be vulnerable to accomplish that goal.

Kris and Silvia put themselves through the same self-reflection in these pages as they ask other contributors to do. They are vulnerable with each other and to readers, they interrogate their experiences of working together and living with others, and they share emotional stories. For example, Silvia tells of the trials of moving from a large metropolitan area to a middle-sized city in Mexico; Kris tells about the challenges and pressures of getting tenure and advising students in service-learning courses and activities, and she shows how identity might be connected to speaking different languages. Together and separately, Kris and Sylvia write openly about the difficulties this publishing venture presented.

I can only imagine the problems they faced in carrying out cross-cultural, cross-geographic, and cross-linguistic writing, teaching, and mentoring—through virtual connections, no less, and with serious technical issues. Most of us would have given up quickly. Kris and Silvia persevered and used the relational, technical, and language difficulties to deepen their understandings and bring forth new insights about cultural communication. Their experiences then add to the stories in this volume about cultural conflict and cooperation. They shed light on power dynamics, subordination and dominance, oppression and submission, and readily examine and acknowledge their roles—cultural and personal—in communication difficulties and the hierarchical positioning that resulted. The editors come to understand each other in deep and complicated ways, viewing understanding as a process, not an end point. Rarely do we have the privilege of seeing the complexities and complications in cross-cultural collaboration, since authors too often focus on the final product and not the process, leading to a sense that all must have been smooth sailing. I learned much from their stories and look forward to and hope for many more joint projects from these two authors.

I have only one reservation to express. Silvia and Kris are too modest in their claims about what they accomplished together and do not take enough credit for having made this project work so beautifully in spite of the difficulties. But then that is who they are—unassuming scholars who care more about the success of autoethnography and their students' achievements than they do about the credit they get for their hard work. They are successful in jointly editing this beautiful book, supporting each other as the sole professors in their respective universities doing autoethnography, and co-mentoring productive students, many of whom are authors in this book. These successes all are evidence of Kris's and Silvia's contributions to humanizing academia through critical autoethnography.

I am touched deeply by this collection of stories, and I predict you will be too. These experiences now have a place in my heart, and I appreciate the vulnerability shown and the insights that writing lives brought forth. These are not victim narratives by any means. They are stories written by people who long to understand their experiences as deeply as possible and convey the nuances, complexities, and multiple meanings to themselves and readers. They yearn to grow and become better people from writing and sharing their experiences, and in the process to offer comfort, companionship, and possibilities to others in similar situations.

So put your feet up and relax a bit. Get ready for an engaging read. What has seemed familiar—such as acceptance of practices in mainstream culture—might suddenly burst into strangeness and what has seemed strange—such as the mass immigration of homeless Syrians into Europe—might now have shards of familiarity. Though I have not experienced personally most of the emotional and traumatic events described in this book, these stories encourage me through example to consider why that is the case. My advantage comes partly from being white and upper-middle class in the United States, the country where my parents and I were born. I have a tenured and well-paying position as a professor in a university, and a stable, long-term love relationship. It is easy to take my lot in life for granted. While my experiences have been privileged, still I am reminded of, and encouraged through these texts to re-examine who I am. I recall what it was like to growing up in a southern, rural, and mountainous community, and then to try to adapt to an academic world of educated cosmopolitan professors.

At times I too worried I didn't fit in this new culture; for a while, I felt concerned about how I sounded and wondered whether I would make it. As Kris wrote recently to me in an email, "Can you believe you grew up in Luray, Virginia, and I grew up in Fayetteville, West Virginia, and we are having this conversation about our commitments in places such as Bangladesh, Panama, and Scotland?" I acknowledged that it amazed me too. Later, Kris continued in another email, "And the mountains live in our hearts, no? For me, they will always be home." "Yes, they feel like home, and yet they don't," I respond now, as I view rural America through the complex lens of the almost fifty years of experience I have had at urban universities and in culturally diverse cities since I left my childhood home. Yes, I have returned to live in the mountains for several months a year; yes they do make me feel cosy and protected; and yes, I continue to be in awe of their beauty and majesty. Yet I also am deeply aware of how I have changed and how I don't quite fit here anymore in terms of some of my values and interests. I have new awareness of the complexities of cultural and political differences both within and outside our borders. Thank you to Kris and Silvia and to all the storytellers in this book for deepening my awareness.

Carolyn Ellis
Franklin, North Carolina

ABOUT THE COVER ARTIST

Yessenia Bautista grew up in Queens, New York, with her mother and five brothers and sisters. She attends college full-time and works part-time teaching in a science museum. This oil and acrylic painting represents the unique talents and perspectives of the diverse group of youth who work with her at the museum. Through art and science she brings joy to those around her.

GRESILDA A. TILLEY-LUBBS AND SILVIA BÉNARD CALVA

INTRODUCTION

SETTING THE STAGE

This is not a book about critical autoethnography per se, but rather it is a collection of stories that use critical autoethnography as a methodological approach to problematize individual experiences through the combined lenses of critical pedagogy and autoethnography. We don't give a step-by-step plan of how to do critical autoethnography; rather we provide an immersive experience for readers who wish to understand the struggles and triumphs that shaped the events the authors write about in emotive and passionate ways (Ellis, 2004). We teach about autoethnography as we present ourselves as vulnerable participants/collaborators/ actors in our own stories. During our co-taught courses on autoethnography and critical autoethnography, the students wrote most of the stories in this volume, and we wrote the others. Along with our students, we examined our words and actions, first as insiders, then as outsiders, and finally as insiders with outsiders' insights (Behar, 1999; Ellis, 2004). Throughout the process, we (Kris and Silvia) tried to replicate some of the experiences we had in a workshop taught by Carolyn Ellis, such as constant writing, followed by peer reading and critique. Just as with any writing that is tied to literary techniques, writing critical autoethnography is experiential, a pedagogy that allowed our students to become immersed in peers' stories, while at the same time understanding their own realities in the light of others' lived experiences. Likewise, readers become participants/collaborators/actors in the stories, making connections to their own lived experiences through their interpretive lenses. There is no generalization to be made; the experiences and experiential reactions are personal, but related to sociocultural aspects of individual worlds.

Despite its connection to autobiography and memoirs, the "auto" in "autoethnography" refers to the examination of self, and the "ethno" indicates a systematic analysis, in this case, through intensive reflection and introspection (Ellis & Adams, 2014, p. 257). The personal experiences form the heart of the story, so we start with our story of collaboration and friendship that emerged from an initial meeting at an autoethnography workshop. We examine the intersections that inform our relationship, bringing together the personal and the political, making research a "socially conscious act" (Holman Jones, 2005a) that brings to light the challenges that face cross-border relationships.

In the sections that follow, we recount our journey together in ways that represent our writers' voices, first in a more distanced academic style, and then, as we talk about a period of discord and growth, in a closer, more vivid and emotional style. Autoethnography can be written in a number of styles, from positioning the self in the text, as we do in the first part of the introduction, to "claiming the conventions of literary writing" (Ellis & Adams, 2014), which we have chosen to do in the critical autoethnographic deconstruction of the tension that grew as we continued to work together. To bring the reader into the midst of the tense moments after the explosion that rocked both our working and personal relationships, we use dialogue and other literary techniques to show, not tell, the story (Ellis, 2004). In contrast with the earlier chronological account of how we met and began working together, we open a space for the reader to experience the conflicts that arose. We "democratize the representational sphere of culture by locating the particular experiences of individuals in tension with dominant expressions of discursive power" (Denzin, 2006), and problematize the sociocultural aspects of our backgrounds that underscored hidden struggles, which, once surfaced, had to be addressed.

"Autoethnography shows struggle, passion, embodied life, and the collaborative creation of sense-making" (Ellis & Bochner, 2006, p. 433), and through dialogue, we trouble the struggles and triumphs two women from different cultural and geographic backgrounds and perspectives experienced in working across linguistic, geographic, and cultural borders. We consider the complexities that occur with cultural differences, causing invisible misunderstandings that can undermine collaborative cross-border projects. We deconstruct those misunderstandings as both cultural and personal issues, depending on autoethnography to narrate the personal, problematizing our reactions and interactions as representations of the social and cultural worlds we live in (Ellis, 2004). Our development as friends and colleagues has been organic, not simply a matter of two scholars reaching out to find a colleague with whom to conduct research, as often happens in the academic world. Just as with any relationship, ours has had its ups and downs, and the deconstruction of our roller coaster ride forms the foundation upon which this book was built.

A SERENDIPITOUS MEETING

We (Kris and Silvia) first met in July 2009 when we attended Carolyn Ellis' workshop on autoethnography. Over two intense days of writing, then reading and discussing other participants' work, we explored autoethnography as a method of inquiry. Through Carolyn's open sharing about the background of pieces we read to prepare for the workshop, we experienced firsthand how Carolyn has revolutionized the world of qualitative inquiry through autoethnography. She shared her struggles while working in non-traditional ways, and then having to justify her methodology in an academic world that regarded "valuable research" in traditional terms. We discussed the importance of regarding the researcher as part of the study, a necessary element for understanding the social, cultural, and political perspectives that shaped both the researcher and the participants in the project. We developed experiential knowledge of autoethnography as a means of making sense of a topic, while providing openings for others to relate their own experiences and contribute to the discussion and the democratization of research findings (Ellis, 2004).

> *Silvia:* I had been writing and experimenting with narrative. I had even written a couple of pieces under a pen name because I didn't feel that what I was doing was the research my university would accept as legitimate inquiry. Then a colleague, César Cisneros, sent me information about a series of workshops on qualitative research that were going to take place in Long Island, New York. I was glad to find methodological approaches that formalized the kind of writing I had done, so I applied for financial support from my university to attend the workshop. I was able to sign up for two different sessions, the first with H. L. (Bud) Goodall on writing narrative ethnography, and the second with Carolyn Ellis on writing autoethnography. At that time I felt an urge to have formal training in doing this kind of work. Before I registered, I wrote to Bud to ask him the difference between the two, and googled both professors to get an initial idea about their research approaches.

> *Kris:* I had been voraciously devouring Carolyn's and Laurel Richardson's autoethnographic work for about a year and a half when I made the decision to take a workshop on autoethnography offered by Carolyn and Art Bochner at the International Congress of Qualitative Inquiry (ICQI) the previous May. When I approached Carolyn after that workshop, she suggested that I participate in the intensive autoethnography workshop she was conducting later that summer. At that time, I had two published articles in which I had experimented with autoethnography as a means of interrogating my pedagogical practices, but I still felt unsure about where my instincts were leading me.

To prepare for the workshop, Carolyn had asked the eight participants to write about an event or situation with which we were struggling emotionally on a deep personal level. We wrote, we listened to each other reading our writing aloud, we cried, we empathized, and we connected—all through writing. Carolyn offered suggestions and comments to each. Due to the short term of the workshop, we left with suggestions and inspiration from Carolyn and our peers rather than with completed pieces. We returned home, Silvia to Aguascalientes, Mexico, and Kris to Virginia, in the United States. During those two short days, we had developed a shared connection.

CONNECTIONS ACROSS BORDERS

Although Kris was from the United States, she felt close to Mexico for several reasons. She had been a Spanish literature major in both her undergraduate and her graduate education at the University of Illinois. Through the years, she had worked extensively in the Spanish-speaking community, most recently interpreting at a public health clinic for Mexican and Honduran women. She had subsequently developed close relationships with them and their families in Mexico, whom she had interviewed for a research project. Silvia felt a similar closeness to the United States, mostly due to her doctoral education at the University of Texas in Austin, but also because her father had worked in the United States after he finished his studies in Canada during the early 1930s.

Kris was drawn to Silvia's warmth and welcoming presence, and Silvia's narrative resonated deeply with Kris since it dealt with family issues they were both experiencing. During the workshop Silvia was moved by Kris's narrative about the shootings at Virginia Tech, where Kris is a professor. As they talked further they also shared their common concerns about social justice, specifically about Mexican immigrants without a legal presence in the United States. Although Kris later published her narrative, *4/16: Public Tragedy Meets Personal Trauma* (2011), Silvia ultimately decided not to publish her piece because of ethical issues involved.

EXPANDING CONNECTIONS

We continued to stay in touch through email until we met again at the qualitative congress in May 2010. Silvia was considering spending her sabbatical year in the United States to deepen her knowledge about autoethnography. She had sought to spend a year with Carolyn Ellis at the University of South Florida, but doing so became complicated. Kris told Silvia she would be welcome to come to Virginia Tech as a visiting scholar. We both knew that autoethnography was not considered a legitimate research methodology either at Virginia Tech or at the Universidad Autónoma de Aguascalientes, but we felt that by working together we could enhance our own knowledge, as well as open up spaces for autoethography within our respective academic realms.

DIFFERENCES EMERGE BESIDE SIMILARITIES

In April 2011, Silvia and her 14-year-old daughter travelled to Blacksburg, Virginia, where they spent four months. During that time, we spent hours talking and working together on autoethnography. That summer, we co-taught a class for doctoral students in Kris's English as a Second Language and Multicultural Education program. As we planned and implemented the course, we became aware of the differences in our formation as scholars, Silvia as a sociologist, and Kris as a pedagogue with a strong background in Spanish and literature. When we prepared the syllabus for the summer class, Silvia wanted to provide a trajectory of autoethnography, including various perspectives, such as those in "Analytic Autoethnography" (Anderson, 2006), and in articles by other critics of autoethnography, such as David Snow. Leon Anderson had been Silvia's classmate at the University of Texas at Austin, and David Snow had been her professor, so she felt a special connection with their work. We agreed that it was fundamental to include authors such as Carolyn Ellis, Laurel Richardson, Chris Poulos, and Ron Pelias. Since Kris's emphasis included writing in a literary style, she wanted to include the art of writing literature, so we included *Bird by Bird* (Lamott, 1995). To enhance students' knowledge about writing narrative, we thought it necessary to include *Writing Qualitative Inquiry* by H. L. (Bud) Goodall (2008).

As we taught the class, we both mentioned authors we had studied as part of our graduate and undergraduate programs. We realized our academic trajectories differed, despite the fact that we agreed on the relevance of storytelling, and the presence of the researcher in the research.

Silvia had studied sociology in the second half of the 1970s at a left-wing university in Mexico City, the Universidad Autónoma Metropolitana, where most of the curriculum was based on Marxist authors. When she engaged in her graduate program at the University of Texas at Austin during the 1980s, she was eager to learn more about classic sociology theory and substantive issues related to meaning and belonging. Her focus on those topics led to her interest in social psychology, more specifically on symbolic interactionism and qualitative methodology.

Kris's undergraduate and master's work at the University of Illinois focused on the literature of Spain and Latin America. Her Ph.D. work was in curriculum and instruction, which led to her career as a professor in a School of Education, where she developed a strong focus on critical pedagogy. Eventually her interests aligned so that she could combine her love for Spanish-speaking culture, her proficiency in Spanish, and her concern with Mexican and Honduran immigrants, with her background in education and critical pedagogy.

Nonetheless, we share certain understandings about qualitative inquiry in general, and autoethnography in particular, which led to this joint venture to enhance knowledge generated under these epistemological and methodological frames of reference within our academic realms in Mexico and the United States. We both strongly agree on the importance of narrating one's story.

Due to our implicit and explicit differences as professors, students during that summer had a long list of readings, as well as significant writing to accomplish. Two pieces that emerged from that first course were Dyanis' evocative autoethnography about her grief as she approached the end of her marriage in "Metamorphosis: A Journey through Grief" (Chapter 9) and the narrative poem of Pamela's story about being a "cross-cultural kid" in "An Invisible Immigrant Made Visible" (Chapter 11).

THE FLUIDITY OF MOVEMENT BETWEEN MEXICO AND THE UNITED STATES

After Silvia returned to Mexico, we continued to communicate by email, staying in close contact, and developing a stronger friendship and collegial relationship as we worked together virtually. During the fall semester of 2011, Silvia asked Kris if she would serve on a student's doctoral committee. We talked about not having colleagues in our own universities who understood autoethnography and who would support our students who were incorporating autoethnography in their dissertations. Silvia was already serving on the committee of one of Kris's students; we were appreciated having a close colleague to would provide support. Soon, Kris received an invitation to visit Silvia's university for her student's end of semester presentation in December.

During that visit Silvia asked Kris to re-read her (Silvia's) developing autoethnographic account of her experience of moving to Aguascalientes from Mexico City, the text which became *Atrapda en provincia* [Trapped in the Provinces] (2014), a deconstruction of her experience of moving from one of the largest metropolitan areas in the world to a middle-sized city in central Mexico. As we sat and worked together in Silvia's office, with Kris reading and commenting, followed by hours of conversation, our differing cultural perspectives became apparent. Kris realized her position as an outsider to Mexican culture, just as Silvia was an outsider to Aguascalientes culture.

In fall 2012, Kris decided to teach an autoethnography class at Virginia Tech, and Silvia skyped with the students. For three hours the students asked questions and Silvia replied and talked about her own work, which had begun with grounded theory before it grew to include autoethnography. She shared details about her process in writing "From Impressionism to Realism" (2012), which was published shortly after her session with Kris's class. The students were fascinated with Silvia's open discussion of the sometimes difficult and painful process of reliving liminal experiences, writing them down, and deciding on the ethical issues involved. Afterwards, students talked about how Silvia had given them more freedom to explore their own experiences in a similar way. They even commented that most professors only talk about the traditional aspects of conducting qualitative research, but they could now give themselves permission to approach research in a more personal way. As we write this piece, Silvia looks at Kris with astonishment and comments, "I didn't feel I had that kind of positive influence on your students. I felt more concerned about whether I had disheartened their efforts to engage in autoethnographic inquiry."

During that class, Kelly started writing the chapter about her experiences conducting dissertation research at a home for adults with developmental disabilities. Whereas her dissertation research relied on more traditional qualitative methods, in writing her personal narrative about how she interacted with Henry, one of the residents at the home, she reflexively interrogated her actions, thoughts, and feelings, which developed into "Henry and Sneaky: Finding Resolution to My Ontological Question about Service" (Chapter 7). On the other hand, Jennifer was in the process of finishing her dissertation for a spring defence. While doing her research, a conversation with a student had caused her to problematize her role as researcher, and during the class she wrote much of the article that emerged from that problematization, "'Were You There?': Critical Autoethnographic Reflections on the Researcher-Participant Relationship" (Chapter 5).

Once again, Silvia invited Kris to Aguascalientes in December 2012 for her student's committee meeting, and once again, our conversations helped both of us to deepen our understanding of, and knowledge about autoethnography. By this time, Silvia had already served on Kris's student Jennifer's committee and at her dissertation defence.

We continued to support each other, still being the only autoethnographers in our respective universities. In fall 2013, we co-taught a course called "Critical Autoethnography," connecting our students virtually so they could learn from each other. The experience was fraught with technical difficulties, to say nothing of cultural and linguistic differences found in disparate university settings, all of which Silvia deconstructs at length in Chapter 3. Her students, David and Marilú, started their chapters. David focussed on social interactions in schools in "Naming in My Present the Past Nameless: Violence at School" (Chapter 3). Marilú wrote about her experiences as an au pair in the United States in "A Reflective Journey through the Experience of an *Au Pair*: From a Cultural Exchange Program to Domestic Labour" (Chapter 15).

Melissa put together her chapter about returning to the United States following her time in Nicaragua with the Peace Corps, "Culture Shock: The New Normal." She examines her re-entry in terms of socially constructed gender roles in both countries (Chapter 14). At the same time, Rong wrote her first drafts of "Never Forget Class Struggle: An Autoethnographic Reflection," her chapter about the complexities of immigrating to the United States from China as an adult. She struggled with the intricacies of constructing a life where language and culture were so different from anything she had previously known (Chapter 12). Kris had been writing her tenure poem, "The Inquisition/Torture of the Tenure Track" (Chapter 6) for some time, and when she brought it to the group, their critique helped her move the poem from a place of anger and frustration toward an analysis of a flawed academic system.

INVISIBLE MISUNDERSTANDINGS

Kris's students had taken one, or possibly two, of her courses in critical pedagogy, and for this course, she combined critical pedagogy and autoethnography to create a new course. The possible paradigm differences between how critical pedagogy was viewed in the United States and in Mexico were not evident to Kris as she planned the course in a way that would be approved by her university. She taught critical autoethnography from her perspective in a dominant culture, and neither she nor Silvia was aware that critical pedagogy was conceptualized differently in Mexico and in the United States. During the first few fall classes, discussions focused on critical pedagogy, and we soon realized that the term represented different theories from either side of the border. In response to these discussions, so Kris decided to write about critical autoethnography in "Critical Autoethnography and the Vulnerable Self as Researcher" (Chapter 1). Silvia problematized the differences by doing research and talking to people in Chihuahua, Mexico, who knew about the two perspectives. She narrates this in her piece (Chapter 3).

In the course of the semester, Dyanis began writing her chapters that interrogated cultural heritage as present in immigrant experiences viewed through the lenses of critical pedagogy and autoethnography in "Decolonization of the Self: Reflection and Reflexivity" and in language and customs in "Watch What Yuh Sayin': The Power of Language" (Chapters 13 and 16).

Two poems, those written by Lisa and Mae, developed from a class assignment in another course Kris taught that same fall, *Topics in Diversity and Multicultural Education*. In "Sojourn," Lisa interrogates her attempts to identify culturally with the Native American tribe that was her birth heritage. Mae, as a Canadian First Nations woman, asserts her cultural identity in "Two Braids." Both poems problematize the dissonance between nature and nurture (Chapters 16 and 17). Jen, who was instrumental in the initial organization of the book, contributed a poem she had written following a trip she made to Joplin, Missouri, with a group of storm chasers. In "What Remains," she interrogates the power and privilege of people who choose to witness a tornado versus those who are forced to lose their lives and belongings as the result of weather (Chapter 10).

TENSION BUILDS AND EXPLODES

Kris went to Aguascalientes for David's presentation of his work in progress in December 2013, and while she was in Mexico, we skyped with her class at Virginia Tech. Up to that point, Kris had not realized how uncomfortable and inconvenient the situation had been all semester for Silvia, David, and Marilú. As Kris participated in the class, the sound was impossible, the noise on the Virginia Tech side was distracting, and the apparent lack of attention on the part of the students was disturbing. After that experience, Kris questioned the wisdom of continuing with the virtual class due to linguistic, cultural, and logistic inconveniences. The situation was disconcerting and there was no resolution. At Kris's university, student evaluations determined merit, so, naturally, she was concerned about negative student reactions to the transnational course. Silvia had felt uneasy for weeks, but she didn't communicate her thoughts and feelings to Kris. We were both unable to work out the problems that had been slowly but steadily growing, partly because neither of us allowed ourselves to focus on the complexities derived from the challenge we had embraced.

Although we had decided to connect occasionally during the following spring semester, we never did. As we write this and discuss that spring class which never happened, we have become aware of the lack of understanding that was occurring on both sides of our socially and emotionally constructed borders, which have resulted in the uneven latitudes that Silvia describes in "Our Will to Construct a Horizontal Bridge over Uneven Latitudes."

We question whether the outcome of the class could have been any different. It has taken time, more than a year, to untangle the issues that entrapped and entangled our friendship after engaging in that video class. Silvia brought back to memory a statement she heard from her professor, Gideon Sjoberg, more than twenty years ago: "You do not get to know someone enough until you realize how s(he) deals with a crisis." And there we were, still months after the semester had ended dealing with the crisis we had naïvely launched into as one more of our many joint ventures. We had come to accept the situation, with its invisible discomforts and pasted on smiles, little realizing our comfort zone would soon be disrupted. In the following section, we choose to present this tension in the present tense, creating a literary style text that invites the reader to listen in as we struggle with bringing together our individual reflection and introspection.

FACING THE UNNAMED PRESENCE

The 2015 ICQI brings us both to our yearly meeting at the University of Illinois, where we sit down to talk to Carolyn Ellis about the possibility of her writing the preface for this book. Suddenly we are confronted with those unresolved issues that have arisen during the previous year and that exploded during the time when Silvia invited Kris to spend a week in Aguascalientes in September 2014.

As we sit in the café at the Illini Union, Carolyn begins the conversation by saying, "I felt some underlying tension in your relationship as I read this. You explored it a bit, but could you take it any deeper?"

"Here we go!" Silvia tells herself, "Carolyn, don't go there!" She closes up and escapes deep inside herself instead of expressing her feelings. At that point Kris goes into her usual mode for coping with unpleasant situations and begins talking about the situation that occurred as a way to understand what had happened. Kris finally stops, reflects, and ends with, "Carolyn, are you sure you are not a counsellor? I'm amazed you could pick up on the tension. We thought we had managed to disguise it."

Carolyn responds, "You've done a great job. Only you two could do such a good job because you are both completely bilingual. Your book can be very significant. If you want to leave the introduction as is, it will still be a good book. However, if you problematize that tension, it can be a great book. It all has to do with your level of comfort."

"Uh, good. That is all I need to know right now," Silvia continues with her internal conversation. "'No more drama,' as my daughter Nana says. Let's get rid of this book and go on with something else."

Carolyn continues: "But I sense unsolved conflicts between you two. You touch on them a little as you describe the process of writing the book in your introduction, but you don't show how you resolved them."

"Resolve them? Carolyn, that's not possible right now. We can't resolve them. Kris and I left them behind and you weren't supposed to notice!" As Silvia silently talks to herself, Kris starts talking to Carolyn about her feelings.

"The problem for me was that for a year and a half, I thought Silvia and I had a solid and deep friendship. I had no idea that Silvia was so angry with me.

When I finally became aware of her anger, I felt as if my self-knowledge had been shaken. I began to doubt my ability to understand relationships, to know what friendship is, to read people and their feelings toward me. I truly had no idea I was doing things that were so upsetting to Silvia. I'm not sure I can revisit those feelings—they're still pretty raw."

Silvia feels like saying, "Don't start, Kris, not again! We already did what we could!"

Then Silvia hears Carolyn's soft and clear answer: "Nothing is more important than your health and your wellbeing. They're worth more than anything else. If you two can work through your introduction, it's okay and, if you can't, just let it stand as it is. No matter what you decide, I'll try to fit writing the preface to your book into my schedule."

We move on to other issues, approaching the end of the conversation, when Carolyn comments, "It may be necessary for you two to sit down and talk about this. I see many similarities between you two. Talk about those similarities, but let us know about your differences as well. You've done a great job!"

"And now what? This was supposed to be the end and look! Now we have to deal with it again!" Silvia continues her internal conversation.

After our meeting with Carolyn, we return to the conference presentations. Kris attends Silvia's presentation where Silvia problematizes her "Mexicaness." What a paradox. When we talked to Carolyn, Silvia commented that Kris, from the United States, often reacts more as a Mexican is expected to react than Silvia, who is Mexican. Kris, Silvia thinks, but does not say, appears to be so much warmer, more expressive, and passionate than she herself.

RESOLUTION … FOR NOW?

The last day at the conference brings the final barbecue that closes the event every year. Kris and her husband Dan originally planned to go somewhere else, and Silvia decided not to go with them, but rather to stay with her student Miguel. Silvia and Miguel are already eating when they see Kris and Dan and approaching. It is a soft Midwestern May evening, a bit chilly at sunset, with the breeze softly blowing, and the blue grass music group playing in the background. Miguel and Silvia are seated on the stone bench Silvia chose as a strategic place from which she could see everybody but not be too close to people to have to mingle all night. Kris arrives and sits next to her. After a few introductory phrases, Kris says, "Silvia, if it were not for Carolyn, I would have never talked to you about this again. I wanted to just sweep all our feelings and words into oblivion, never to be resurrected. You were so mad at me in Mexico that I just assumed we would never collaborate, and that I would never visit you or the university in Aguascalientes again."

Silvia says, "It's true I was mad, but I didn't say a word about that to you at all."

"Yes, but when you picked us up at the hotel to drive us to your house, you drove as if you wanted to kill us all. You wouldn't speak to us. You gripped the steering wheel and drove on as though to remove our presence."

"Well, I was under a lot of pressure. Our other guests were coming to my house soon. The food you and Dan were going to help me prepare was not ready because it was so late. Now you talk to me as if you were the one who was mad at me and not the opposite. You told me that you wanted to return home early. I felt that you were telling me you were not going to talk to me again."

Kris replies, "I didn't know what to say. I was embarrassed that I had gotten caught on a conference call that made us so late. I wasn't mad. I was so taken aback and so crushed to have that reaction from such a dear colleague and friend whom I trusted so much. I was discombobulated and beside myself. I just wanted to return to Virginia. I have never been very good at handling conflict—my way of handling conflict is to escape from it."

Silvia continues, "And all those days in Aguascalientes that we had to work on the book, you were busy with a thousand things other than what we had to do."

"Silvia, you were the same. You had to go to class, talk to students, and deal with many other things as well. You were also doing other things at the same time."

Of all the people who could be sitting around the table right in front of us, it has to be Carolyn. She is talking to someone else, but she see us as we spend such a long time talking, and sitting together, sometimes in silence, and other times crying. Then Kris suggests that we all go to a restaurant since she and Dan haven't eaten and the barbeque food has been cleared away. We all leave together and crowd into Dan's car: Silvia, Kris, Dan, Miguel, and Rebecca, one of Kris's students.

After they order food, Kris and Silvia go to the bathroom together, then as they return to the table, Kris spontaneously says, "Silvia, *te perdono* [I forgive you]," and Silvia responds, "*Yo también,* Kris (me too)." We hug. Later, as we sit with the rest of the group back at the table, Silvia says in Spanish, the language we use to communicate unless we are with non-Spanish speakers:

"I talked to Nana and she asked how I was getting along with Kris. Nana said, please, don't argue."

Kris says, "That's what my daughter Eowyn asked about when I talked to her on the phone a few hours ago."

We laugh. We can finally laugh together again as we enjoy a huge dessert.

We resolved the discord that finally erupted into full anger in Aguascalientes in September 2014, but this process also served as a growth experience in our relationship. We are still friends. We are still colleagues, but we are different. Our hope is that this relationship, which has changed, will not hinder further research and educational endeavours. Being open with each other and communicating at such a deep level was a new experience for both of us, one that never could have occurred without the process of writing this book.

ACKNOWLEDGEMENTS

We would like to acknowledge with gratitude four people without whom this work would not have been possible. First we would like to thank the two translators who made a bicultural book possible. Aline Bénard Padilla translated Marilú's chapter, "A Reflective Journey through the Experience of an *Au Pair*: From a Cultural Exchange Program to Domestic Labour." Dyanis Popova translated David's chapter, "Naming in My Present the Past Nameless: Violence at School." Finally our thanks go to Jennifer Wagner, who worked tirelessly and tediously on formatting the entire book. She graciously accepted all the changes as they occurred, and her eye for detail guided the entire process. And last, but certainly not least, we acknowledge the thoughtful and intuitive editing done by Kris's husband Dan, who witnessed much of this journey. This was a collaborative work in every sense of the word, and we would not have had it any other way.

REFERENCES/BIBLIOGRAPHY

Anderson, L. (2006). Analytic autoethnography. *Journal of Contemporary Ethnography, 35*(4), 373–395.

Behar, R. (1996). *The vulnerable observer: Anthropology that breaks your heart.* Boston, MA: Beacon.

Bénard, S. (2014). *Atrapada en provincia. Un ejercicio autoetnográfico de imaginación sociológica* [Trapped in the provinces: An autoethnographic exercise in sociological imagination]. Aguascalientes, Ags, MX: Universidad Autónoma de Aguascalientes.

Denzin, N. K. (2006). Analytic autoethnography, or déjà vu all over again. *Journal of Contemporary Ethnography, 35*(4), 419–428.

Ellis, C. (1993). "There are survivors": Telling a story of sudden death. *The Sociological Quarterly, 34*(4), 711–730.

Ellis, C. (2004). *The ethnographic I: A methodological novel about autoethnography.* Walnut Creek, CA: AltaMira Press.

Ellis, C. S., & Bochner, A. P. (2006). Analytic autoethnography: An autopsy. *Journal of Contemporary Ethnography, 35*(4), 429–449.

Ellis, C., & Adams, T. E. (2014). The purposes, practices, and principles of autoethnographic research. In P. Leavy (Ed.), *The Oxford handbook of qualitative research* (pp. 254–276). New York, NY: Oxford University.

Goodall, H. L. (2008). *Writing qualitative inquiry: Self, stories, and academic life.* Walnut Creek, CA: Left Coast.

Holman Jones, S. (2005). Autoethnography: Making the personal political. In N. K. Denzin & Y. K. Lincoln (Eds.), *Handbook of qualitative research* (pp. 763–791). Thousand Oaks, CA: Sage.

Lamott, A. (1994). *Bird by bird: Some instructions on writing and life.* New York, NY: Pantheon.

Tilley-Lubbs, G. A. (2011b). 4/16: Public tragedy collides with personal trauma. *Qualitative Inquiry, 17*(2), 144–147. doi:10.1177/1077800410392334

Gresilda A. Tilley-Lubbs
Faculty of Teaching and Learning
School of Education
Virginia Tech
Blacksburg, Virginia, USA

Silvia Bénard Calva
Departamento de Sociología y Antropología
Universidad Autónoma de Aguascalientes
Aguascalientes, Aguascalientes, México

SECTION 1

THEORY OF CRITICAL AUTOETHNOGRAPHY

GRESILDA A. TILLEY-LUBBS

1. CRITICAL AUTOETHNOGRAPHY AND THE VULNERABLE SELF AS RESEARCHER[1]

ABSTRACT

This chapter presents critical autoethnography as an innovative approach to conducting research in marginalized, vulnerable communities. Combining autoethnography, ethnography, and critical pedagogy, the researcher becomes a participant in the study, turning inward to examine the Self and the complexities of cultural perspectives through the lens of critical pedagogy. Intense reflexivity and introspection undergird this study of Self as participant, going beyond recounting facts as objectively as possible, as occurs with autobiography, to acknowledging that the researcher is interpreting the facts through cultural perspectives formed through years of sociocultural, socio-historical, socio-political, and socioeconomic events and circumstances. Subsequently, the researcher, more than likely a member of the dominant culture in some categories, is able to understand herself as an oppressor.

CRITICAL AUTOETHNOGRAPHY

Critical autoethnography combines ethnography, autobiography, and critical pedagogy to shape a methodology that allows me to examine myself as a qualitative researcher who works in vulnerable, marginalized communities. As a member of the dominant culture, it is crucial that with every research project I come to understand my own cultural perspectives and that I communicate those perspectives to the people who read my research. I can write autoethnography that only investigates an event in my life, or I can integrate my autoethnography into an ethnography that investigates that same phenomenon within the context of the group being researched. In either case, I present myself as a participant in the study so that I can internalize the researcher gaze and thus examine my Self in the same way that I examine others. That is, with autoethnography, I situate myself as researcher within the study, whether as a separate study or integrated as another participant in an ethnographic study (Blanco, 2012). Intense reflexivity and introspection, examined through the perspective of critical pedagogy, help me to understand some of the cultural complexities that have shaped me as a researcher and a pedagogue.

Since I don't believe it is possible to function without preconceived thoughts and beliefs, nor to maintain a completely objective position for recounting events, such as occurs with autobiography (Blanco, 2012), I make it explicitly clear to the reader that I am interpreting the data according to my own perspective. I openly expose my presence in the study, without trying to disguise it under the pretence of objectivity. Then those who read the work can form their own ideas, knowing that I am a participant in the study and that my interpretation reflects both my selection of the data to include and my decisions about how to present those data. With this methodology, as a researcher who is a member of the dominant clase and culture, I can understand the danger of being, or in some cases acting as, an oppressor. This awareness can influence my positionality as I conduct research in communities that are not considered part of the dominant culture.

Other researchers have used critical autoethnography as a way to connect "evocative personal narrative to cultural criticism" (Ellis & Bochner, 2014, p. 10), or to connect autoethnography and intersectionality (Boylorn & Orbe, 2014). Robin Boylorn combines cultural and social phenomena to comment on personal experience from a "raced, classed, gendered, sexed, positionality, identifying the distinctions between her lenses for viewing the world and those of others" (Boylorn & Orbe, 2014, p. 13), using critical standpoints as a way to theorize about lived experiences contextualized in intersectionalities. In combining autoethnography and critical pedagogy, I examine intersectionalities, but rather than positioning myself as a member of a marginalized community, I acknowledge the insidious, pervasive power and privilege I possess due to my race, socioeconomic status, religion, education, and countless other cultural perspectives that have shaped me, regardless of the marginalization I sometimes experience due to gender and age. Like Boylorn and Orbe, I also acknowledge my subjectivity and positionality, but I also claim the possibility of my position as an oppressor when working in vulnerable community. In addition, whereas they position themselves within Communications as a home discipline, and I position myself in Curriculum and Instruction, which lends different focuses to our work as well. In other words, while our concepts of critical autoethnography share certain characteristics, they do differ in others.

AUTOETHNOGRAPHY

Autoethnography has its roots in qualitative inquiry (Ellis, 2004), specifically in the branch of ethnography. As with any qualitative inquiry, the epistemological premise of autoethnography posits that reality and science are interpreted by human beings, focused on explaining some phenomenon and its interactions aside from numbers and statistics, with an emphasis on the quality rather than the quantity of the data. I can provide the reader with a human face, not only the statistics of the phenomenon. I use ethnographic methods such as observation, participation, and interviews to collect data. Autoethnography also combines ethnography with autobiography, "writing about the personal and its relationship to culture" (p. 37). With autoethnography, I include the data that emerge from my own reflexivity and introspection as a researcher. I can write this as a personal narrative, but by combining this personal story with the ethnography, I can examine the meaning I give to the phenomenon, while at the same time trying to understand it from both the individual and the group perspectives.

As a researcher, autoethnography allows me to examine an event, a practice, or a circumstance in my own life. Autoethnography is "research, writing, story, and method that connect the autobiographical and personal to the cultural, social, and political" showcasing "action, emotion, embodiment, self-consciousness, and introspection" (Ellis, 2004, xix). This method is "self-narrative that critiques the situatedness of self with others in social contexts" (Spry, 2001, p. 710).

Since I use literary forms, such as narrative, poetry, and drama, autoethnography permits the intersection of art with science (Ellis, 2004) to present what I learned as a researcher by practicing deep reflexivity and introspection. I use writing as inquiry (Richardson, 2000) to help me understand the sociocultural reasons that explain the situation I am examining. With autoethnography, I interpret the narrative according to my perspective, without the pretext of having eliminated myself as a participant in the study. With autoethnography, I am an actor and participant in the study, and in my other role as author, I write to "understand the significance of what [I think and feel and do]" (Ellis, 2004, p. 68) and the "significance or meaning that [I] give to [my] experience" (Tarrés, 2001), which allows me to deepen the knowledge I discover through reflection and introspection.

CRITICAL PEDAGOGY

Critical pedagogy provides the theoretical framework that helps me in my efforts to push against the grain of sociocultural, socioeconomic, socio-historical, and socio-political influences that have shaped me and have caused me to perform and interpret life as I do. Like the rest of the world, I have my origins in a temporal and spatial context, which influences the way I construct the nature of the world (Kincheloe, 2005); that is, my race, ethnicity, socioeconomic class, religion, gender, etc., have shaped my way of thinking and living. Of course, my way of thinking and performing life have changed through the years, but situations still occur when my reactions reflect previously forgotten and/or hidden beliefs from my cultural past. In other words, I examine some phenomenon and I reflexively interrogate my own relationships with the phenomenon, focusing on my own power and privilege compared with those of the group in which I am conducting research. Therefore, while I investigate the social, political, and economic contexts that have shaped my perspective, I can recognize myself as a potential oppressor, an important revelation that influences me as a researcher, especially in vulnerable communities.

Freire (1970) developed the concept that the oppressed need to come to a critical consciousness of the causes of their oppression. In this essay, I propose that as researchers, we must recognize our own cultural perspectives and how they are influenced by the dominant culture. Possibly we are not even conscious of our potential for participating in oppression. Such conscientization of my role as oppressor resonates with the plea of Freire (2005) that teachers be educated as cultural workers, but here, my suggestion is that we think in the same way about ourselves as researchers—as cultural workers who have the intention of including those voices that are often not heard, or even worse, that are ignored.

To conduct research that pushes against the grain of cultural norms that create oppression, it is necessary to recognize the people with whom we conduct research not as subjects or informants, nor even solely as participants, but rather as our collaborators in the research. This epistemology opens the opportunity to participate in emancipatory research (Street, 2003) in which we conduct research as a participant *with* other participants instead of *for* them. This causes us to have a counter-hegemonic and counter-institutionalized ethic that doesn't exacerbate inequalities, and that permits the documentation and denunciation of injustices in the same words as the other participants. In this way, research serves to problematize the representation of Others, and to create a bridge between the excluded and the included at the same time that it erases the separation between subject and object (Street, 2003).

CRITICAL AUTOETHNOGRAPHY IN MY OWN WORK

Combining the methodology of autoethnography with critical pedagogy permits me to push against the grain of norms established by the dominant society, problematizing my own actions and practices from a sociocultural perspective. Since I conduct research with vulnerable and marginalized populations, it is important to incorporate a methodology that forces me to examine my own cultural perspectives as a member of the dominant society, and critical autoethnography permits me to do it, examining myself in a systematic and transparent way.

To arrive at a state of critical consciousness regarding my own cultural perspectives, I need to examine how I position myself within socially constructed categories (Banks & Banks, 2012) that create or erase power and privilege: race/ ethnicity, religion, class, gender, sexual preference, language, etc. I can recognize myself as a member of the dominant and powerful culture only by first analysing how social norms position power and privilege, and then by understanding my own cultural heritage within the dominant culture. Through intense reflection and introspection, I can understand the insidious nature of power and privilege, and the way they "reach into the very fibre" of my being, and that "are inserted in [my] actions and attitudes" (Foucault, 1980, p. 39). Through critical autoethnography, I can position myself in the research (Behar, 1996) to critically examine my own practices as a researcher, navigating the vulnerable spaces that require me to examine my own words and actions with the same care that guides me as I examine those of the other participants in the study. My vulnerability also causes me to be more conscious of other people, which many times guides my selection of the data I want to include in the narrative. As the result of this intensified awareness of vulnerability due to my role as a participant in the study, I feel the necessity of obtaining the permission of each participant to publish the results of the inquiry and to present them in public venues. Ethics are integrated into the very fabric of study.

This methodology emerged organically as I was writing an article to examine my own pedagogical practices. My work includes poetry and narrative, as well as more traditional research. In the examples that follow, I include illustrations that demonstrate how critical autoethnography allows me to interrogate my research as well as my pedagogical practices. Conducting research and writing within the theoretical framework of this methodology has caused me to become aware that conscientization is not a static state. At the same time that I arrive at a state of conscientization in one aspect of my work, my perspectives based on my heritage in the dominant culture surge forth in another situation, and once again I act from that ingrained perspective. While I interpret my own work, I visualize conscientization as a process that occurs repeatedly insofar as we remain open to being vulnerable through introspection and to admitting our roles as oppressors. With these illustrations, I show the potential of critical autoethnography for helping us as researchers to distance ourselves from the perspectives of the dominant culture that shaped our beliefs and practices as oppressors. This perspective leads the way for listening and hearing words and their diverse meanings that are based on the cultural context from which I come and against which I push.

GOOD INTENTIONS PAVE THE WAY TO HIERARCHY

I began to combine autoethnography and critical pedagogy without knowing that I was inventing an innovative methodology. That is, I knew I was using autoethnography as a methodology and critical pedagogy as a theoretical framework, but it had not occurred to me that this combination was a different methodology. I had already read extensively about both autoethnography and critical pedagogy, and when I began to write my text, it seemed natural to refer to both to establish my methodology. The text emerged from three liminal moments over a seven-year period. The first occurred in the context of the research study that informed my doctoral dissertation. I had been working as an interpreter in a public health clinic for Spanish-speaking women for their prenatal care and their family planning appointments. I was spending 20 hours a week working with them, and since I was the only English speaker they knew and trusted, they called me constantly to ask for help with doctor appointments or teacher conferences, or to ask if I could help them with getting some basic support. I attended a church where people were always ready to share, and they donated mountains of clothes, furniture, etc. I stored everything in my garage, and after a while, I realized that this project was more than I could handle alone, especially with my fulltime work in the university, my work at the clinic, and my doctoral students. The idea occurred to me to design a course that would include service-learning. After a year of listening to class discussions and reading student reflections, I decided to examine the reciprocal friendships I observed developing between the students and the families with whom they spent

50 hours per semester. I also decided to establish a work day on the first Saturday of the semester when the students came to my garage to separate and divide the donated articles and to deliver them to the families, who referred to this as *la dispensa* [gifts of help and love].

The second semester that I did it, the students reacted less than favourably. They told me they had not liked the practice because it was "like observing animals at the zoo" when we went in a truck to deliver the items. As part of the narrative for my dissertation, I included the story of the workday without mentioning the students' comments. Then when I defended my dissertation, two committee members questioned the practice. One commented, "Kris, I don't think you understand what you are doing with this practice." You are establishing social hierarchy, with the students as the "haves" and the families as the "have-nots." Her words shocked me. They caused my second liminal moment.

The third moment occurred at the end of my first semester as a tenure-track professor when I had my end-of-year evaluation. The Director of the School of Education and my Department Head had read an article (2003) that I wrote based on my dissertation research (2003). In the article, I presented only the positive aspects of the service-learning experience, and they asked me about the "dark side" of the program. Then I remembered the words of my students and my doctoral committee members, and once again I felt the shock of a liminal moment. So I began a period of reflection and introspection, and from that time came two articles, both of which examined the practice of the workday using the lens of critical pedagogy: "Troubling the Tide: The Perils and Paradoxes of Service-Learning in Immigrant Communities" (2009) and "Good Intentions Pave the Way to Hierarchy: A Retrospective Autoethnographic Approach" (2009). Since I was already familiar with autoethnography as a methodology, I wrote both articles from a personal perspective, examining my practice and trying to understand my actions through a detailed examination of the sociocultural environment that had caused me to establish the workday. This article was my first experimentation in combining autoethnography with critical pedagogy, which I presented as two distinct methodologies.

4/16: PUBLIC TRAGEDY COLLIDES WITH PERSONAL TRAUMA

I continued experimenting with autoethnography as a methodology that did not intersect with critical pedagogy. I wrote about the shootings at Virginia Tech, the university where I teach and where I am an Associate Professor, in order to understand what had happened. I was in my office when 4/16/2007 occurred. The event affected me in an unexpected way, leaving me desolate and inconsolable, almost at the point of not being able to function in either my personal or professional life. After spending time trying to understand why it had affected me so gravely, I began to read the work of Carolyn Ellis and Laurel Richardson, and I realized it was possible to write as a way of understanding my situation. From that period of intensive reflection and introspection, I came to understand that I was suffering from having not taken time to grieve the death of my mother, who had died in January 2006. I used the literary techniques of narration and poetry to write a text about my personal experience (2011), which served as a cathartic experience that led me into a state of peace and consolation. "[I] narrated my own experience, because through it, [I] could understand more deeply what had seemed incomprehensible [to me]" (Bénard Calva, 2014, p. 18), and thus I could resume a normal life. As it has turned out, many people who have read this essay have written to tell me that it helped them to understand their reactions in the face of some tragedy, whether public or personal. As Stacy Holman Jones (2005) says:

> Autoethnography is a blurred genre …a response to the call …it is setting a scene, telling a story, weaving intricate connections between life and art … making a text present …refusing categorization …believing that words matter and writing toward the moment when the point of creating autoethnographic texts is to change the world. (p. 765, cited in Denzin, 2006, 420)

I said in my own text:

> Therapy and healing through powerful academic writings.
> I dissected the things I didn't do but should have, the things I did but shouldn't have.
>
> Trips to conferences: Tampa, San Juan, San Francisco, Mexico.
> To the tune of the death dirge that accompanied every thought every day.
> Too much busyness.
> I lived in yoga clothes. I ate organic food. I followed the workbook's advice and detoxed my system. I practiced serenity. I breathed so deeply I felt light-headed.
> The emptiness filled with peace. (p. 147)

Only after the publication of my text, "4/16: Public Tragedy Collides with Personal Trauma" was I able to move on.

THE COAL MINER'S DAUGHTER GETS A PH.D.

My next autoethnographic text, which once again uses the lens of critical pedagogy, resulted in a poem, "The Coal Miner's Daughter Gets a Ph.D." (2011a). Using poetry, I examined my trajectory as a coal miner's daughter who through the years came to be an associate professor in a university. Through the methodology of performative autoethnography, I examined the influences that had caused me to perceive myself as an outsider in the university community. I also examined how the mystory has influenced my work with the Latino community. I questioned how I position/reposition the essence of my Self as I move with certain fluidity between my roots and my academic position:

I write to understand mystory.
To grapple.
To struggle.
To accept.
To release
Notions of self-doubt.

…

I am a coal miner's daughter.

…

Conducting research in the Latino community.
Still …
Interrogating power, privilege, and whiteness.
I am now a university professor.
Reflecting, writing, and performing as inquiry. (Ellis & Bochner, 2001; Richardson, 1998)

Just as with my text about the shootings, many people have told me that reading this poem has helped them to know that other people were able to obtain professional position in the academy despite their working class backgrounds. I have performed this poem in Mexico, Chile, and the United States, and in each place, people have commented to me, "That was my dad. He was a miner/migrant worker…."

CROSSING THE BORDER: (AUTO)ETHNOGRAPHY THAT TRANSCENDS IMMIGRATION/IMAGINATION

The next text in which I used autoethnography in combination with critical pedagogy has an ethnographic context. I presented and interpreted what I had learned from a research trip to Mexico. I interviewed the families of five women whom I had been interviewing for the seven years they had been living in my city. I collaborated with those women to design a study to investigate the impact their immigration had on the families that stayed behind. The women gave me the questions they wanted me to ask their families, and they spoke with their families to pave the way for the interviews. Their families opened their homes and their hearts to share with me the pain of losing a daughter/sister/aunt, because without legal immigration documents, it was not possible for them to return to Mexico to visit their families.

First I wrote a narrative essay about the research, and when I submitted it to *Qualitative Inquiry,* I received a letter from Norman Denzin, telling me "There is too much telling and not enough showing. I want a manuscript that enacts its own reflexivity as your poem does [The Coal Miner's Daughter Gets a Ph.D.]," just as

Bud Goodall (2008) tells us in his advice for writing qualitative inquiry narratives. I returned to the essay, and I removed all the words that weren't necessary for communicating the power of the data and interpretations that had emerged from the transcribed manuscripts. As I did so, I became aware of my own power and privilege as compared to the women and their families, which I include throughout the resultant poem, "Border Crossing: (Auto)Ethnography that Transcends Immigration/ Imagination" (2011b):

Lina left San Juan Bautista, Oaxaca;
Marisol left Ciudad Juárez, Chihuahua;
Lupe left Tonalá, Jalisco.
Laura left Santa Fe, Jalisco;
Gisela left Santa Fe to join her sister Laura;
Me. I never left anywhere I couldn't return to.
Never. (pp. 386–387)

I also gave the details of my encounter with the immigration guard at the airport in Ciudad Juárez, Chihuahua, which is on the border with El Paso, Texas, because I wasn't carrying with me the paper I had filled out on the plane and in which I gave information about my stay in Mexico. The guard cancelled my passport, saying:

"My people need them to travel to your country
So you need them to travel to mine."
…
Two cancelled passports.
"Illegals.
You can go to jail for being in Mexico without papers."

The same as Lina, Marisol, Lupe, Laura, and Gisela,

Never in jail
Except the prison of their own fear
Of getting caught
And put in jail.
Not the same at all.
I do have rights.
I do have papers.
I do have power and privilege.
I can cross the border whenever I want
From north to south to north to south to north ….
One angry border guard.
Two cancelled passports.
Not the cancellation or negation of our rights
As human beings
As US citizens

Our white selves free to roam anywhere in Mexico
Or the US
Or almost anywhere else. (p. 395)

While I was changing the narrative to a poem, more questions than answers appeared. I began to articulate the doubts that had been bothering me since the time I began conducting research in the Latino community. I realized that I don't have the right to speak for anyone, and even my right to interpret the words of anyone is limited:

(Auto)ethnography
The auto is correct.
I can try to analyse/understand/interpret
My own words/thoughts/perceptions
But I can't even be sure of that.

Ethnography.
I can report what I heard/translated/interpreted
When I heard/translated/interpreted it.
Would they have said the same the week/month/year before?
Would they say the same next week/month/year?
I can only report what I heard/translated/interpreted
At that specific time.
And nothing more.
I can't determine what people mean
By their words.
Their subtexts
Filtered
By my perspective.
My subtexts.
I can only report what I heard/translated/interpreted.
At that specific time
In my life and theirs. (p. 400)

I realized it wasn't possible for me to ever know the Truth, since for me, a single Truth doesn't exist. I became aware of the complexity of the human being and of my inability to interpret the words of other people. I can report what someone says in an interview, and of course, I am the researcher who chooses what to include in the text, but for me, fixed interpretations don't exist.

This text represented a liminal moment in my development as a researcher. Since the time I began to study for my doctorate, the idea of being an expert with the right to interpret the words of others, of analysing their actions and coming to conclusions regarding their true motives, had bothered me greatly. This text served to help me realize, in an unforeseen way, that by combining autoethnography and critical pedagogy, it's possible to interrogate and problematize any situation or circumstance.

THE BAPTISM/EL BAUTIZO

After writing "Border Crossing," I continued to think about my positionality in the Spanish-speaking community, especially after my Mexican American grandson was born in 2010. Once again I wrote as a way of conducting research, this time to examine my own positionality/power/privilege, but also to interrogate socially constructed borders. Throughout the text of "*The Baptism*/El bautizo," (2013), I refer to the friendships/relationships that I described in "Border Crossing," contrasting my position as mother/surrogate grandmother for the women with whom I collaborated to conduct that research project with that of being the grandmother of my daughter's baby. Although I had attended the baptisms of those grandchildren of my heart, this time I was attending the baptism of my grandson by blood:

Insider-outsider.
Surrogate grandmother/mother.
Friend.
This time, there's no surrogate status.
This time, I am the grandmother.
By blood.
Not just by heart.
This time, Dan and I
Witness the baptism of our grandson

David Isaac Hernández. (p. 2)

Thus I was able to connect "the autobiographical and the personal with the cultural and the social" (Ellis, 2004, p. xix).

During this time, I have developed my desire to write as inquiry, and I have also developed my passion for writing in literary forms, probably the result of my specialized studies in Spanish literature. When I write my poems, I hear in my mind the voices of Miguel de Unamuno, Pablo Neruda, Gabriela Mistral, Federico García Lorca, and many more, drowning me in a deluge of words and images, at the same time that critical spirit becomes reality with the combination of autoethnography and critical pedagogy. As T. S. Eliot says:

We shall not cease from exploration
And the end of all our exploring
Will be to arrive where we started
And know the place for the first time. (Eliot, 1971, p. 144)

NOTE

1 This chapter is based on and adapted from an earlier version which appeared as Tilley-Lubbs, G. A. (2014). La autoetnografía crítica y el Self vulnerable como investigadora. *REMIE: Multidisciplinary Journal of Educational Research, 4*(3), 268–285. http://dx.doi.org/10.447/remie.2014.014. Also in Spanish: Tilley-Lubbs, G. A. (2014). La autoetnografía crítica y el Self vulnerable como investigadora. *Astrolabio, Nueva Época, 14* (with permission). Translation into English by the author.

REFERENCES/BIBLIOGRAPHY

Banks, J., & Banks, C. (Eds.). (2012). *Multicultural education: Issues and perspectives* (8th ed.). Hoboken, NJ: Wiley.

Behar, R. (1996). *The vulnerable observer: Anthropology that breaks your heart.* Boston, MA: Beacon.

Bénard Calva, S. (2014). *Atrapada en provincia: Un ejercicio autoetnográfico de imaginación sociológica.* Aguascalientes, Ags: Universidad Autónoma de Aguascalientes.

Blanco, M. (2012). ¿Autobiografía o autoetnografía? *Desacatos, 38,* 169–178.

Denzin, N. K. (2006). Analytic autoethnography, or déjà vu all over again. *Journal of Contemporary Ethnography, 35*(4).

Eliot, T. S. (1971). Little Giddings. In *T. S. Eliot* (Ed.), *The complete poems and plays 1909–1950.* New York, NY: Harcourt, Brace & World.

Ellis, C. (2004). *The ethnographic I: A methodological novel about autoethnography.* Walnut Creek, CA: AltaMira Press.

Ellis, C., & Bochner, A. (2001). Autoethnography, personal narrative, reflexivity: Researcher as subject. In N. Denzin & Y. Lincoln (Eds.), *Handbook of qualitative research* (2nd ed., pp. 733–768). Thousand Oaks, CA: Sage.

Foucault, J. (1980). *Power/Knowledge: Selected interviews and other writings.* Brighton, UK: Harvester.

Freire, P. (1970). *Pedagogy of the oppressed.* New York, NY: Continuum.

Freire, P. (2005/1997). *Teachers as cultural workers: Letters to those who dare to teach.* New York, NY: Continuum.

Holman Jones, S. (2005). Autoethnography: Making the personal political. In N. K. Denzin & Y. S. Lincoln (Eds.), *Handbook of qualitative research* (3rd ed., pp. 763–792). Thousand Oaks, CA: Sage.

Kincheloe, J. L., & McClaren, P. (2000). Rethinking critical theory and qualitative research. In N. K. Denzin & Y. S. Lincoln (Eds.), *Handbook of qualitative research* (2nd ed., pp. 923–949). Thousand Oaks, CA: Sage.

Richardson, L. (1998). Writing: A method of inquiry. In N. K. Denzin & Y. S. Lincoln (Eds.), *Collecting and interpreting qualitative materials* (pp. 345–371). Thousand Oaks, CA: Sage.

Richardson, L. (2000). Writing: A method of inquiry. In N. K. Denzin & Y. S. Lincoln (Eds.), *Handbook of qualitative research* (2nd ed., (pp. 923–949). Thousand Oaks, CA: Sage.

Spry, T. (2001). Performing autoethnography: An embodied methodological praxis. *Qualitative Inquiry, 7*(6), 706–732.

Street, S. (2003). Representación y reflexividad en la (auto)etnografía crítica: ¿Voces o diálogo? *Nómadas, 18,* 72–79.

Tarrés, M. L. (2001). *Observar, escuchar y comprender: Sobre la tradición cualitativa en la investigación social.* Porrúa, Mexico: Facultad Latinoamericana de Ciencias Sociales, El Colegio de México.

Tilley-Lubbs, G. A. (2003). Crossing the border through service-learning: The power of cross-cultural relationships. In J. A. Hellebrandt, J. Arries, & L T. Varona (Eds.), *JUNTOS: Community partnerships in Spanish and Portuguese* (pp. 36–56). Boston: Heinle.

Tilley-Lubbs, G. A. (2009). Good intentions pave the way to hierarchy: A retrospective autoethnographic approach. *Michigan Journal of Community Service Learning, 16*(1), 59–68.

Tilley-Lubbs, G. A. (2009). Troubling the tide: The perils and paradoxes of service-learning in immigrant communities. *International Journal of Critical Pedagogy, 2*(1), 67–87.

Tilley-Lubbs, G. A. (2011a). The coal miner's daughter gets a Ph.D. *Qualitative Inquiry, 17*(9). doi:10.1177/1077800411420669

Tilley-Lubbs, G. A. (2011b). 4/16: Public tragedy collides with personal trauma. *Qualitative Inquiry, 17*(2), 144–147. doi:10.1177/1077800410392334.

Tilley-Lubbs, G. A. (2012). Border crossing: (Auto)Ethnography that transcends imagination/immigration. *International Review of Qualitative Research, 4*(4).

Tilley-Lubbs, G. A. (2013). The baptism. *Qualitative Research in Education, 2*(1), 272–300. doi:10.4471/qre.2013.02

Gresilda A. Tilley-Lubbs
Faculty of Teaching and Learning
School of Education
Virginia Tech
Blacksburg, Virginia, USA

SECTION 2

AUTOETHNOGRAPHY AS PEDAGOGY
(OR HOW IT TEACHES)

SILVIA BÉNARD CALVA

2. OUR WILL TO CONSTRUCT A HORIZONTAL BRIDGE BETWEEN UNEVEN LATITUDES[1]

ABSTRACT

This chapter presents an analysis of a course taught in the fall semester of 2013 simultaneously in two countries, Mexico and the United States, through videoconference. Its purpose is to explore through a critical lens issues regarding language, technology, and how participants—one professor from Virginia Tech and one from Universidad Autónoma de Aguascalientes, and eleven students, two from Mexico and nine from the US—performed multicultural interactions among themselves. This reflection is framed within the two theoretical and methodological approaches that informed the course itself: Autoethnography and critical pedagogy.

THE INVITATION

On Skype:

"Silvia," said Kris, my friend and colleague from Virginia Tech, "we should teach a critical autoethnography class together. We could have students from Mexico and from the United States and meet every week on videoconference. Then we can edit a book with articles from the participants, part of them written in English and part of them written in Spanish. Wouldn't that be great?"

"Yes…. Let me see if we can arrange it here so that students from the graduate program, and even undergrads, can take the class"

"Great!"

***

Oh, Kris! Publish a book with our contributions? That's so much! Yet, teaching an autoethnography video class together, sounds interesting. We could do a good job and also through the class I can make this approach better known in Mexico, at least in my university. Also as so many years have passed since I took my graduate courses at the University of Texas in Austin, it would be interesting for me to compare and contrast the dynamics of the graduate seminars here in our doctoral program and those taught in the two different universities from the USA. That would be a good reference for me, as I very often wonder about the differences among universities in Mexico and those in the USA, particularly regarding their quality.

I should give it a try.

G. A. Tilley-Lubbs & S. B. Calva (Eds.), Re-Telling Our Stories, 19–32.

***

A few days later, I talk with the Head of the Graduate Program in Cultural Sociology:

"I'm organizing a videoconference graduate course with my colleague from Virginia Tech on autoethnography, to be taught simultaneously in both universities. Do you think it could be part of the courses taught in our program?"

"Our students cannot participate in any other courses besides the mandatory ones. The program is not flexible enough to allow for such an option."

Then, I talk with the Head of the Sociology Department:

"Could we offer a videoconference course on autoethnography as an option for our undergraduate students?"

"Yes, that sounds like a very good idea. But you have to talk to students and make sure that there are at least ten willing to register for the course. Otherwise the university will not agree to either offer it as a regular course, or for you teach it as part of your workload."

There are not ten undergraduate students that would be willing to take the course and fewer if the readings are in English. Besides—as I remember Yvonna Lincoln's comment at a workshop at the International Congress of Qualitative Inquiry (ICQI) a couple of years ago—younger people may not have enough to tell yet using autoethnography.

I decide to go ahead and teach the course "informally," having two "students" from Mexico: My research assistant, Marilú, who has been reading articles on the topic and who began translating some of them to Spanish, and a graduate student, David, for whom I am chair and Kris is a member of his dissertation committee. David is interested in the topic because he has decided to use autoethnography as a research strategy. They both have agreed to take the seminar, also "informally."

Kris designs the syllabus and sends it to me a couple of days before the first day of class. It is mostly organized around the *Handbook of Autoethnography*. I'm glad I bought it at the last ICQI and was willing to carry it all the way back to Mexico. I get so tired from traveling that I really consider what to carry with me so that I can successfully get back home.

THE FIRST DAY OF CLASS

A day previous to the start of the class, our technician in the *universidad*, Néstor, calls me to find out the CODCE number from Virginia Tech. I write an email to Kris requesting the number. She doesn't know what that is about, but promises she will ask her assistant. The assistant doesn't know either. Marilú goes to Néstor's office to ask what that is: "It means codifier de-codifier, but ask them by the brand, ask them for their Polycom number." That is how we establish our understanding of the key to open remote communication through Internet, at least for the following day.

The video room is in a building different from that of my office in the Department of Sociology. It is a small classroom, probably six by eight meters, with a wooden table surrounded by chairs and a big television on one wall. There we are, the three of us with our computers turned on, and Néstor, all ready to start the videoconference once we hear the phone call from Virginia Tech.

"It is a nice place," I mention.

"Yes" replies Marilú "I didn't know about this facility."

"Neither did I," says David.

"I was in a doctoral exam," I say, "with one of the four professors participating through videoconference and it worked out perfectly. It felt almost as if he were sitting at the table with us!"

They are calling. I feel my heart beat fast. I want to see Kris. I want to reencounter the students I met and worked with when I was a Visiting Scholar at VT. There, I see them all sitting in the classroom.... Suddenly the image is fragmented and we cannot hear clearly what they say. It is all frozen.

Then, we listen to the technician on the other end, speaking fast, loudly and clearly:

"How many megas do you have?"

"One," replies Néstor, simply and quietly.

"One mega?!" With eyes wide open the lady on the Virginia Tech remote side asks.

Just as it disappeared, the connection starts again and works out for a while. We see them clearly; we can listen to what they are saying:

"Hi Silvia" says Kris.

"Hi Silvia" say Rong and Kelly.

"*Hola* Silvia" say Pam and Dyanis.

"Hi everybody!" I say.

"Let's get started," says Kris "why don't we each introduce ourselves?"

***

Whatever happened during the class at the beginning, including the issue about what the one mega issue means technologically, doesn't make us look good. I can sense an abyss between this highly technological university in the USA and our Mexican public university.

My doubts are present all semester long, jumping up every time the connection goes wrong, which is quite often. Nevertheless, it is not until I begin writing this chapter that I go to the videoconference area and talk to Néstor, who kindly explains to me some of the issues we faced during the semester.

"Do we really have only one mega?"

"Nooo, the university has much more than that, but I was talking about that specific piece of equipment, which can hold no more than one mega."

"So that was not the problem?"

"The problem with us now is that the authorities have recently decided that whatever comes into the university, it has to pass through the firewall, which operates as an antivirus barrier, verifying that the information is safe and thus will not harm the university. So, if there is too much information coming in, it gets stuck in the firewall."

"Oh! So that is the reason why, many times during the semester, you called the systems department people, and asked them to jump the firewall?"

"Yes, exactly."

"And how can we tell which side of the videoconference has to fix the transmission when things go wrong?"

"If they are receiving a frozen image, or the words are cut, it is on their end; and the same for us."

W. Thomas' (1928) well-known premise comes to my mind: "Regardless of whether they are true or false, what people think has real consequences" (p. 572). We carried on the burden of being at fault because of our lack of technological aids; regardless of whether there were problems on both sides of the videoconference, or that the participants at VT had similar concerns when communication was cut, Marilú, David, and I often thought it was due to the technological and/or bureaucratic flaws at our university.

THE FOLLOWING CLASS

This time we are communicating fluently. "This is great," I tell myself. "Now we can have a regular seminar." The classroom at VT looks very big; it is five or six times bigger than ours. Students are scattered all over the place, some of them talking among themselves, others participating as Kris asks questions. Nevertheless, we now have a hard time listening to what they are saying, and we cannot easily understand their English.

As I position myself closer and closer to the screen to be able to follow the class dynamics, Marilú and David seem to get further away from my view, from my attention, from the other crowd. They, on the other side, are very many, eight or nine, different accents, different types. "Why doesn't David speak louder? Why don't he and Marilú try to participate more, and include themselves in the discussion?"—I think to myself, but I do not tell them. "Please, I need a class break!"

At the end of the class, assuming the remote side of the class is unplugged, I comment in Spanish "¡*Estoy exhausta*! (I'm exhausted!)" "Silvia, I heard you!" Pam, one of the students on the other side says. "It is true," I reply. "Don't you get awfully tired during class as well?"

TALKING PAST ONE ANOTHER[2]

Kris and I taught Autoethnography in a summer course when I was a Visiting Scholar at Virginia Tech during my sabbatical year in 2011. We met in Long Island in a workshop with Carolyn Ellis, where I discovered autoethnography and began to use it as method in 2009. In 2013, when Kris invited me to teach this second edition of the course, called Critical Autoethnography, I did not pay enough attention to the first word in the class name. To my understanding, autoethnography was critical and that was it.

Then, when I reviewed the syllabus, Freire's name, together with those of other critical pedagogues, came up during the first section of the class. I did not pay too much attention. I just overlooked it as I thought Kris included him as a reference, the same as in Long Island when having a conversation about critical pedagogy with César Cisneros and me. We were having a hard time figuring out why she still considered this author to be so important as we had grown further and further away from him. In Mexico, Freire's *Pedagogía del oprimido* [*Pedagogy of the Oppressed*], together with the work of many Marxist authors, was in most of the social sciences' undergraduate curricula, at least during the seventies. Thus, at the beginning of the eighties, when Cesar and I got our undergraduate degrees, many students like us had usually read more radical literature than we were willing to take on.

Years later, I taught the action-research class many times at my university in the sociology undergraduate program. This was because for several years before I entered the university, I had been organizing developmental programs with peasant women and inhabitants of a suburban locality in a northern municipality from the city where I live in Aguascalientes.

It is not until after five or six classes when Freire and critical pedagogy are mentioned on the other end of the conference class that I say:

"Freire = *Investigación – acción* [action research], right?"

"No, Freire = critical pedagogy. Action-research is more practical and critical pedagogy can be completely theoretical."

"Critical pedagogy, Freire? .... "

"Yes, critical pedagogy. Besides Freire, it relates to authors such as Habermas, Adorno...."

"Oh! The Frankfurt School."

"Yees, but not only. Also, and most importantly, Joe Kincheloe, Peter McLaren...."

"Oh-oh, I'm in trouble," I think to myself. "How could I have passed through half of the content of the seminar? That is serious, I can't believe it!"

With urgency, once the class session is over, Marilú, David, and I get together in my office and discuss the topic, search for texts through the virtual library, and decide to contact a researcher from the department of education in our university so that she can help us fill such a void ASAP. My colleague recommends someone else to talk to. Our Education Department is a very good one, but not only that; it has also been the major architect of the evaluation tests for students and teachers in Mexican elementary and middle schools. In fact, the first head of the *Instituto Nacional de Evaluación Educativa*[3] (National Institute of Education Evaluation) was from our university, and some of his colleagues have collaborated with the *Instituto* since then. That indicates how far they position themselves from the critical pedagogy perspective.[4]

We keep searching and come to realize how little has been done using the critical pedagogy perspective in Mexico. Besides, whatever we find about the topic, it is not in either of our disciplines, sociology or psychology, but of course, in education, and mostly at a national university system in Mexico called *Universidad Pedagógica Nacional*.[5]

Then, in the following class, Kris gives us the name of a professor at the University of New Mexico in Las Cruces, Luis Huerta, a Mexican scholar who has been working from the critical pedagogy perspective and who can give us a view of its development in Mexico. We contact him through Skype and he narrates to us, corroborating what we have found, a short history of critical pedagogy in Mexico, and how little research has been done in our country within that perspective. He also confirms and makes it clear to us, that there is a group of researchers in Chihuahua, Mexico, who began offering the first doctoral degree on critical pedagogy in the world. They have created the *Instituto de Pedagogía Crítica* (Institute of Critical Pedagogy), where the doctoral program is now in fact being offered.

So, Freirean thought and its uneven impact on our disciplines and countries, turns out to be another area in which the understandings between the group from Virginia Tech and those of us in Mexico have to catch up.

ANOTHER CLASS

A couple of hours before the seminar is scheduled every week, Kris e-mails all of us an assignment for the class.

"Silvia" Marilú suddenly shows up in my office and asks, "Did you see Kris's e-mail? She wants us to do that for this class!"

"It's too late for that!" I think to myself. Then I tell Marilú, "I think it's too late for assignments, but let's see if we can do it before the videoconference."

A couple of hours later, in the videoconference room and being connected to the VT class, I hear a lot of noise. Students are talking more than usual.

"Hi Silvia," says Kris.

"Hi, what's going on? They are all talking...."

"*Están bicheando* (they are bitching), they are mad because of the assignment I e-mailed earlier."

"Well, they are not the only ones" I say.

I hear no answer. Is it because she doesn't listen to me? Should I say it again? No, that is something we have to talk about away from students.... I wonder, I'm puzzled: Is it because she was planning the class and she thought it was a good idea.... And it is.... But aren't we supposed to plan the assignments together? .... So, I am not the co-teaching professor of this seminar. I am not, and in the students' eyes, I fear, it confirms that I am not a professor in the same terms.

***

The differences in the institutional status given to the class at Virginia Tech and at the *Universidad Autónoma de Aguascalientes*, becomes more and more noticeable as they shape our interactions throughout the semester. At VT there is a formal graduate seminar with a professor and nine students. In the UAA, on the contrary, we participate as volunteers in an informal relationship, not just among ourselves in Mexico, but also with the class members in Virginia. This is particularly relevant in my case because I had assumed I was supposed to be another professor in the classroom, but I had no institutionalized authority. And last but not least, the readings and the class are both in English, which is not our mother tongue. Finally, because the class is not included in my scheduled activities in the university, I feel torn between what I am expected to do, and what I am doing "informally."

AND ANOTHER CLASS

"Ok, we will review the chapters assigned for today from the *Handbook*. They were 16, 17, 18 and 19, right?" We hear Kris asking, and many students agreeing from the other side of the videoconference.

I turn my head towards Marilú and David with a puzzled expression on my face. Marilú quietly laughs and David quietly says, "I didn't know that!"

We are talking quietly and in Spanish so that just we can hear: "Nooo we didn't either, did Kris mention it last class?" Marilú asks. "Darn, it was in the syllabus!" I say. "Look, it was marked in the syllabus, and I complain to my students when they don't check their syllabus to make sure what the next class assignment will be, ha, ha, ha, I feel like a student again."

Incidents such as those narrated above open our paths as classes develop toward the end of the semester. It seems more and more that they have their class and we have ours. We are less active in the assignments; more tired in our attempts to be part of the class, and less present during the seminars due to technological problems.

INTERLUDE

I am wondering which approach to take in writing this chapter and feeling a bit stuck, so I ask my good friend and colleague at the university to take a break and go for coffee. We sit down outside and start talking about Nana, my daughter who has been living in Brazil for nine months.

"I talked to Nana on Skype," I say, "and she got mad at me. She asked me if I had any gossip from Aguascalientes and I remembered something, told it to her, and at the end I said, "So this is some gossip from your *pueblo* [town]. And she said: "It is your pueblo too and people are the same all over the world."

"I agree with her for getting mad at you," my friend said. "You always talk about Aguascalientes as if you disdain us, as if you coming from the capital are superior."

"But I'm critical of Mexico City as well, and it is an expression to say *en tu pueblo* to refer to one's own hometown. Besides, I do not consider myself to be us from the capital as against you, people from Aguascalientes. I don't really feel part of any 'us,' you know?"

"Well, but when you criticize Aguas, we feel that you do, that you think people from the capital are superior."

And as I talked to my friend I wondered: Is that really true? Is it really the case that I have no parameters to refer to as being better than the ones I criticize in Mexico or when I observe and analyse other countries? Well, I ought to be honest enough to say no. That is not true. I have struggled with issues related to those parameters since I settled in Aguascalientes. I even wrote a whole book trying to figure out why living in a middle size city in the interior of Mexico was so traumatic to me (Bénard, 2014), and something similar happens to me when I think about cultural practices, in this case, in academic circles as I compare Mexico and the USA.

***

David comes to my office once and I mention that the students from Virginia Tech have made a very good poster about the class to present in the 2014 Conference of Higher Education Pedagogy in VT.

"Those VT women students are amazing," I said. "They finished a poster from one day to another. They are so good! We are really far behind in our productivity as compared to them. No wonder we are always behind in measurements of international standards."

"If we want to be productive in those terms, as neoliberals are dictating, yes we are. But is that what we really want?"

I don't know, I don't know.... That's another life struggle of mine. I did my graduate studies at the University of Texas in Austin, having a very modest scholarship, which I supplemented by working as a research assistant. I had to study like I never had before in my life. I read tons of books and photocopies in English, and worked ten hours a week, which became twenty when my scholarship ended two years after I started the program. I lived alone most of those first four years of graduate school, when I didn't do much more than study and work. I can still remember Gideon Sjoberg, my master's thesis advisor, telling me "Ms. Bénard, you can't afford to have many friends. You don't have time," and I thought he was right.

That probably made sense to me because of my father's influence—a son of European immigrants in Mexico, my French grandfather and my German grandmother—who studied in Canada. He became an engineer at McGill University. Right after that, he got a job at a General Electric plant in Wisconsin in 1929, and he was deported to Mexico in 1931 due to the Depression.

When I was studying my undergraduate degree in sociology in Mexico City, I told him about the assembly line in the Charlie Chaplin movie we had seen in class. Then he said: "I worked on one of those, and I tried to help the woman next to me when she couldn't make it on time, but she got mad at me. I don't know why!" I kept silent. I decided not to answer that I thought she was probably feeling threatened about her ability to accomplish the job, and therefore she feared she could get fired.

Given my father's background, we were brought up being constantly asked to do something all the time, to either study or work or exercise, anything, but never at rest. That included the eight of us brothers and sisters, and my mother. My father just couldn't stand to even see us sitting round the table after we ate our main meal at three in the afternoon.

So my life in Texas as a graduate student followed my father's path. That is why my adviser's comment made perfect sense to me at that time.

Those ideas and guilty feelings about not always being at work have come and gone, well, for all my life. These last twenty some years, all of which I have lived in Aguascalientes, I have confronted myself with the need to change my working habits; first because I got pregnant before I finished my dissertation, and then, I had a new-born when I moved to Aguascalientes, with practically no informal support networks. At that time, I had to learn to revalue other parts of life, and to adjust myself to working mostly during the time my son was at the day-care centre, six hours a day. It was through him that I learned life was more than working all the time.

I still sway between the desire to work more, deeply admiring those who do so, and trying to balance out my life with other activities, multiplying my interactions, and having some free time. So when David questions me about productivity, I realize I am again flirting with my Anglo-Saxon roots.

When I met Kris, and still up to this time, I wonder how she manages to work so hard. And as I read accounts of USA professors, such as Carolyn Ellis (2011) and Leon Anderson (2011), about the way they kill themselves working and struggling to "have a life" at the same time, I tell myself: "Silvia, you are not being serious enough. You will never be as good as they are. Leon was your classmate in Austin, and see how far he's gone, not just academically, but even trying to do serious leisure activities." And Carolyn, who loves her dogs, writes:

> Zen chases Buddha around the room. When the two dogs connect, they roll and topple in play. I watch them and think about how I'd like to be more with them. Then, "in a minute," I tell them as the ping sound and flashing icon at the bottom of my screen tells me another message has arrived.

> Checking e-mail of course takes more than an hour, and now it's too late to walk. In the dark of my office, the dogs lie quietly at my feet. I can feel their disappointment. (2011, p. 163)

At this point in my life, I realize I honestly don't want to and can't work to the point of exhaustion and elimination of everything else, and as much as I admire Leon for his achievements and for being as good a person as he was in grad school, and still appears to be in his article, I just refuse to multitask whether at work, with family, or even while being at leisure, as he loves to practice sky diving. He writes:

I have graded papers while waiting for clouds to clear at the DZ. I spent a daylong "wind hold" at Skydive Arizona reading David Karp's *Is It Me or My Meds*? And I put together the syllabus for my sociology of mental illness course after sunset at the Bent Prop Café. (2011, p. 151)

Besides, as my university has become more and more bureaucratic, the same as other universities in Mexico, and also in the USA, and in many other countries, at least on the American continent, I wonder whether my job as it is now is what I really want. It seems like we academics have become so concerned with productivity, and with hundreds of other bureaucratic issues in our daily workloads, that we have forgotten, at least very many in my generation in Mexico, that we studied social sciences because we strongly believed we could contribute to building a better world, an issue certainly not very commonly discussed among us in academic debates anymore.

Following my dilemma, I read *The Gifts of Imperfection* by Brené Brown (2010), as well as other books by her. She connects me with that part of myself that refuses to be what I do. But when I'm trying to survive in my job, I tend to escape from her suggestions: "Silvia," I tell myself, "Brené could decide to work half time at the university because she's already very successful and her books and workshops are very popular. Besides, she has a husband and you don't. Careful there, once you make the move, you won't be able to go back and will probably never recover."

AND CLASSES GO ON

I more and more feel off base as a professor.
I view myself as not being taken seriously by students at VT.
I know I do not speak English as well as native speakers,
I have not done all the reading assignments.
It is like being a Mexican graduate student again:
Not good enough,
Not having done it all,
Struggling with my English skills.
Again, as it was thirty years ago,
Feeling systematically at a disadvantage.

AND ON

Okay, I will accept that I am in a peculiar situation. I will also accept that I am imperfect and show myself to be vulnerable, as Brené Brown suggests we do. Besides, I do have certain strengths. I am a professor and whether or not I participate on their grading, I do have a doctorate degree and they don't.

Try again.
Do your best.

Humbly accept what you know about the topic of the class.
Speak English as well as you can.
Make comments to their chapter drafts.

AND ON

In a video class:
"What's the difference between autoethnography and autobiography?" Kris asks. Long silence. I answer.
"The former is about a specific topic and the latter is about a whole life."
"That is, according to my training as a creative writer," a student says, "a genre called memoir."
"A Mexican author, Mercedes Blanco, has argued that autobiographies intend to be "objective," while autoethnography argues that the author is positioned in the narrative," I reply again.
"I have never heard of such a thing," she says.
That is it. Period. So, following my humble mandate, I say, "Thank you."

AND ON

"I also need to assume my responsibility as a professor and review each of the drafts students sent us to read," I command myself. "I will do my part."
It takes me about five or six days of work to go through the manuscripts. I decide not to make comments on the texts, but instead, write an e-mail including suggestions and encouraging their good work. Most students answer right away and thank me very politely for the work I did, and for my comments. They mention that they will consider my suggestions to review and resubmit their papers. Only one student, the next class day, says: "I'm not in the stage for general comments yet."

LAST DAY OF CLASS

Kris comes to Mexico and we have the last class with the group of students at Virginia Tech with Marilú, David, she, and I here in the conference room at the *universidad*. As soon as we connect with VT, Kris says: "Silvia, how could you follow the class all semester like this? They look so far away, and it is so difficult to understand what they are saying! You should've told us, we could've done something about it!"
That makes me mad, again. I have been all semester long making an effort to listen and to pay attention to the other side of the videoconference, I have lost contact with David and Marilú, but instead of voicing my discomfort, I have spent all semester long assuming there was nothing to be done about it, and assuming that I had to put up with those inconveniences.

Then, we decide to talk to the students through Skype from my office once we review each of their final drafts, and to see David and Marilú in person. The perspective of talking with students after reviewing together their papers, gives me more confidence, and it makes me feel again considered as a professor.

In what would be our last class, Kris and I talk to four students through Skype. We spend far more time with them than we had expected. That is particularly true with two students who are not willing to consider the possibility of exercising a more serious introspection process such as we think they need in order to question certain domain assumptions present in their sociocultural background as they were growing up, and that appear to still be quite prominent in their present worldviews, and consequently in their drafts.

As weeks pass, and months pass, and we do not hear from them again, I many times worry and wonder: "Was I too hard on them?" It was probably very difficult for one of the students to listen to us saying that there must have been something not so perfect on her Southern upbringing in a Baptist family, or to another one listening to me arguing that domestic workers are okay and that they may like what they do.

AND IN THE END

Well, in the end, we probably took the roles we knew on each side of the bridge. They acted as a professor and a group of students in a graduate seminar. They were fairly active, did their assignments, and engaged in discussions. We assumed a more passive role. We were there, we listened, and we kept rather silent.

At the end, the class for me felt like a showcase where they were acting and we were spectators. Their presence became more evident as we stayed in the margins. I think that this was not a voluntary and fully conscious attitude from either of us, it developed as we constructed our day by day class interactions according to the type of roles and interactions we knew from before, the definition of the situation, the bureaucratic realms of our academic institutions, the technological facilities on each side of the screen. Anyway, those are the issues I have tried to convey as I write this chapter.

I truly believe that we all made an effort to engage in alternative interactions, making them horizontal, dialogic, and respectful of our cultural differences and our understandings of power and privilege. This is the reason why, as I took notes during the semester about our dissonances and communication difficulties—made most evidently clear through language and technology—I realized how hard it was going to be writing a critical reflection about our seminar. In fact, many times I thought about escaping from such a sensitive task by proposing an alternative topic for this edited book. As that did not happen, I find myself making comments that can appear to many as unfair and biased, but my concerns are concentrated on us as participants. That is certainly possible, but how can I really be critical of our pedagogy if I do not practice introspection and am not strong enough to show myself as vulnerable? How can I truly talk about an intercultural class pretending everything went smoothly and pleasantly?

This exercise of writing my experience during this multicultural videoconference seminar has clearly showed me that autoethnography is an essential research approach to make a critical pedagogy practice possible. If I had not implicated myself in the happenings as an autoethnographer, and had I not written as a way of knowing (Richardson & St. Pierre, 2005), reaching out for contact with my feelings, my doubts, and my differences with others, it would have been impossible for me to practice the capacity to be critical. I wish I had been more proactive as the course went on, and that I had clearly expressed myself through the semester as issues developed, but I did not articulate my ideas more clearly until I sat down and found the courage to write this chapter.

NOTES

[1] First published in Spanish: Tilley-Lubbs, G. A. (2014a). La autoetnografía crítica y el Self vulnerable como investigadora. *REMIE: Multidisciplinary Journal of Educational Research, 4*(3), 268–285. http://dx.doi.org/10.447/remie.2014.014 Tilley-Lubbs, G. A. (2014). Also in Spanish: La autoetnografía crítica y el Self vulnerable como investigadora. *Astrolabio, Nueva Época, 14*. Reprinted with the permission of the author and the editors. Translation to English by the author.

[2] I use this phrase paraphrasing Manheim (1954).

[3] The INEE was created in 2002 and its major goal is to evaluate the quality, the performance, and the results of the whole national education system from k-12 to high school.

[4] McCloud (2013) makes a good revision of how standardized tests respond to the neoliberal model of education.

[5] This university system trains teachers and it has 70 campuses all over the country.

REFERENCES/BIBLIOGRAPHY

Anderson, L. (2011). Time is of the essence: An autoethnography of family, work, and serious leisure. *Symbolic Interaction, 34*(2), 133–157.

Bénard, S. (2014). *Atrapada en provincia. Un ejercicio autoetnográfico de imaginación sociológica.* Aguascalientes, Ags.: Universidad Autónoma de Aguascalientes.

Blanco, M. (2012). ¿Autobiografía o autoetnografía? *Desacatos, 38*, 169–178.

Brown, B. (2010). *The gifts of imperfection: Let go of who you think you're supposed to be and embrace who you are.* Center City, MN: Hazelden.

Ellis, C. (2011). Jumping on and off the runaway train of success: Stress and committed intensity in academic life. *Symbolic Interaction, 34*(2), 158–172.

Holman Jones, S., Adams, T., & Ellis, C. (Eds.). (2013). *Handbook of autoethnography.* Walnut Creek, CA: Left Coast.

Manheim K. (1954). *Ideology and Utopia. An introduction to the sociology of knowledge.* New York, NY: Harcourt, Brace, & Co.

McCloud, J. (2013). *Storied lives: Exploring English language learners' school experiences* (Unpublished dissertation).

Richardson, L., & St. Pierre, E. A. (2005). Writing: A method of inquiry. In N. Denzin, & Y. Lincoln. (Eds.), *The sage handbook of qualitative research* (3rd ed., pp. 959–978). Thousand Oaks, CA: Sage.

Thomas, W., & Thomas, D. (1928). *The child in America. Behavior problems and programs.* New York: NY: Knopf.

Silvia Bénard Calva
Departamento de Sociología y Antropología
Universidad Autónoma de Aguascalientes
Aguascalientes, Agualcalientes, Mexico

DAVID CASTILLO-ARCEO

3. NAMING IN MY PRESENT THE PAST NAMELESS

Violence at School

ABSTRACT

When the author presented his dissertation proposal on violence in secondary schools, he didn't consider what the problem had to do with him. In this chapter, he examines how he perceives his experiences with school violence and bullying differently and, perhaps, more clearly.

LITTLE MORE THAN A YEAR AGO

"Why do you research school violence? Were you bullied as a child?" said Kris through the screen.

"No! Why would you think that?" I answered right away and blushed.

In truth, I had never thought that this was a possibility. Why did this question make me uncomfortable?

I am sitting facing Kris's image on the TV screen along with my colleagues in Virginia, USA, while trying to participate in an intercultural course in critical autoethnography. After various communication problems, both technical and due to our own cultural differences, we are finally talking more or less continuously. Silvia, Marilú, and I are on this side "of the pond."

I have only been doing autoethnography for a few months. Not only am I trying to learn something new, I have to struggle to understand those on the other side of the screen, and in spite of reading it daily, I didn't know how limited my spoken English was until I had to express myself. I feel embarrassed by my stammering and try not to speak much in class.

So much has changed in just over a year and I have studied authors who once were alien to me. I also never imagined that I would read Paulo Freire again now that I am doing my Doctorate and that I would end up talking about critical pedagogy. The first time I read him, eight years ago, while pursuing my psychology degree and rummaging through books in the university library, he was an unknown to the educational psychology students at my university. I remember being fascinated with his suggestions for literacy stemming from real problems within a community and the oppression of the students. At that time though, I had no one to talk to about

G. A. Tilley-Lubbs & S. B. Calva (Eds.), Re-Telling Our Stories, 33–50.

it. Now, it amuses me to see how a cycle that remained unclosed has come back around with such force. I am passionate about critical pedagogy.

"I believe that writing about your experiences in school is a good activity. Perhaps this will give you new ideas for your research," Silvia said to me after class.

"But I don't know where to start."

"Then write down everything you can think of and it will come to you."

I have now spent a year writing and editing, wondering about the relevance of it all. How do I decide what's important? To name the unnamed. To find, within my experiences, a critical understanding that considers the proper context, culture, and structures of my society has not been an easy task. At first, I didn't really know that my experience had been tinged with violence. In her comments on the theme of bullying in my recent drafts, Kris remarked:

"Why don't you accept that you were a victim of bullying? Is it because of a fear of vulnerability? Because of shame?"

This is probably true. It is difficult to accept myself as a victim and, of course, to render myself vulnerable. This is perhaps the greatest challenge I have faced while writing autoethnography: working through my emotions, recognizing my mistakes, showing the human side that I often hide.

To give it a name and to use a concept that wraps up the story, that explains and pinpoints the problem, has in reality been something that I have tried to avoid, at least partially. I start by understanding violence not only as a straightforward expression of power coercively imposing personal wishes – direct violence – but also, in agreement with Galtung's (2003) perspective, I see violence in the cultural character, which reproduces injustice through internalized social norms and in the structural character, where antidemocratic, hierarchical institutions impose a particular social order, reproduce it, and sustain relationships of the oppressor and the oppressed (Freire, 1970).

My story, like looking through stained glass windows, tells the story of my path through middle school and focuses on my social education. It is written in the present tense to emphasize its everyday nature, created by those around me. These social lessons are rarely considered in the teaching curriculum – focused on developing competencies, however, their daily presence tends to form the basis of our future relationships more than what is being taught through the standardized curriculum.

I have placed my interpretation of my story at the end of the chapter, this reconstruction of my past nameless. This is one of many decisions I made in writing about my life and I believe the risks that come with this decision are a necessary part of the process.

I agree with Peter McLaren (2005) that "all thought, actions and relationships are political in an ideological sense" (p. 74) and it is in this sense that my decision has at least two implications: (1) that my words can be read from different perspectives, and (2) although my analysis of the account is postponed, the story I present, the experiences that I choose, and the way that I describe them are in themselves an interpretation of my lived experience, an ideological perspective: the narrative is an epistemology – "a way of knowing" (Goodall, 2008).

Therefore, in the chapter below, I am not looking to make a positivist argument about life removed from "real" data and the related analysis. Instead I mainly want to connect emotionally with my readers, to offer up my experiences as motivation to recall their own, and to be open to the fact that there will be multiple interpretations of my story.

Autoethnography as a method that clearly sets forth the researchers' active role in the interpretations of what he/she lives and studies, contributes to the demystification and democratization of the written, and furthers open dialogue beyond researchers' desktops and disjointed academic logic: "Critical pedagogy lives, relevant and effective, in the contemporary world and should be at the same time intellectually rigorous and accessible to the general public [...] I stress the profound importance of writing and speaking about critical pedagogy in a way that is engaging to all" (Kincheloe, 2008, p. 26). I believe[1] that language focused on evocative emotions and experiences creates this space.

1997

Stained-Glass Windows

We are sitting in a hallway at school. We are holding hands and learning to kiss. My hand sweats in hers: she is my first girlfriend. I look at her lips. The memory of her mouth and her tongue playing with mine remains etched in my mouth for a few moments. My breath returns and my blood races through my body. What is she saying while her lips are moving? And if I start to kiss her? I get closer. She avoids my mouth and smiles at my distress, leans in quickly and bites my lower lip, moves away again, and returns to kiss me. This back and forth, like ocean waves, moves my emotions in the same way: anguish and joy, wonder and terror. It is February. I am twelve years old, she is thirteen. I began middle school six months ago, met her two months ago, we began to meet after classes to walk three weeks ago ... it's been one week since we've been dating.

This motion is her favourite game, approaching and retreating time and again. I still don't know how to play it. I despair with each retreat, smile with each approach. There is so much I don't know about her and that she doesn't know about me; a week ago I didn't even know she liked me. Everything is new with her. Even becoming boyfriend and girlfriend began with the same motion:

"Don't you like me?" Sitting on a garden bench, her question took me by surprise.

No. That should be the proper response to her question. She is my cousin's ex-girlfriend and that alone was enough to see her only as a friend. But her question has changed the way I see her.

"Yes, yes I like you." I hang my head and blush, with thousands of feelings passing through me. I am paralyzed.

"Then why haven't you said so?" I am at a loss for words. In my confusion, she changes the topic, gets up and suggests we walk to the bus stop. She takes my hand and it starts to flow like a river.

"Goodbye" she tells me while she kisses me very close to my lips and gets onto the bus.

How do I say, "Be my girlfriend?" Why didn't I ask her at that moment? The truth is that I wanted to, but my mouth wouldn't open.

The following day, I looked for her at the start of the dressmaking workshop.

"Teacher, may I speak with Cindy?" I say with a red face and on the verge of exploding.

Her classmates laugh at me: "Oooooh, your boyfriend is talking to you! When's the wedding?! He wants to cry! He wants to cry!" The teacher shouts, "Silence!" and Cindy leaves the room, closing the door behind her.

"I want to know if you want to be my girlfriend," I say stuttering. Maybe I should have started with a "Hi, how are you doing?" She stares at me and smiles, amused by my awkwardness.

"I don't know. Let me think." My heart beats rapidly. Could she say no?

"All right," I say, hiding my anguish.

"I'm going," she says, and as she holds the door open, "I'll talk to you at recess. I'll see you behind the room where we have history class," amidst the shouts and jeers of her classmates.

Why didn't I notice her penetrating black eyes, dark face, long hair, and those big, full lips earlier?

At recess, I wait behind the classroom. And what if she says no? I think as my body struggles to stop moving forward.

"And then?" I say anxiously, and sit next to her.

"Then what?"

"Well what do you think?" My stomach writhes and my legs beg to flee.

"Of what?" She says on the verge of laughter, "All right, I'll be your girlfriend," she answers immediately, while taking my hand a second time and opening the flood gates, saving me from despair.

So here we are, sitting in the hallway of the dressmaking class, on the second floor of a building that faces the electrical workshop where I take classes. Neither my teacher nor hers has arrived yet. My classmates are waiting below for us. I hope the teachers never come!

Little by little .... First as a murmur and then more clearly, I hear this word. I begin to hear it all week, the same laughs, the same tone and rhythm: "Imanol! Imanool! Imanool!" Recess ended several minutes ago and in the hallways around us all you can hear is the chorus and the laughter. She has stopped talking and kissing me and looks below us to see what is going on, knowing it has to do with us. I try to position my body between her curious eyes and my classmates' shouts.

"What are they yelling?" she asks, trying to get around me. She has the same smile as when she is thinking of playing a prank or when she sees my anguish at the back and forth rhythm of her kisses.

"They're shouting 'Imanol'!" I respond angrily, giving up my attempt to hide it.

"Why are they shouting that?" she says light-heartedly.

"It's the waiter from the show "*La Otra Cosa*," I tell her, with my head lowered, my face red, my frustration and anger contained.[2]

She looks at me long and hard. I see in her face the way she will remember me. She studies my face, my hair, my entire body; I am frozen like a mannequin before her. A moment goes by and when she finishes and expresses approval at my likeness, she starts to roar with laughter and my friends' mocking grows louder: Her voice is so rough and her laughter so loud!

I run furiously toward the stairs, I dodge her, she tries to hold me back. In this moment she corners me between the bars of the railing and holds me firmly. Why doesn't she stop smiling? She tries to kiss me while I sidestep her and try to escape. Finally, she has found my lips....I let her kiss me, my anger eases, and all that remains is frustration.

"Hey! It's not that bad! Anyway, it's not true. You have a girlfriend right?" she says, smiling and caressing my hair.

She doesn't stop smiling. While looking at my face and reconciling my likeness with my personality, her caresses no longer ebb and flow. Her embraces completely comfort me and help me forget her own guffaws.

Now, the hallways are silent. The teacher has arrived, ordering my classmates to be quiet and to enter the workshop. Her teacher has also arrived, comes up the stairs, scolds us for our embrace, and orders my girlfriend to come into the classroom.

Upon entering the room I continue to hear whispers of the name that they have given me: "Imanoool. Imanoool," like crickets rubbing their feet in my ear. The teacher demands silence again and begins to teach class.

I'm 12 years old. My body is thin and fragile and plain. My hair is much longer than average and untidy ...and I am an effeminate boy, "mild-mannered." My voice has not changed; it's high-pitched. The way I walk and express myself is similar to girls my age. I am not a typical adolescent, boasting about every beautiful part of my body, with short hair, a deepening voice, and a strong, rugged body. I seem homosexual to my classmates, and at that time and in the context of my school, to be a gay teenager has serious social consequences. Being different is the first trait – sometimes the only one – you need to suffer bullying in school.

***

I have been raised by women. My father wasn't around. Most of the time he was traveling, selling whatever he could, and he was not a male role model. When I was 15 years old, my mother divorced him and his absence was then almost complete.

Since childhood, I have been raised by my mother Lola, by a great-aunt who died in May earlier this same year, and by my mother's sisters. My mother worked all day – as a cashier, secretary, or office assistant. She also had to travel a lot as my sister Cecy, three years younger than I, was born with a heart ailment and had treatments and operations in various hospitals throughout the country until she was six years old. In my mother's family, my uncles were not part of the everyday dynamic and we only saw them on birthdays. There was no one close to me from whom I could learn to be a man.

This didn't mean that there weren't examples of machismo in my social education. Not long ago, an aunt said casually and loudly, "Another *mandilón!*"[3] to refer to the times I prepared meals. I remember my grandmother telling my aunts to cook for my uncles and to wash their dishes. It was the same when my mother took charge of the economic livelihood of the house, also ironing, cooking, washing, and tidying up the house, while teaching my sisters to "do what had to be done," until when divorced and tired of the burden, she announced that everyone was responsible for these things.

I say this without complaint. I was a child well loved by all my mothers.

What I didn't learn about walking, speaking, moving, (not) expressing affection, "treating" a woman…like other men in my society, was replaced by a profound respect for women and their daily lives, their strength, solidarity, sensitivity, affection, and courage in raising children, their own and others. I was raised by women and, as such, the realm of women was my comfort zone, what I knew, and where I could be myself. Yes, I was an effeminate boy.

***

Because of these taunts and my nickname, proving my manliness has become a priority. In May, I began smoking and drinking in secret after the death of my godmother Lola and after giving in to peer pressure – all my cousins my age drank. But, to my classmates, I have become interesting again. I am breaking the adults' rules. Besides, I have a girlfriend, and as such, it's easy for me to talk to girls my age, something that my classmates can't do. I am like Cupid in the class. In one way or another, this has saved me from harassment, and the nickname they gave me has been forgotten little by little. Already, I no longer hear it in the hallways.

Although I keep having conflicts with my classmates for being different since I hardly fit into their conversations, I have other places to be, other social circles. I turn to the girls. I have many more female friends than male.

The problem now is that one of my female friends has a jealous boyfriend.

"I don't understand why Alan gets so pissed, as if I was going to steal his girlfriend" I tell Yugos while we're eating during recess.

"Well he says that he doesn't want you to go near Emma anymore".

"That's fucked up! She's my friend!"

We sit in alphabetical order in class and Alan sits behind me. He is cheerful and outgoing, tall with dark hair. He has many suitors, and is the son of the chemistry teacher. On the other hand he is overbearing, rough, and comes off as being full of himself.

The first argument we've had is about our space. He wants to be close to his friend and I am in the way. He has yelled at me to take his seat but I don't want to. Yugos, mediating the dispute, asks the person in front of him to switch seats with Alan and they agree.

A few days later, I find out that Alan likes my friend Emma, so I ask her. The two like each other. Trying to remedy my clashes with him, that same day I introduce them, and the following week they are dating. Now he's jealous of me.

Emma is very pretty, slim, fair skinned, blond, shy, and quiet. Her group of friends, my friends too, is small – four or five girls who meet up in stenography class.

Friday. We are playing basketball in P. E., the last class of the day, and Alan is on the other team. I am at the three point line, with the ball in my hand, looking for someone to pass to. He comes running, pushes me, and pulls me. Everyone stops to see what's going to happen. The teacher turns his back to scold some students.

We stare at each other....

"What?!" He says defiantly, a few meters away from me, smiling and showing off in front of the others.

I throw the ball at his face.
   I spring up.
      He covers up his face,
         A trickle of blood slips out between his hands.

The teacher notices what's happening at this point:

"What's going on here?" He yells while standing between us, keeping us apart with his hands.

"He knocked me down when I was going to pass the ball," I say in my defence, confused and agitated.

"Can't you see? He hit me in the face with the ball!" he says showing him his bloodied nose and hands.

"Let's go to the principal," shouts the teacher and pulls us along with him.

In the principal's office, I received my first complaint. Alan didn't stop looking at me from his chair, holding a rolled up piece of paper to staunch the flow of blood from his nose. I looked at him sporadically too, with mixed feelings moving between anger and guilt for making him bleed.

"I don't want to find out that you were fighting outside," says the school counsellor. Her comment distresses me. I hadn't thought of that! She looks at us, thinks a bit, and corrects herself. "David, go straight home!" Does she see my fear?

I leave the principal's office and head to the door. From there I run to the bus stop. I don't want a fight at the exit either. I have never gotten into a fight at school. At home, my brother and sister's arguments, both younger than I, are frequent. We spend too much time alone and it seems like arguments have become the most common way we interact. At home I am domineering and rough, the older brother who has the privilege of doing or not doing whatever he wants. At school, it's a different matter. It's not about watching TV shows or about who uses the computer, and the fight won't end after my mother's threats. I am afraid.

Monday.   I have arrived at school late even though Friday's fight has faded from memory, and if not for the desire to be with my girlfriend, I probably would not have gone to class that day. I'm almost sure that they will not let me enter school because almost two hours have passed since the opening bell rang. At this time they should be starting the ceremony to salute the flag.

"Go to your room, David" the counsellor tells me while opening the door.

The feeling in school is different. There's no sign of the ceremony going on, and there are more people in the hallways that I would expect to see if they had finished. The rooms are very quiet and students are hanging around the doors whispering among themselves.

I arrive at my room and from the door, I see them in small groups hugging and sobbing.

"Can I come in?" my classmates turn around to see me and burst into tears.

Yugos, also crying, says as I get to my seat, "Alan is dead."

The teachers have said that he had an accident with a rope while playing with his two year old cousin and choked. The majority of us believe, without knowing with absolute certainty, that he had killed himself, but there is no reason to believe this. No one had seen that his temperament had changed. He was the same outgoing boy, teasing and rude as always.

I leave the room and race toward my friend Emma. Upon seeing me, she hugs me and cries bitterly. I am unable to cry. My emotions are stuck in my throat like in a funnel, pushing and shoving as they go. From one moment to the next, a classmate's life is gone. Why did we fall out? Suddenly, I no longer remember.

Emma has been pulling away from her friends little by little, and after several weeks has decided not to talk to me anymore. I haven't reacted to her decision. I accept it. We don't need to talk about it, she simply avoids eye contact when she approaches me and now won't come close to me anymore. I want to distance myself from anything that has to do with Alan's death and to not think about him anymore. "Alan has gotten his wish," I think ironically each time I see her pass.

During the next few months, I am overcome with guilt. There is neither logic nor reason; however, I feel responsible for his death. Little by little, the happy, outgoing David from my childhood is changing, and with it comes a delusional belief that explains the injustice of his death. Influenced by television, I think that I have magical powers that hurt those who hurt me.[4] I become withdrawn and irritable. At recess or between classes, I meet up with other classmates to play with a Ouija board and cast spells we read from magazines we got at the flower market. In the evenings, I lock myself in my room, write letters to my girlfriend, and read about magic.

We are four, two girls and two boys. Playing with magic makes us different. Again, I have become the target for harassment by my classmates: they regard us with suspicion and fear. But this doesn't last long. A month later one of my friends has come with her wrists with cuts in form of a circle and a cross in the centre.

"I spoke with an aunt and she told me that this protects us from the things we do with the Ouija board. I don't want to keep practicing witchcraft," she says anxiously.

We all agree. That day at home I engraved the same symbol with the tip of a needle on my wrists.

Alan returns a couple times in my dreams. When this happens, the feeling of guilt returns and days go by before I can sleep well.

***

"The truth is that I wanted to '*madrearte*'⁵ Esteban admits several months later."
"I asked to be moved because I knew that Alan had unfinished business with you."

"He told you?"

"Yeah. I talked to him a day before he died and he told me, 'Monday I'm going to get him.'"

Esteban was Alan's cousin. He was in Emma's class last school year, then he switched to my class. After several months, we've become friends which, in the face of his confession, sounds unbelievable. He's an outgoing guy, different from the others. His comments are usually inappropriate and confused, and his humour is not well received by others. Also, he has trouble making friends in class. They call him *lelo.*⁶ It took me several months to realize that he and Alan were cousins and when I found out, I only remember thinking that they were very different.

"And why didn't you do it?" I asked him while picturing Alan telling his cousin.
"I don't know. Not everyone liked you: Luis, Ernesto, Mota, that dude that you blocked from Cindy," he tells me and roars with laughter. "You were damn stuck-up, and well, I don't know, you acted like a chick. One day Luis was going to fuck you up in the middle of the field. He started running to fight with you and I went up to him and said, 'That one is mine, Dude,' and well, then he left."

"But, why didn't you do it?" I insisted, surprised.

"I don't know. Then I liked you," he says and laughs again.

Esteban is an only child. He lives with his mother in a small house near the middle school—two rooms, a bathroom between them, a space that serves as both living room and dining room, a kitchen, and a small laundry area. She is a single mom and even though he knows his father, he is a forbidden topic in his house. He never took care of the family or acknowledged his son. She is very indulgent with Esteban and their relationship is quite strange. They argue about everything, "Like brothers," he tells me when I mention my impression of their fights. "Including having the same last name!" I say light-heartedly, rounding off his comment.

"Hey Mom, go to your own fucking room!" he yells at her when she pokes her nose in our conversation.

"Straighten up this room, Dumbass," she responds while closing the door and leaving us alone.

The house is filled with mountains of objects. Everything is everywhere: dishes and plastic containers, boxes that were closed and sealed or half open and showing blankets and clothes, cookbooks, school papers scattered in the dining room, appliances on the chairs. It is difficult to sit anywhere. "We are reorganizing the house," was the first thing she said the day I met her.

Little by little this place has become our hideout. We spend the days we play hooky here watching TV or playing on the computer until his mom arrives and whips up dinner, usually sandwiches or salads.

It's December. It's the first time that Ulises, another classmate, and I stay at Esteban's house. At night, we plan to go to a *Posada*[7] and to come back to his house afterward. The plan is to drink without our parents finding out – Ulises' and mine. Esteban's mother is amused by our plans, even offering to speak to our parents to get permission.

I am feeling sad because it's the second time that I have broken up with Cindy; the first time upon discovering that she wanted to be my girlfriend to make my cousin jealous and this time because of problems we've had since getting back together. We will get back together one more time for about eight months but this time she won't be my only girlfriend and I will hide my other relationships and dalliances from her while showing off to my friends and cousins. When she finds out she will end our relationship.

At the *posada* I have decided to drink punch mixed with tequila and to listen to everyone's conversations. I am not in the mood to talk. The neighbour's dad finds us drinking and ends our party. We go back to Esteban's house. Once in the room, having lost the coin toss, I have to sleep on the floor. I find space near the entrance to the room with my feet toward the half open door.

We are laughing and, with mixed emotions, my laughs turned to tears and I hide my face in the pillow. Ulises and Esteban don't realize what's happening.

Esteban's mother comes in because of the noise to see what's going on, looks at all of us, and sees me crying.

"What have these dumbasses done to you?" She shouts from the doorjamb. There is silence and all that remains after the question is the crying I can no longer stifle.

"What's wrong, Bro" Esteban asks me anxiously, with his hand reaching for my shoulder.

"Nothing's wrong," I say between sobs with my face still buried in the pillow.

"What happened, Esteban?" insists his mother. She tries to turn me around to see my face.

"Nothing's wrong!" I yell furiously as I get up and leave the room, avoiding her hands.

I am sitting in the dining room with my face lying on the table and my arms covering my head, still crying: I miss Cindy. A moment later Esteban's mother comes out of the room, sits next to me stroking my hair, and asks again.

"What's wrong?"

"Nothing! I already said nothing. I just want to be alone. Leave me here."

"I'm not going, tell me already. What did they do to you?"

"They didn't do anything to me! I just want to be alone," I shout and push her hand from repeatedly stroking my hair. Her caresses make me uncomfortable, but resigned and still crying, I am no longer fighting them off.

Suddenly, her body surrounds mine in a smothering embrace. I feel her lips and her breath on the back of my neck. She holds me with her hands while putting an arm around my back and pushes me against the cold glass of the table. Finally, after struggling, frightened, and without stopping to figure out what is happening, I move away from her.

"Go already! What don't you understand?" I shouted angrily. She gets up, turns around, and goes to her room.

Hours later, the house is silent again and with my emotions calmed, I decide to go to sleep. I enter the bathroom and look at myself in the mirror, my red, haggard eyes, my dishevelled hair, my gaunt skin and sparse moustache. I feel tired.

I leave the bathroom and there she is again. Without warning, she lunges at me again, embraces me tightly from behind while kissing my neck, and pulls me toward her room. With my arms trapped against her body, I try desperately to free myself, afraid of the silence in the house but also of waking the others. Why am I afraid to wake them? Then an idea pops into my mind, the only way out:

"I'll scream!" I tell her in a whisper that strives not to be a shout. She squeezes me tighter. "I'll scream and tell Esteban everything!"

I get free. She looks at me with a strange expression, somewhere between a smile and annoyance. I run to the room and push the door behind me, smacking it into her as she tries to grab me again. I push with all my strength and finally get it closed. I hide under the shelter of the bedding on the floor. And what if she has keys? Little by little my body detaches from the exhaustion and fear. I fall asleep.

The following day, she leaves early, and I use the opportunity to leave before she returns.

I try not to go to Esteban's house alone. Maybe I shouldn't go back; but it's our hideout, where my friend is, where we party, where we can do things we can't do at my house. Each time I go, I'm afraid to be alone with her. But Esteban has a nasty habit of taking naps in the afternoon, and she won't stop harassing me.

One day, three years later, I risk talking to Esteban.

There are several of us at a party at his house. His mother, no longer trying to hide what she is doing, has come up to me from behind and cut a lock of my hair while I am playing the guitar and singing, like a personal trophy! Closing my eyes while I sing is such a bad habit!

I leave the room running after her, shouting all the hatred I feel. You can't hear anything in the house above both my yells and hers trying to drown out mine. Behind me, Norma, my close friend, and Esteban try to catch up.

With exasperation, she yells hundreds of things from the door of her house. I manage to hear one over all the others and it slips into my ears, changing to ice inside my body.

"No one is going to believe you!"

***

We wander aimlessly through the city.

"You saw what your mom did and I only have one question to ask you, but I want you to answer me honestly," I say to Esteban after we sit on a sidewalk. "Did you know all this?"

"I don't know," he said after thinking for a long time. "Maybe I did know, but I didn't want to believe it."

"That's why you were taking naps?"

"Yes."

Those were the last real words that we spoke as friends.

RECONSTRUCTING THE NAMELESS PAST

Now, almost 20 years later, I have been able to recognize myself inside a culture and society where I reproduce their stereotypes and interactions. This would not have been possible if, on the way, I didn't have open, honest dialogue with those that read and commented on my writing. My preoccupation with school injustice and violence emerged strongly when I taught high school. As with Peter McLaren (1980), at this time I had genuine concern for my students and the daily injustices they faced at school, depoliticized and without contextual awareness of their lives. Reclaiming my childhood experiences, studying forms of violence beyond direct acts of aggression and the ideas that arose from critical pedagogy has given me the opportunity to contextualize my life experiences, to find meaning beyond a psychologisation of the problem. I should say that for me, this is a big step, considering my training in psychology.

What do you learn in school? As educators and researchers concerned with student development, we often focus our attention on the knowledge and skills[8] our students should develop, and we disassociate ourselves from the emotions and social learning that takes place every moment. We forget the importance of being an adolescent within the complex socialization process that exists in the context of schooling.

How do you think of school as a place where you can acquire the knowledge necessary for life when academic programs set up each reorganization with a major emphasis on the economic demands of our capitalist society and less on peaceful coexistence and the development of engaged and conscious citizens? The emphasis on the market and the production of efficient, competent, and low cost human capital has trickled down little by little into school discourse and the reforms it calls for (McLaren, 2005).

Long ago Freire (1970) suggested a solution to the problem of the disconnect between curriculum and actual social issues, focusing teaching curriculum on the specific needs facing student-teachers, in my case, those of the youth.

If we believe that school is a place of possible change, and we are looking for reform, to approach it from a humanist perspective, to connect it to both the historical context and the one in which we now find ourselves, I believe that there are at least two fundamental problems that we must acknowledge and address. Connecting these problems provides an interpretation of my story about my past in school as a teenager.

1. Schooling is Disconnected from Our Current Social Reality and Political Outlook

As critical researcher-teachers it is absolutely necessary to believe that school is an exceptional place to foment social change, to have hope. This can't begin with naïve viewpoints regarding what's taking place: In school we learn, produce, and reproduce ways of relating to others with culturally accepted behaviour.

The education of young people that takes place in the hidden curriculum of schools (McLaren, 2005) looks to cultivate future adults according to the norms of the established school culture, with their social images, stereotypes, and roles. This education is not explicit probably because its silence and namelessness are needed for the continuous and effective reproduction of the hegemonic culture (Bourdieu, 1981), so there is no opportunity for criticism, dialogue, and transformation.

Considering Berger and Luckmann's (1972) suggestions regarding the cycle of creation and reproduction of social reality has, in my experience, connected with the implicit social rules that shaped the events I have shared, in particular, about gender and age-related roles and stereotypes. In all this, I find myself faced with a basic need to fulfil: the feeling of community, supporting the other, being part of "us." Without this need to "support the other," the stereotype has no strength. I would not have suffered and tried so hard to eliminate it. Starting from a basic need to describe direct, cultural, and structural violence is one of the great skills for conceptualizing violence that I found in Galtung's (2003) work.

Through stereotypical expressions I will give a name to these unspoken rules that, in view of my need to belong to a group, frame my daily interactions.

A man can't seem feminine. It is clear that my behaviour, different from what is expected from a man, was a trigger for the harassment and teasing I endured from my classmates. Being an effeminate teenager was not a problem for me until others noted the difference. I wanted to be recognized as a man and they viewed me as not fitting the stereotype of manhood, a crystallization of gender differences

45

that dichotomizes strict boundaries between the in-group and out-group (Tajfel & Turner, 1979).

Driven by the need to belong, to be perceived as a man within my social group and culture, I reproduced the stereotypes demanded of me and created/formed a violent and womanizing persona that I was moved to revisit while I read farewell cards that I received when I left middle school.

> "[…] I hope you get more chicks. P.S1 = you're a player/P.S2 = you're a scoundrel". "You're a crazy drunk and half fag, I'm joking. You're so cool". "You talked me into getting the most wasted I have ever been in my life". "You're a big slacker, but very cool, so charming and bad-ass, I'm joking, and you know how to make friends […]". I hope your dreams come true, maybe you'll be a famous singer or quit smoking. It causes lung cancer". "[…] I wish you a lot of success with music and that you overcome your vices (you know what I'm talking about)."

Women belong to men. In this account, the objectification of the other takes shape, not only as a need to belong, but to own the other, to establish ownership: private property. On the other hand, to own a woman, as an unconscious object/private thing, supports the macho stereotype of men in my culture. The fight with Alan in my story seems to be a clear example of this stereotype erupting in violence in school: "He says he doesn't want you around Emma." In my later experiences, this has been repeated frequently when a female friend's boyfriend sees her as property, watching her, wanting us to end our friendship. Unfortunately, sometimes they have succeeded.

From all of this, it cannot be assumed that jealousy satisfactorily explains the assumptions of private property, within which the anguish experienced through losing someone we love is quite clear. Nor can we be certain that this is unique to machismo in my society or to men and the way they behave. What is unique about this jealousy is reflected in the statement that "women belong to men" is found in the power relationship and the ways of expressing this jealousy. I'm afraid to lose you so I forbid you – or manipulate the explanation to convince you – from seeing him or from others seeing you.

This covetous behaviour is not the only example. Cindy's questions were justified using this same statement, but in a different way.

Cindy made a camouflaged and cautious pass at me, in a way that departed from her role as a woman and that shouldn't have strayed from the way things are done. "Women should wait and men should pursue" is a form of machismo in our society that sees women as passive, submissive, and waiting for men's wishes. Her caution was not unwarranted. There was a real danger of being seen as "easy" if she didn't follow this practice, that is to say, being seen as a girl that isn't worth having. I assert that this behaviour stems from the same need to belong that I was experiencing, to be considered a woman in terms of her culture. In my society, you often hear expressions for controlling this behaviour and reproducing the women's roles and stereotypes, "She's a whore," "bitch," "slut." In contrast, for me as a man to be a "scoundrel" and a "charmer" that "gets girls/chicks" are qualities to be admired by my friends.

Finally, it is under this same expression of private property, of the objectification of women, which at first dictated that I couldn't see Cindy as someone I liked. As an internalized rule, she was someone else's possession. She was my cousin's ex-girlfriend. To be the ex didn't necessarily mean that you were no longer the other person's property as, later on, an ex-friend of mine made it clear when he strongly asserted, "You cannot date my ex-girlfriends."

Adults have the last word. Esteban's mother telling me "No one is going to believe you!" echoes in my head while I try to identify the role of adults relative to teenagers. The sexual harassment I experienced is important, not only as part of the relationships that emerged from my fight with Alan, including my friendship with Esteban , but rather because it is impossible to understand school violence isolated from the broader social context, in this case, adult-youth relationships

The fear that this constant harassment caused, the many moments in which I felt helpless, without the strength to save myself from her caresses and attempts to kiss me, resurface with the phrase: "No one is going to believe you!" which expresses quite clearly the place in the world of adults commonly occupied by teenagers: Teenage arguments are not reliable. Their concerns and suffering "are teenage things," that is to say, transient, and as such should not be taken so seriously.

Where are the adults in school in my story? Cindy's teacher saw our kisses and embraces as "teenage things" that she should put a stop to, according to school rules and the moral values of my culture, without noticing the harmony and comfort being experienced at that moment. My teacher, who arrived late to class, could not have known about the harassment from my classmates, and the urgency to maintain silence was perhaps only in terms of managing student behaviour for the purpose of class. Cindy's teacher asked for the same thing when I went to ask Cindy to be my girlfriend. The P. E. teacher and the counsellor, in the same way, saw my fight with Alan as "teenage things" without putting too much effort into understanding and resolving the conflict. The given solution correlated with the rules imposed on teenagers like us.

It could also be, as I touch on in the following point about the problems that we must acknowledge and address, that the teachers preferred to stay out of our issues and let us fix our "teenage things." In any case, they have the final word in their classroom, in school, and at home. That final word has long been "maintain quiet" and punish those who deviate from the rules.

Silence is not commonly studied in schools. For adults, silence in school represents order and takes a huge effort resulting, in some cases, in more than 30% of classroom time to achieve, maintain, and restore this silent order (Vasquez-Bronfman & Martinez, 1996).

Silence as a theme refers to another important "skill" to teach, the ability to listen. The student is not usually encouraged to listen to others, just, in fact, to the teacher. It is not due to the need to listen to each other and discuss what's happening, but rather because of the student's obligation to pay attention to the teacher, what Freire (1970) described as banking education. The teacher is the keeper of the last word and of knowledge, and the students in turn receive this knowledge passively and acceptingly, in silence.

2. Schooling as Synonymous with the Acquisition of Intellectual
and Work-Related Talents is Disconnected from Existing
Emotions in Social Relationships

I started teaching classes at the high school level just after finishing my degree. In staff meetings I heard teachers again and again try to justify this disassociation between standardized education and students' emotional needs:

> "I can't teach class and worry about students' problems at the same time."
> "I try to keep my distance when they approach me to tell me something. I don't want to get involved in legal or parental problems." "We're in charge of their education. We're not their psychologists."

These justifications place us in an employee-employer relationship, as worker bees in an educational factory that in turn produces future workers, where one should dedicate oneself exclusively to the process for which we are paid: that students learn to do what the program dictates.

The curriculum focuses on acquiring knowledge and skills and not on the needs of young people. It reproduces injustice in our society, and incorporates a hidden curriculum (McLaren, 2005). This is based on a stereotypical image of teenagers, rebellious, impulsive, unaccomplished, immoral, at risk, etc., and is couched in terms of what they should become in an idealized and pre-designed future. It negates their immediate, daily present. It's a curriculum that distrusts their ability to make decisions, that decides for them what they need to know and who they need to be.

Faced with this obstacle against deciding about their future, it doesn't seem strange that, having the opportunity, they switch roles from the oppressed to the oppressor, something that Freire (1970) observed long ago in his literacy work. We can think about bullying as an example of these oppressive relationships, as part of their daily interactions not necessarily only between adolescents but as internalized cultural norms, and as the reproduction of the established social order. This does not exhaust the explanation, rather it compounds it, but we could also go beyond psychological explanations that assume that the aggressor is a deviant person with "intellectual-emotional disorders" and the person being bullied is someone with learned helplessness. Injustice spawns frustration, resentment, hatred, and a natural need to overcome and transcend it.

Finally, social relationships are emotionally charged, not just for adolescents but also for adults as we interact with them. Education in schools, that we believe will be significant and will transcend the classroom as well as institutional barriers, cannot be restricted to intellectual pursuits. Learning that transcends lives in the exchange between individuals, between the satisfaction of being for and with others, and in the frustration of not being so, in a dialog for building realities. As such, meaningful education that seeks to facilitate this cannot distance itself from the love that we feel toward others and with which we create our sense of being. It should be liberating.

> Founding itself upon love, humility, and faith, dialogue becomes a horizontal relationship of which mutual trust between the dialoguers is the logical consequence. [...] Conversely, such trust is obviously absent in the anti-dialogics of the banking method of education. (Freire, 1970, p. 91)

Educators who love the work they do must also develop love for those with whom we construct learning, our students who in turn teach us. Why are we afraid to acknowledge our love for our students and the satisfaction that we feel in witnessing their development? Perhaps it is the same fear that I feel in writing this, fear of vulnerability, of being hurt. Perhaps it is anxiety over not being in control, of casting doubt on my knowledge as a teacher and an adult. Who is the teenager we think we know? Why are we so afraid of them creating their own pathway? What hinders our capacity to establish an open dialogue with them?

NOTES

[1] I use "believe" with the same need to demystify research. I argue that what is investigated, and even more so, the decisions made throughout about how to research our theme is fundamentally independent of the assumptions, prejudices, and beliefs about the world in which we live. I dispute the possibility of being neutral or of rejecting our beliefs for the sake of research, and I acknowledge that in the end, what we do is hide or take for granted that our position is legitimate and/or universal. This, on the other hand, does not mean that said assumptions, prejudices, and beliefs can't be re-expressed and/ or modified when articulated and are in contrast with other beliefs and points of view, not with a far-away reality beyond our perception.

[2] Imanol is the name of a character played by Mexican comedian Hector Suarez on the show "La Otra Cosa," which was shown on Mexican television from 1995-1997. It's the parody of a gay waiter with long, unruly hair who serves customers complaining of foreign objects in their food, such as flies or hair. Watch minute 5:27 of the video: https://www.youtube.com/watch?v=QAoQ0C9-2Qs

[3] This comes from the word for the apron used at home to protect your clothes from dust and cooking stains. "Mandilón" is used to refer to men that do household work that is typically carried out by females, and even more so, it is used as a crack at men who do what their female partner asks, and not vice versa, I should add.

[4] In 1997 the movie The Craft (1996) played in Mexico, retitled Young Witches, that tells the story of four teenage girls who acquire supernatural powers from charms and rituals that they practiced in secret. The main character is protected from attack from her friends by magical powers inherited from her mother. http://es.wikipedia.org/wiki/The_Craft_(pelicula)

[5] To hit someone with force, in general causing injury. It is interesting that this word entomologically comes from the word mother. http://enciclopedia_universal.esacademic.com.

[6] This word is used disparagingly to refer to someone who is intellectually delayed or is a slow learner.

[7] In Mexico there are celebrations every weekend in December before Christmas where traditional food is served – fruit punch usually with tequila, mescal, or brandy added, tamales and buñuelos (a traditional fried dough ball usually with a topping or filling), and piñatas. The tradition represents the passage of Joseph and Mary as they went door to door seeking shelter before the birth of Jesus.

[8] In recent years, the country's educational programs were developed under a skill-centered approach that places emphasis on students' abilities to solve daily problems, based on the knowledge acquired and built in the classroom.

REFERENCES/BIBLIOGRAPHY

Berger, P., & Luckmann, T. (1972). *La construcción social de la realidad.* Buenos Aires, Argentina: Amorrortu.

Bourdieu, P., Passeron, J. C., Melendres, J., & Subirats, M. (1981). *La reproducción: Elementos para una teoría del sistema de enseñanza.* Barcelona, Spain: Laia.

Freire, P. (1970). *Pedagogía del oprimido* (2nd ed.). Madrid, Spain: Siglo XXI.

Galtung, J. (2003). *Violencia cultural.* Guernika-Lumo. Gernika Gogoratuz No.14.

Goodall, H. L. (2008). *Writing qualitative inquiry: Self, stories, and academic life.* Walnut Creek, CA: Left Coast.

Kincheloe J. L. (2008). La pedagogía crítica en el siglo XXI: Evolucionar para sobrevivir. In P. Mclaren & J. L. Kincheloe (Eds.), *Pedagogía crítica: De qué hablamos, dónde estamos* (pp. 25–69). Barcelona, Spain: Graó.

Mclaren, P. (1980). *Cries from the corridor.* Toronto, Canada: Methuen.

Mclaren, P. (2005). *La vida en las escuelas: Una introducción a la pedagogía crítica en los fundamentos de la educación* (2nd ed.). México: Siglo XXI.

Olweus, D. (1978). *Aggression in the schools: Bullies and whipping boys.* Washington, DC: Hemisphere.

Tajfel, H., & Turner, J. C. (1979). An integrative theory of intergroup conflict. In W. G. Austin & S. Worchel (Eds.), *The social psychology of intergroup relations* (pp. 33–47). Monterey, CA: Brooks-Cole.

Vásquez-Bronfman, A., & Martínez, I. (1996). *La socialización en la escuela: Una perspectiva etnográfica.* Papeles De Pedagogía (1st ed.), Barcelona, Spain: Paidos.

David Castillo-Arceo
Centro de Ciencias Sociales y Humanidades
Universidad Autónoma de Aguascalientes
Aguascalientes, Aguascalientes, México

GRESILDA A. TILLEY-LUBBS

4. GOOD INTENTIONS PAVE THE ROAD TO HIERARCHY[1]

A Retrospective Autoethnographic Approach

ABSTRACT

I explore certain complexities of partnering university students with members of the Mexican and Honduran immigrant community[2] through service-learning. I reveal how my "good intentions" inadvertently created social hierarchy and deficit notions of the community, establishing the students as "haves" and community members as "have-nots." Critically examining my practices, I reflect on the service-learning instructor's role in fostering reciprocal relationships based on non-hierarchical constructs when bringing seemingly disparate groups together in service-learning partnerships.

***

In the body of literature that situates service-learning within social justice or critical pedagogy, researchers and practitioners have written about the role service-learning plays in students' journeys from privileged, dominant culture backgrounds to an understanding of the lives people lead in non-dominant communities (Arries, 1999; Camacho, 2004; Dunlap, Scroggin, Green, & Davi, 2007; Kiely, 2004, 2005; Mitchell, 2008; Pompa, 2002; Rockquemore & Schaffer, 2000). Researchers have also tackled the thorny topic of service-learning's role in reinforcing students' hierarchical perceptions and attitudes toward non-dominant partner communities (Boyle-Baise & Kilbane, 2000; Eby, 1998; Morton, 1995; Pompa). Furthermore, with critical service-learning students examine social constructs that create inequalities while encouraging them to accept responsibility for implementing social justice-oriented change (Mitchell, 2008). However, I suggest that similar critical examination of faculty's own practices as service-learning practitioners is equally important, so as to constantly monitor our own attitudes and behaviours, which students and community participants may regard as models for their own interactions.

Therefore, in this chapter I document my own transformative journey, exploring my role as the instructor of an academic course for Spanish and education students, Crossing the Border through Service-Learning (CTB). As the person who designed

G. A. Tilley-Lubbs & S. B. Calva (Eds.), Re-Telling Our Stories, 51–67.

and implemented the course that brought students in contact with a hitherto unfamiliar population, I realized I was unconsciously creating social hierarchy and patronization through a workday each semester when university students delivered material goods to partner families while meeting each other for the first time. My situation was particularly perilous since I had gained insider-outsider status in the immigrant community by collaborating and serving in various capacities for more than 30 years, always secure in the assumption I had "figured out" my role in the Spanish-speaking community, with the accompanying supposition that my actions were good for all concerned, students and families alike.

BACKGROUND

I initially designed CTB to partner university students with immigrant women for whom I had been serving as interpreter at prenatal and family planning clinics at the Health Department for two and a half years. I often spent hours with the women in clinic waiting rooms, and we had become friends. Consequently, they began to request my aid as a cultural mediator and interpreter in other venues, often asking if I knew where they could obtain clothing and furniture for themselves and for other family members immigrating to join them. I continually solicited items from my university colleagues, church members, and various friends and acquaintances to honour their requests for assistance.

Because time did not permit me to keep up with their requests for assistance, I decided to involve my Spanish students in the endeavour, responding to their interest in meeting and interacting with the families about whom I spoke in class. CTB resulted, offering a setting for reciprocal opportunities for the women to learn to speak English and navigate in a new culture, and for students to practice spoken Spanish and experience Mexican and Honduran cultures.

In addition to their academic readings, class discussions, and journaling about Spanish-speaking immigrants in the United States, the students spent 50 hours per semester in the home of partner families. During their time with the families, the students concentrated on helping the women develop the ability to navigate in a new culture. They practiced English with the family, tutored school-age children, made phone calls to obtain information or appointments, provided transportation, interpreted when sufficiently proficient, and generally responded to requests made by families. In turn, the families enjoyed helping students practice Spanish and learn their customs, often over a meal or while watching television. This simplistic view of reciprocity initially guided the course as I followed a path inspired by my own belief in the values of community service and cross-cultural relationships (Tilley-Lubbs, 2003a, 2007).

Early in the morning on the second Saturday of each semester, the students arrived at my garage to sort mounds of donated clothing and furniture to deliver to their partner families. Each student received the names, ages, and sizes of partner family members so they could choose items they deemed appropriate and suitable. Once everything was bagged and ready to go, we loaded cars, vans, and trucks for our cross-city trek to the families' homes. Because all the readings and class discussions up to this point focused on social justice issues in service-learning, I felt the students were well prepared for this experience.

However, regardless of the thoroughness of the foundational readings and my preparation of the students, Othering still seemed to occur as a result of the workday (Fine, 1998). In fall 2002, the semester that serves as the context for this chapter, in the class following the workday, student criticism raised questions regarding the appropriateness of "cramming a bunch of university students" into people's private spaces. From then on, my growing unease about the event caused me to critically examine the workday in terms of the social hierarchy I suspected I was unintentionally creating.

LITERATURE INFORMING THE COURSE

In CTB, service-learning defines a method/pedagogy that joins three concepts: community action and academic knowledge, with deep reflection on the intersection of the two (Eyler, Giles, & Schmeide, 1996). In planning the course, Dewey's work (1929/1997) echoed my belief in experiential learning as an integral component of education. Similarly, Freire's (1970) concept of emancipatory education resonated with my desire to co-create educational opportunities with/for Mexican and Honduran community women while facilitating an understanding of the power of praxis for students. Exploring funds of knowledge residing in the homes of Spanish-speaking families (González, Moll, Tenery, Rivera, Rendon, González et al., 1995; Greenberg & Moll, 1990) also informed the students' so as to challenge deficit notions regarding non-dominant groups.

Noddings' (1999) work on caring and competence underlined a class discussion on the virtues of caring. Eby's (1998) and Morton's implied (1999) cautions about service-learning and Nava's (1998) heartfelt portrayal of the pain of receiving charity also contributed to the foundational understanding of service-learning as opposed to volunteerism or community service. In all, I mindfully chose readings for the early weeks to facilitate an understanding of service-learning in the community.

GUIDING PERSPECTIVES

Feminist poststructuralism refers to "renewed interest in writing a critical history that emphasizes diacronic (changing over time) analyses; on mutation, transformation, and discontinuity of structures" (Peters & Burbules, 2004, p. 24), providing "critiques and methods for examining the functions and effects of any structure or grid of regularity that we put into place" (St. Pierre & Pillow, 2000, p. 6). Implicit in any structure are power issues that reach "into the very grain of individuals, touches their bodies, and inserts itself into their actions and attitudes, their discourses, learning processes and everyday lives" (Foucault, 1980, p. 39). To reflect on these power issues, I use self-reflexivity, basing my authority on my own engagement with the class and the community, a view consistent with Lather's (1991) situating of self as "a first-world woman—white, middle-class, North American, heterosexual—my self-described positionality" (p. xix). Nonetheless, I realize that my position of power and privilege in society by no means provides answers (Kirsch, 1999) in regard to working with families from traditionally non-dominant communities, particularly as I weave the families into partnerships with university students.

Critical theory also provides a lens for examining the asymmetrical power structures inherent in any program involving university students in a non-dominant community (Camacho, 2004; Darder, 1991). From the perspective of critical theory, critical consciousness frames my examination of practice (Freire, 1970). Furthermore, critical pedagogy informed the class that provided the context for this autoethnography, recognizing the importance of "the social, cultural, and political in shaping human identity" (Kincheloe, 2005, p. 6).

ANALYTICAL PROCESS

I teach at a Land Grant Research I University, and although the students I teach represent a variety of socioeconomic backgrounds, their university attendance usually reflects a more privileged economic situation than most partner families enjoy since the latters' socioeconomic situations make them eligible for public prenatal and family planning healthcare. From the outset I sought to establish a space where two seemingly disparate groups of people could relate to each other through their shared humanity, rather than simply as representatives of different socioeconomic, ethnic, educational, or linguistic backgrounds. I acknowledge the perils involved in such a "colour-blind" approach, but at the time it made sense to me, and my initial qualitative research provided evidence that students and families do come together and develop relationships of varying depths that cross, or at least straddle, these barriers (Tilley-Lubbs, 2003a, 2003b, 2007).

Nonetheless, the initial data analysis suggested a need for re-examining the practices of the workday. I reread student journals, and I reanalysed countless hours of informal time spent in the company of the students and families as recorded in my field notes. Actual words are quoted from the journals of two students who questioned the workday and from my personal journals[3] regarding the workday *conscientização* and student reactions to the event. That semester [conscientization] (Freire, 1970) began, causing me to question my established practice.

The self-reflexivity that guided this chapter allows me to "be known and seen by others, …to open up the possibility of learning more about [my] topic, and [myself], and in greater depth" (Etherington, 2004, p. 25). Through self-reflexivity, I can reflect on and become more fully conscious of my own "ideology, create a "dynamic process *and* of interaction within *and* culture, and politics," going beyond self-awareness to between…[myself] … the data that inform decisions, actions and interpretations," addressing "ethical issues and power relations" (p. 36) between myself and the participants in the class and the community. I could step away and "reflect on [my] actions through the eyes of the 'other's" actions (Rhoads, 2003, p. 239), acknowledging "response data" from participants who forced me to "significantly reconstruct [my] interpretation" of my actions as I engaged in the process (St. Pierre, 1997, p. 184). In a text informed by "deconstructive reflexivity," I am able to be confessional and critical of my own actions in interacting with a university class and an immigrant community (Denzin, 2003, p. 236). My commitment to using a critical lens to examine my practice intersects with my commitment to develop a theory of praxis "guided by critical refection and … revolutionary praxis" (McClaren, 1997, p. 170), informed by my "positionality as both [subject] and [object] of the gaze" (p. 149) of critical self-reflexivity.

Similarly, autoethnography presents "research, writing, story, and method that connect the autobiographical and personal to the cultural, social, and political" (Ellis, 2004, xix). I examine my perspectives on working in non-dominant populations through the lens of the world that shaped me, but at the same time, I present a meta-ethnography that revisits my original critical analysis of practice (Tilley-Lubbs, 2003b), allowing me to alter the frame in which I wrote the original story, ask questions I didn't ask then, consider others' responses to the original story, and include vignettes of related experiences that happened since I wrote the story and now affect the way I look back at the story (Ellis, 2009, p. 13). I first addressed the issue of the workday in my dissertation (Tilley-Lubbs, 2003b), but in this chapter I reconsider the event six years later, viewing the experience through the lens of my current perspectives about power and privilege.

EARLY TIMES

Where to park? As I followed my husband who was manoeuvring the Ryder moving van, I clutched the steering wheel and hoped for the best. All the cars following behind cautiously edged their way past the numerous cars and trucks in the parking lot. There were some 20 of us, so many of the students had to park out in the street. It was a warm September

Saturday afternoon, so there were people outside milling around, creating a vibrant atmosphere. We finally managed to park and get out of all the vehicles to make our way to the families we had come to visit for the workday.

When we arrived at Isabel's[4] we had to wait outside while she finished negotiating with the vendor parked outside her apartment. He had backed his truck up to the sidewalk, and the pop-top was open, showing neatly arranged shelves filled with brightly coloured vegetables and boxes of Mexican food. Yaneth was hopping around licking a sucker, stopping only long enough to run up and hug me.

After a brief wait, we went inside, some twenty students crowding into the one-bedroom apartment. The minute I sat down on the couch, Isabel said, "Permiso," [Excuse me.] and disappeared into the bedroom. She returned with a bag of papers, and within ten minutes, as the students stood observing, we had glanced at all the school papers and the doctor bills.... I was finally able to break into the litany of requests for help interpreting the stacks of papers to introduce Isabel to Kathy, the student who would be her partner for the semester. Each nervously uttered greetings, and as I moved away, they began their negotiations for their weekly meetings. By the time we left, they were excitedly making plans for Kathy's twice-a-week trip to Roanoke. (Journal, fall 2002)

I present this excerpt from my journal about a typical workday to aid in understanding the situation and mind-set that guided my work at the time, to provide a baseline for the rest of the story. Looking back at this vignette, I am aware of the implicit social hierarchy being established, but at the time I wrote this, my only concerns focused on responding to perceived community needs and providing an opportunity for everyone to meet. I enacted historian Wise's (1980) words: "[A]n ironic situation occurs when the consequences of an act are diametrically opposed to the original intention," and "when the fundamental cause of the disparity lies in the actor himself, and his original purpose" (p. 300).

HOW IT ALL STARTED

From the inception of the workday to the student interrogation of the practice, it never occurred to me that I was creating a hierarchical situation between two groups of people whose life circumstances and socioeconomic status differed significantly. I was just doing what I had always done, trying to respond to people who asked for help of any kind. The only difference was my inclusion of students and families in the process.

Up to that time in my life, my way of being in and serving the world included beneficent acts in response to requests from the community. Inadvertently, through my sense of empathy, I converted my sense of caring into perceiving need among the families, subconsciously developing a deficit notion about the families. In so doing, I failed to appreciate their demonstrations of strength as evidenced by their ability to cope adequately and independently in a new and often alien society (Nieto & Bode, 2008). In other words, I was practicing kindness propelled by emotions and a sense of service (Morton, 1999), completely oblivious to the ramifications of my actions in regard to students' interpretations of the event:

The service-learning workday has already helped me on my journey to understanding the impact of the little things that people can do to help others. By simply donating clothes, shoes, and household items, we were able to brighten several families' lives. From house to house I learned the real need for our services. Each household had different needs and wants from the students, but they all needed our guidance. (Tina, September 2002)

At the time I read this reflection, I focused on her empathy, but in rereading the words through the deconstructive lens of conscientização (Freire, 1970), her word choices epitomized Eby's (1998) cautions about service-learning. A young university student placed herself as a role model providing "guidance" to adult parents responsible for their families' livelihood, demonstrating her deficit notion regarding non-dominant groups.

This journal, which I posted to the class listserv, represents my thinking at the time:

As several of you pointed out, we are very different from the Lions Club[4] described by Michael Nava (1998) in *Charity*. The most important difference in my opinion is that I know and love each and every one of the folks we work with, and they know that. They know also that the students who work with them come to have a similar feeling about them, and they respond in kind. We are not simply buying anonymous gifts for anonymous people; we are sharing the bounty of our world with those whose material blessings are fewer than ours. Every item of clothing that was selected yesterday had a face or name behind it. Our gifts were for persons, for individuals. (Journal, fall 2002)

My discomfort lies not only in my patronizing attitudes, but also in the knowledge that my attitudes shaped the thinking of groups of students and community members, my tone of beneficent charity attempting to justify behaviour about which I already felt uneasy. I include this embarrassing passage because I suspect I am not alone in having reacted this way as a service-learning instructor shaped by a life of service in the community.

STUDENT UPRISING

I was not prepared for the class discussion that ensued following the actual workday as students questioned their own feelings and those of the families we visited, to say nothing of my role in facilitating the event. Some expressed discomfort at our middle class co-opting of another's space and privacy. Liz referred to "dragging a huge group of university students to people's apartments," which Bill called "tourism of the marginalized." Liz said, "How would you feel if a big ole Ryder moving van pulled up to your apartment and then a bunch of students swarmed out and crowded into your apartment to stare at you like animals in the zoo?" She also stated that she felt quite uncomfortable with my picture taking as if the families were exhibits. I never had thought along those lines; I simply wanted to create archives for the class.

The entire three-hour class was fuelled by conversation about the workday, charity, and the true meaning of service-learning. I felt defensive and irritated, defending my actions by stating that the families still needed help getting established and the workday provided the opportunity to deliver clothing and furniture people continued to give me. However, the two most vocal objectors did not buy my explanations. Truth be told, at the time, I was not acknowledging, even to myself, that it also provided an opportunity for me to empty my garage of the mountains of goods people constantly donated, probably also taking advantage of the opportunity to clean out their own closets, drawers, houses.

For the first time class members critically questioned my practices, and the ensuing discussion was heated and controversial. As the conversation swirled around me, I observed the class, watching the varied emotions and opinions. Thinking I had it figured out, I explained to them that although I am an only child, I grew up in a large extended family that constantly passed clothes around depending on each person's current size or needs. I felt so close to the local families that sharing with them was simply an extension of what I have always done. Whoever had more shared with the one who needed help, but I failed to see that my family did not include a great variation in social or economic status, and that our clothing exchanges tended to be reciprocal, vastly different from the dynamics of a large group of students taking clothes and furniture to newly immigrated families whom they were meeting for the first time, creating structures of power and privilege that would extend throughout the semester. I felt as if I had been pushed into a "disturbingly vulnerable place where I was forced to confront my ineptitude" (Vacarr, 2001, p. 286). Unlike Vacarr, however, I was unable to move away from my disequilibrium to create a teaching moment. I allowed my annoyance to prevent my revealing my humanity that framed an error in my judgment. I opted instead to maintain the "all-powerful Super Teacher" (p. 290) stance. Up to this time, I had resided comfortably in my position of power and privilege, believing that if I chose to ignore their existence, I could create an environment in which the societal constructs of race, class, and other hierarchical concepts could be blurred by my "goodness." At that point, I subconsciously began to confront my motives, but I chose to remain cloaked in denial and irritation, unable to acknowledge the situation I had created. Fortunately, I had created a class that encouraged questioning, even if I had not intended to be the object of the questions.

My journal from the following week demonstrates change taking place in my thinking:

> In a way, the workday is a powerful agent in providing a means of taking the first steps toward erasing Otherness by allowing the students and the families to meet each other, but at the same time, it is a day fraught with the danger of embedding Otherness in the students' and the families' consciousness/ subconsciousness. (Fall 2002)

I was accustomed to reading journals submitted by students who, charged with explaining their reasons for taking the class, wrote about wanting to "help people out" or to "help the less fortunate," familiar phrases that frame the altruism of the middle class. However, that class shook my beliefs about the rightness of the workday as students critically evaluated the practice. I describe the experience as the critical point of *conscientização* (Freire, 1970) that first caused me to feel self-doubt about the practice.

Up to that point, my vision included facilitating a class to foster change within students, causing them to become agents of change in society. I never once considered they could serve as agents of change for me through what I perceived at the time to be probing, hurtful criticisms and accusations directed toward me. My idealistic notion saw the students as:

[L]eaven in the evolution of a critical mass of those who, whatever their profession or status in society, will have the compassion, conscience, and competence to act in solidarity with the poor and most neglected members of society as critically thinking agents of change committed to the fashioning of a more humane and just world (Wood, 1998, p. 192)

Nonetheless, when the students acted in unconscious solidarity with the community by questioning my practices, my knee-jerk reaction was irritation and defensiveness. The journal entries for the week reflected student protests, but because I read them wearing blinders of caring (Noddings, 1999) about/for the community, I did not hear the student voices until I reanalysed the journals.

The following spring, I defended my dissertation based on research conducted in fall 2002. Two committee members knew reaction papers I wrote for their courses indicating that through CTB I sought to provide an environment that would foster reciprocal relationships between university students and community members. When one committee member asked, "Kris, do you realize that you are setting up a situation in which all the participants involved will perceive the students as the 'haves' and the community members as the 'have-nots' of society?", I was so shocked that I could not reply. I knew she was correct; she confirmed what the students had said and I had ignored.

Although I passed the defence, I spent weeks reading social justice literature and critically examining both my practice and theoretical framework prior to publishing the research on the university's electronic dissertation library (http://www.lib.vt.edu/find/etds.php). After that semester, I continued the workdays for two more semesters, before finally conceding that the practice reflected theory inconsistent with my beliefs about hierarchy (Boyle-Baise & Kilbane, 2000; Camacho, 2004; Eby, 1998; Morton, 1995; Pompa, 2002; Ransford, 2000).

GAINING AN UNDERSTANDING

As my academic life continued, I became consumed with other concerns, but the issue of the workday stayed in my mind as a bothersome topic I needed to address honestly and openly at some point, if for no other reason than my certainty that I was not the only service-learning practitioner whose practices were inconsistent with her beliefs. As I reflected on the world I grew up in, I realized I am the product of a paternalistic, hierarchical society that socialized me to believe in altruistic behaviour (Wildman & Davis, 2000). As a member of the dominant culture, I am often unable to recognize my privilege. By unintentional actions with good intentions, I have the ability to perform hurtful acts, and I questioned whether that was the case with the workdays.

Eby (1998) posits that although service-learning is a transformative pedagogy that helps students develop social responsibility toward the community, a lack of understanding about underlying societal situations may leave students with the impression that need exists in a marginalized community, and that they can "fix" the need by their presence or "help." According to Eby, such simplistic views of social problems lead to an emphasis on deficiencies in the community, rather than fostering appreciation for their strengths. Although I agreed with Eby's arguments, only after I began to question my practices did I completely understand his concerns regarding involving students in a non-dominant community.

The irony of this narrative is that the continuum of my transformational journey was precipitated by student questioning, a journey that changed me from enacting a deficit notion of the community, which I in turn implicitly had been communicating to the students.

Similarly, in designing a course in which members of a non-dominant community serve as text, teachers, students, and collaborators for a course whose mission espouses a social justice precept, my responsibility lay in facilitating relationships that would not reinforce existing societal constructs based on inequity and Othering. However, "random, individual acts of kindness" underscored my practice as I worked from "emotional response and not [my] head" (Morton, 1999). While pushing students to deeply examine societal practices that caused immigrants to live in marginalized circumstances, I interposed my own previous acts of random kindness, described by some of my colleagues in my department as my "missionary zeal," as a model for the relationships which would frame the CTB experience. Rather than fostering reciprocity through shared language and culture, I created a deficit notion regarding the community.

The patriarchal society in which I grew up promotes charitable acts as beneficent and virtuous. I am a member of a church that considers service to humankind to be of the highest calling, whether in manual labour to build a house through Habitat for Humanity or in donations to Heifer Project.

International. My code for moral behaviour is similar to Kant's moral philosophy that extolled a life seeking how to comply with my ethical obligations, precipitated by the question: "What ought I to do?" (Johnson, 2004, p. 1). Perhaps Lamott (2005) best sums up the guiding principle that has framed my life for as long as I can remember: "You do what you can, what good people have always done: you bring thirsty people water, you share your food, you try to help the homeless find shelter, you stand up for the underdog" (pp. 307–308). However, CTB indicated the first time I included students and families in my efforts and beliefs.

I grew up in an environment probably typical of a generation of baby-boomers who were affected by Martin Luther King's "I Have a Dream" speech in 1963. We joined hands in sisterhood and solidarity. I was appalled to recognize that my entire perspective about the world and the workdays contributed to the oppressive behaviour I abhor. I was blatantly exercising my White privilege to create invisible racism (Tatum, 2000) and classism (Ransford, 2000). At this time of self-searching, Behar's (1996) voice also resonated with my discomfort as she talked about the vulnerability of the researcher placing herself in the research. I felt I could not leave out this revelation of my own transformation and remain true to the beliefs that shape who I am, not only as a researcher, but also as a person.

THE CONUNDRUM

Nonetheless, just as I was contemplating letting my friends and church family know that I could not accept any more items for the families, I received a call from Aracely, who had been in the program for the first three semesters, letting me know she had returned from Mexico after a year and a half back home with her family, and she had no clothes or furniture. Could I help her? Once again, the van and pickup truck made their way across town to deliver the clothes and furniture stored in my garage, this time with the assistance of my family and one student whom I called to ask if he could bring his pickup truck to help with the delivery. That occasion represented the final large delivery we made, either through the class or personally.

Even today the need still exists for sharing or charity or serving or whatever else we want to call this complex concept, although it has a different shape than it had when CTB began. Many of the families with whom we collaborate have become fairly well established and do not suffer from the desperate need that shaped their lives when they first immigrated. Needs continue to exist with increasing frequency, mirroring the economic downturn the world is experiencing. The conundrum is how to address appeals from people who have fewer financial resources and subsequent needs. A recent phone call made me realize anew the imponderability of the situation, causing the end of the story to touch the beginning.

Marta called to check on me, beginning with her usual, *"Quería escuchar su voz."* [I wanted to hear your voice.] Her husband quit his job at a local dairy, tired of constant abuse from the owner, but he continues to face great difficulty finding constant, consistent work in construction, a reflection of the general economy. I knew they had moved in the spring from the trailer provided by the dairy into a small house in a nearby town, and I had accepted her excuse of the move for terminating her relationship with the CTB students who visited her weekly. Not until we talked last week did she share that the reason she could no longer host the students was due to the fact that she had no food in the house to offer when they visited, a fact that embarrassed her greatly. Now they are feeling more secure, but their budget is still tight and she tentatively inquired if we could loan them some money. Her call was one of several, reflecting the recent lack of work many immigrants face.

61

IF I HAD KNOWN THEN …

Reflecting on these conversations, I am confronted anew by the proposition of how to provide assistance without deepening the divide of the "haves" and the "have-nots" of society. On a personal level, I continue to operate from the point of view Behar (1993) described in talking about her dealings with Esperanza, a Mexican peasant whom Behar interviewed over a period of years: I remain honoured to serve as their *comadre* [friend who has more and thus can share].

By starting the placements with a workday, I was overtly, albeit unconsciously, establishing the students and myself as dominant members of society and the families as the marginalized. At the same time, I recognize that "[s]ervice-learning is a way of building relationships; not hierarchical relationships that are top-down, helper-helpee, but non-hierarchical relationships in the sense that each partner has something to gain and each has something to give" (Jackson & Smothers, 1998, p. 113). Additionally, I acknowledge that the "served [should] control the service[s] provided," thus making them "better able to serve and be served by their own actions" (Sigmon, 1979, p. 3). Keeping in mind these two basic precepts of service-learning, I seek creative ways to involve students with families in empathetic relationships that foster attitudes of concern for social justice and equity not based on deficient notions but rather on a realization of their responsibility to help people meet their basic needs (Eby, 1998). I intend to place more emphasis on the literature and class activities that deconstruct societal contexts that affect immigrants to promote an understanding of the economic hardship involved in immigration both in leaving the home country and in living in the host country as well as the discriminatory practices that restrain many immigrant lives, affecting their opportunities for earning a living wage.

When I receive random calls from people asking for help, I will devise ways to involve students personally in the process of reaching out to people in their moments of authentic need. If a time comes when economic necessity determines a need for re-establishing the wide scale distribution of food and clothes, I will abandon the role of trying to "fix" the situation single-handedly. I will invite students and women to come together and discuss the possibilities for identifying and addressing community needs. I play with the idea of returning to the Nava (1998) piece, having the students and women work together in small groups to read the story and deconstruct the impersonal charity that framed the event. I would suspect that by brainstorming together they might come up with solutions that would be far better than any I could devise. I can envision resulting reciprocity, which would then form the basis for critically thinking about ways for the families to address their needs. Through dialogue, the students should be able to recognize connections between the families' situations and the social contexts in which they are rooted as they move through the "cycle of theory, application, evaluation, reflection, and then back to theory" (Freire, 1998, p. 75) and thus into *conscientização*. The bottom line is the imperativeness of involving the women in the process of praxis to transform charity into collaboration.

THE AFTERMATH

After I discontinued the workday, some changes occurred. The students and families still needed an opportunity to meet prior to beginning their partnerships, so we began having a Meet and Greet as the third class meeting. These potluck social times took place in my church fellowship hall, providing neutral ground for two seemingly disparate groups of people to meet without automatic assumptions regarding power and privilege. Also, because the students no longer spend 8–10 hours on the workday, I cut the required hours back to 40. As more of the children began attending elementary school, the need for tutoring and homework help has increased, so the students tend to spend more time working with the children than with their former service-learning activities that focused on the women's needs for interpretation and social navigation. I now incorporate more literature about multicultural education, such as Nieto and Bode (2008), as we challenge the deficit notions that frame public schooling for immigrants.

In recent years, the women stepped into leadership roles with the students, constantly making suggestions about the partnerships, whether regarding scheduling, course content, or expectations for students. The women now lead busier lives that include jobs, church, children's school activities, and friends, so they determine their availability based on their convenience, rather than accepting whatever time the students suggest, as was the case in the beginning. Initially, the students and women did a final collaborative media project talking about the women's lives in their home countries, their immigration, and their lives in the United States. The women expressed boredom with repeating the story every semester, and they now determine a new topic each semester, choosing topics such as the difficulty of living in the United States and not speaking English. They also take responsibility for holding the students accountable for their commitments, informing me of any infractions they are unable to resolve. From the way the women speak and behave, I believe they perceive themselves to be stakeholders with a "voting voice" in the program. Their enacted freedom to direct their experiences reinforces my belief in the power of critical pedagogy to effect emancipatory attitudes and performances (Freire, 1997/2005; Kincheloe, 2008).

Would these changes have happened if the workdays had continued to place them in the role of recipients of charity? I don't know.

A WORD OF OPTIMISTIC CAUTION

In my exploration of the implications of placing university students in a traditionally non-dominant immigrant community, I reinforced my belief that such partnerships are rich and meaningful for most participants, but the instructor who chooses to engage an immigrant community in such a partnership needs to exercise extreme caution in regard to fostering Othering and reinforcing social hierarchy, concepts that are diametrically opposed to the precepts of service-learning (Jackson &

63

Smothers, 1998). The necessity of constantly including the community members in decisions and policy-shaping is imperative, which I do by meeting periodically with the women to seek their input about their goals regarding the program and how the students and I can best help them achieve those goals. As service-learning instructors practice critical examination from a variety of disciplines, pedagogical practices, methods, and theoretical frameworks, the challenge is to begin/continue to examine our efforts through the crucible of self-reflexivity. This critical examination of my practices seeks to engage in dialogue with other service-learning researchers and practitioners as we consistently interrogate our own practices.

ACKNOWLEDGEMENTS

I would like to thank the editor, Jeffrey Howard, and the three anonymous referees for their most helpful comments as well as Jennifer McCloud, who now serves as the graduate research assistant for the service-learning experience and who tirelessly reads my work and provides valuable insights as I critically examine my practice.

NOTES

[1] First published: Tilley-Lubbs, G. A. (2009b). Good intentions pave the way to hierarchy: A retrospective autoethnographic approach. *Michigan Journal of Community Service Learning, 16*(1), 59–68. Reprinted with permission.

[2] Although I refer to the Mexican and Honduran community, in actuality in the locale where my work is situated, the two groups do not often intersect. Nonetheless within the confines of CTB, the context of this chapter, the two groups do intersect and interact frequently. I avoid using "Latino" in an attempt to circumvent generalization and stereotyping of Spanish speakers who immigrate from south of our border. In addition, the women whom I interview as part of my research self-identify as Mexican or Honduran. In certain places, I do use the term "Latino" when quoting or referring to statements made by students. In this chapter, journal and field notes will be used interchangeably to refer to my personal writings.

[3] All names used in this chapter are pseudonyms to protect the participants' privacy.

[4] In preparation for the workday, the students read a memoir about being the recipient of the generic beneficence of the Lions Club at Christmas time when he was a young child whose family had recently emigrated from Cuba.

REFERENCES/BIBLIOGRAPHY

Arries, J. (1999). Critical pedagogy and service-learning in Spanish: Crossing borders in the freshman seminar. In J. Hellebrandt & L. T. Varona (Eds.), *Construyendo puentes (Building bridges): Concepts and models for service-learning in Spanish* (pp. 33–48). Washington, DC: American Association for Higher Education.

Behar, R. (1993). *Translated woman: Crossing the border with Esperanza's story.* Boston, MA: Beacon.

Boyle-Baise, M., & Kilbane, J. (2000). What really happens? A look inside service-learning for multicultural teacher education. *Michigan Journal of Community Service Learning, 7,* 54–64.

Camacho, M. M. (2004). Power and privilege: Community service-learning in Tijuana. *Michigan Journal of Community Service Learning, 10*(3), 31–42.

Darder, A. (1991). *Culture and power in the classroom: A critical foundation for bicultural education.* New York, NY: Greenwood.

Denzin, N. (2003). *Performance ethnography: Critical pedagogy and the politics of culture.* Thousand Oaks, CA: Sage.

Dewey, J. (1929/1997). My pedagogic creed. In D. J. Flinders & S. J. Thornton (Eds.), *The curriculum studies reader* (pp. 17–23). New York, NY: Routledge. (Reprinted from Journal of National Education Association, 18, 291–295, 1929.)

Dunlap, M., Scroggin, J., Green, P., & Davi, A. (2007). Michigan Journal of Community Service Learning, 13(2), 19–30.

Eby, J. W. (1998). *Why service-learning is bad.* Retrieved May 10, 2006, from http://www.messiah.edu/external_ programs/agape/service_learningarticles/wrongsvc.pdf

Ellis, C. (2004). *The ethnographic I: A methodological novel about teaching and doing autoethnography.* Walnut Creek, CA: AltaMira.

Ellis, C. (2009). *Revision: Autoethnographic reflections on life and work.* Walnut Creek, CA: Left Coast.

Etherington, K. (2004). *Becoming a reflexive researcher: Using our selves in research.* Philadelphia, PA: Jessica Kingsley.

Eyler, J., Giles, D., & Schmeide, A. (1996). *A practitioner's guide to reflection in service learning: Students' voices and reflection.* Nashville, TN: Vanderbilt University.

Fine, M. (1998). Working the hyphens: Reinventing self and other in qualitative research. In N. K. Denzin & Y. S. Lincoln (Eds.), *The landscape of qualitative research: Theories and issues* (pp. 130–155). Thousand Oaks, CA: Sage.

Foucault, J. (1980). *Power/Knowledge: Selected interviews and other writings.* Brighton, UK: Harvester.

Freire, P. (1970). *Pedagogy of the oppressed* (M. Bergman Ramos, Trans.). New York, NY: Continuum.

Freire, P. (1997/2005). *Teachers as cultural workers: Letters to those who dare to teach.* Cambridge, MA: Westview.

Freire, P. (1998). *Pedagogy of hope.* New York, NY: Continuum.

González, N., Moll, L., Tenery, M. F., Rivera,.A., Rendon, P., González, R., & Amanti, C. (1995). Funds of knowledge for teaching in Latino households. *Urban Education, 29*(4), 443–470.

Greenberg, J., & Moll, L. C. (1990). Creating zones of possibilities: Combining social contexts for instruction. In L. C. Moll, (Ed.), *Vygotsky and education: Instructional implications and applications of sociohistorical psychology* (pp. 319–348). Cambridge, UK: Cambridge University.

Jackson, S. A., & Smothers, T. L. (1998). The Southern Volunteer Corps at West Virginia Wesleyan. In J. L. DeVitis, R. W. Johns, & D. L. Simpson (Eds.), *The spirit of community in liberal education* (pp. 102–120). New York, NY: Peter Lang.

Johnson, R. N. (2004). Kant's moral philosophy. *Stanford Encyclopedia of Philosophy.* Retrieved November 7, 2007, from http://plato.stanford.edu/entries/kant-moral/

Kiely, R. (2004). A chameleon with a complex: Searching for transformation in international service-learning. *Michigan Journal of Community Service Learning, 10*(2), 5–20.

Kiely, R. (2005). A transformative learning model for service-learning: A longitudinal case study. *Michigan Journal of Community Service Learning, 12*(1), 5–22.

Kincheloe, J. (2005). Foreword. In L. D. Soto & B. B. Swadener (Eds.), *Power and voice in research with children* (pp. 1–6). New York, NY: Peter Lang.

Kincheloe, J. (2008). *Critical pedagogy* (2nd ed.). New York, NY: Peter Lang.

Kirsch, G. E. (1999). *Ethical dilemmas in feminist research: The politics of location, interpretation, and publication.* Albany, NY: State University of New York.

Lamott, A. (2005). *Plan B: Further thoughts on faith.* New York, NY: Riverhead.

Lather, P. (1991). *Getting smart: Feminist research and pedagogy with/in the postmodern.* New York, NY: Routledge.

McLaren, P. (1997). *Revolutionary multiculturalism: Pedagogies of dissent for the new millennium.* Boulder, CO: Westview.

Mitchell, T. D. (2008). Traditional vs. critical service learning: Engaging the literature to differentiate two models. *Michigan Journal of Community Service Learning, 14*(2), 50–65.

Morton, K. (1995). The irony of service: Charity, project and social change in service-learning. *Michigan Journal of Community Service Learning, 2*, 19–32.

Morton, K. (1999). *Starfish hurling and community service*. Retrieved July 5, 2008 from http://www.mncampus compact.org/

Nava, M. (1998). Charity. In E. Santiago & J. Davidow (Eds.), *Las Christmas* (pp. 51–58). New York, NY: Vintage.

Nieto, S., & Bode, P. (2008). *Affirming diversity: The sociopolitical context of multicultural education.* Boston, MA: Pearson, Allyn, & Bacon.

Noddings, N. (1999). Caring and competence. In G. A. Griffith (Ed.), *The education of teachers: Ninety-eighth yearbook of the national society for the study of education* (Part I) (pp. 205–220). Chicago, IL: University of Chicago.

Peters, M. A., & Burbules, N. C. (2004). *Poststructuralism and educational research.* New York, NY: Roman & Littlefield.

Pompa, L. (2002). Service-learning as crucible: Reflections on immersion, context, power, and transformation. *Michigan Journal of Community Service Learning, 9*(1), 67–76.

Ransford, M. E. (2000). Two hierarchies. In M. Adams, W. J. Blumenfeld, R. Castañeda, H. W. Hackman, M. L. Peters, & X. Zúñiga (Eds.), *Readings for social diversity and social justice: An anthology on racism, anti- Semitism, sexism, heterosexism, ableism, and classism* (pp. 412–418). New York, NY: Routledge.

Rhoads, R. (2003). Traversing the great divide: Writing the self into qualitative research and narrative. In N. K. Denzin (Ed.), *Studies in symbolic interactionism* (pp. 235–259). Boston, MA: Elsevier.

Rockquemore, K. A., & Schaffer, R. H. (2000). Toward a theory of engagement: A cognitive mapping of service learning experiences. *Michigan Journal of Community Service Learning, 7*, 14–25.

Sigmon, R. L. (1979). Service-learning: Three principles. *Synergist*, 9–10.

St. Pierre, E. A. (1997). Methodology in the fold and the irruption of transgressive data. *International Journal of Qualitative Studies in Education, 10*(2), 175–189.

St. Pierre, E. A., & Pillow, W. S. (2000). *Working the ruins: Feminist poststructural theory and methods in education.* NewYork, NY: Routledge.

Tatum, B. D. (2000). Defining racism: "Can we talk?" In M. Adams, W. J. Blumenfeld, R. Castañeda, H. W. Hackman, M. L. Peters, & X. Zúñiga (Eds.), *Readings for social diversity and social justice: An anthology on racism, anti-Semitism, sexism, heterosexism, ableism, and classism* (pp. 79–82). New York, NY: Routledge.

Tilley-Lubbs, G. A. (2003a). Crossing the border through service-learning: The power of cross-cultural relationships. In J. A. Hellebrandt, J. Arries, & L T. Varona (Eds.), *JUNTOS: Community partnerships in Spanish and Portuguese.* Boston, MA: Heinle.

Tilley-Lubbs, G. A. (2003b). Crossing the border through service- learning: The power of cross-cultural relationships (Unpublished doctoral dissertation). Virginia Polytechnic Institute and State University, Blacksburg, VA.

Tilley-Lubbs, G. A. (2007). The intersection of the academy and the community: Researching relationships through community-based education. In A. Wurr & J. Hellebrandt (Eds.), *Learning the language of global citizenship: Service-learning in applied linguistics.* Bolton, MA: Anker.

Vacarr, B. (2001). Moving beyond polite correctness: Practicing mindfulness in the diverse classroom. *Harvard Educational Review, 71*(2), 285–295.

Wildman, S. M., & Davis, A. D. (2000). Language and silence: Making systems of privilege visible. In M. Adams, W. J. Blumenfeld, R. Castañeda, H. W. Hackman, M. L. Peters, & X. Zúñiga (Eds.), *Readings for social diversity and social justice: An anthology on racism, anti- Semitism, sexism, heterosexism, ableism, and classism* (pp. 50–60). New York, NY: Routledge.

Wise, G. (1980). *American historical explanations: A strategy for grounded inquiry* (2nd ed, rev). Minneapolis, MN: University of Minnesota.

Wood, W. J. (1998). Santa Clara University's Eastside project: A pilgrimage toward our own humanity. In E. Zlotkowski (Ed.), *Successful service-learning programs: New models of excellence in higher education* (pp. 189–209). Bolton, MA: Anker.

Gresilda A. Tilley-Lubbs
Faculty of Teaching and Learning
School of Education
Virginia Tech
Blacksburg, Virginia, USA

JENNIFER SINK MCCLOUD

5. "WERE YOU THERE?"

*Critical Autoethnographic Reflections on the
Researcher-Participant Relationship*

ABSTRACT

While conducting qualitative research in an English as a Second Language classroom
in a high school, the author increasingly struggled with her researcher position as she
interacted with JanCarlos, a 15-year-old research participant from Honduras.[1] In this
chapter, the author shares the discomfort and resistance that she felt when JanCarlos
subverted the researcher-participant relationship by asking her questions about her
own school experiences, namely her memories and feelings about the tragic school
shootings at Virginia Tech on April 16, 2007. She critically examines this moment,
raising questions about ethics, researcher-participant relationships, school violence,
and the positioning of students in research and actual school spaces.

INTRODUCTION: "WERE YOU THERE?"

"JanCarlos, thanks for meeting with me for a follow-up interview." I remove the
portable microphone from my computer and fastidiously save the interview audio
file. Later I would return to transcribe, code, and analyse his ongoing school story,
fraught with failing grades, troubles with teachers, and bullying.

"Yeah," he shrugs.

The interview is over, but he stays put. Baggy jeans and extra-large T-shirt engulf
his five-foot frame. He looks at me through big brown eyes framed by thick lush
eyelashes. His striking baby face belies his 15 years. We sit in silence as I wrap the
cord around the microphone and gather my computer from the empty desk in the
empty quiet office in the guidance department. I hear a clock ticking. He interrupts
the silence:

"So, were you there when that kid killed all those people?"

I stop fiddling with my stuff. My hand holding the microphone suspends in
mid-air. My eyebrows knit together as I pull myself from my mundane task and
focus on his question. Perplexed, I ask, "Where? What kid?" Then it hits me. Hard.
"The kid at Virginia Tech? Do you mean the April 16 shootings?"

"Yeah," he says.

I nod silently.

G. A. Tilley-Lubbs & S. B. Calva (Eds.), Re-Telling Our Stories, 69–84.
© *2016 Sense Publishers. All rights reserved.*

He looks me in the eye, earnestly and intensely. "Were you like…scared?"

I break our eye contact and look back down at the microphone in my hand.

Was I like scared?! My breath quickens and my heart thumps. The memories, so carefully and deliberately tucked away, clash against my carefully constructed researcher façade. Claustrophobia confines me as I remember how a 9:00 a.m. Monday morning ethnographic methods course turned into a period of lockdown[2] in a windowless classroom while first responders helped victims and police searched for a shooter (or shooters) on campus. Sharp metal fills my mouth—the taste of adrenaline, vulnerability, and fear—as I remember not knowing where Jonathan, my husband and fellow graduate student was on campus that day: Where had the shootings occurred? Was Jonathan in that building? Are other buildings targets? Is a shooter at large? Is there one shooter or are there more? The panic and isolation of intermittently being blocked from making phone calls from that windowless room, due to overloaded circuits, settle into my muscle tissue, making my legs and arms heavy. Thankfully, the tidal waves of re-lived memories also remind me that I did make contact and learned that Jonathan was safe and on lockdown in another building on the other side of campus. Others were not that fortunate. An "are you ok?" email sent to a friend, to be forever unanswered, haunts me and reminds me of this fact. My mind races with these memories and other thoughts that interrupt and trip over each other—why is JanCarlos asking me about April 16, 2007? What does he want to know? How does he even know about that morning when Seung-Hui Cho, a Virginia Tech student, killed two students in a dorm and then chained shut the doors of a classroom building, killing 30 students and faculty and wounding more than two dozen in body and thousands in spirit?

As an immigrant from Honduras, JanCarlos did not grow up in the shadow of the Hokie Nation. He does not idolize the football players or dream of becoming a Hokie. I had talked frequently with JanCarlos and his classmates about how I conducted dissertation research through Virginia Tech. I had spent a lot of time in his English as a Second Language (ESL) classroom conducting interviews and ethnographic observations to understand how JanCarlos and his classmates experienced school. During that time, I told them about Virginia Tech. I tried to define a dissertation with K-12 concepts that they understood—"It's a big final paper that counts a lot." I talked to them about my program. Yet, there was so much they never seemed to understand, no matter how many times I explained it. They had never been to Virginia Tech. They never fully grasped its location in relation to their town. I had shown them a map of the university. In awe, they couldn't believe that it more resembles a sprawling town than their previously held notion of a single building, much like that of their own high school. They were surprised to learn that I could be both a "teacher" (supervisor of university students seeking teaching licensure) and "student" (doctoral candidate). I realize that JanCarlos had been paying attention.

But when did he connect the April 16 tragedy with me? How long has he wanted to ask me about it? How do I answer him? Then the awful, guilty thought: Does JanCarlos, a bullied and depressed kid, identify with the shooter, also depressed/

mentally ill? What is the appropriate "teacher" response? "Researcher" response? "Human" response? Before I can answer him, or myself meta-conversation style, another thought rushes in, scolding the others:

*   I'm asking him to tell me about his school experiences, isn't it only fair that I tell him about mine?*

REVISITING A SUBVERSIVE RESEARCH MOMENT TO CONFRONT MY RESEARCHER SELF

Backstory/My Research Beginning

I did not set out to conduct an autoethnographic project. However, I did set out to conduct a critical exploration of experience. Influenced by scholarship that challenged "reductionist" (Kincheloe, n.d.) explanations of student experience, such as the work of Carger (1996) and Kincheloe, I resisted reducing immigrant students' school experiences to problems and deficits with markers like math achievement, graduation rates, and English language proficiency. Instead, I wanted to understand the complex school experiences of immigrant students. I wanted to know about the social and academic challenges they faced, but also to learn about moments of joy, success, and agency. I wanted to hear their stories and learn about their complex identities and experiences through those stories, as story both creates and makes sense of experience (Clandinin & Connelly, 2000; Goodall, 2000). Therefore, I designed a qualitative study (McCloud, 2015) using narrative inquiry and ethnographic methods (Clandinin & Connelly, 1994, 2000; Connelly & Clandinin, 1990). I relied on positioning theory (Davies, 2000; Harré & van Langenhove, 1999) as the theoretical frame for capturing the fluid, emergent, and creative nature of identity. I began my research with an ethic of care (Noddings, 1984) that respected the autonomy and agency of young people (Moinian, 2006; Thorne, 2004). Finally, as a matter of personal ethics, I began the research knowing that I needed to be reflexive about my own identity and positionality, especially since my life experiences were and are so starkly different from those of the participants.

    In most ways, I could not be more different from the adolescent Mexican, Honduran, and Chinese immigrant students that participated in my study. I am a white, middle-class woman in my thirties. English is my first language; Spanish is my second language. I am a U.S. citizen by birth. With the exception of extended study abroad experiences in Spain and Mexico during college and graduate school, I had lived within a 200 mile-radius of my hometown and family until I was 35 years old. Conversely, the student participants had moved; rather, had been moved by the adults in their lives, thousands of miles away from their hometowns and families, at young ages. Most were unable to travel back due to immigration status or financial constraints. Like the participants, I attended a mostly white high school; unlike them, I was part of the ethnic majority. Instead of ESL classes, I took college-bound courses like AP English and AP Government. I attended a private liberal arts college. At the time of the research, I had a master's degree and was completing the final stages of my Ph.D. degree in Curriculum and Instruction with an emphasis in ESL and Multicultural Education. Higher education remains a distant opportunity for JanCarlos and his classmates.

My undergraduate and graduate studies had turned me on to social justice issues. I had learned the importance of continuously reflecting on my material, cultural, racial, and political privilege. I also understood the importance of recognizing the ways in which those very markers of privilege/power systemically create and reinforce inequality. As a holder of a state-issued driver's license, a U.S. passport, and other legitimizing documents, I am able to move freely throughout the world. I have never been perceived as suspicious, untrustworthy, or dangerous due to the colour of my skin or the language I speak. JanCarlos and his classmates do not live with these same privileges. Neither my study abroad experiences nor my experience as a curriculum coordinator for a bilingual family literacy program for Mexican and Honduran families could ever provide experiential common ground with the immigrant students in the high school of my study. So I understood the importance of reflexivity, at least in part. By being white, adult, middle-class, U.S. citizen, a former high school teacher, and university affiliated, I knew I would affect and alter the research space (Davies 1999, as cited in Anderson & Glass-Coffin, 2013, p. 73). I knew that these positions would shape what I saw as data in the field and would influence how I interpreted that data (Davies et al., 2004; Goodall, 2000). Thus, I intentionally worked at keeping my researcher positionality and my privilege at the forefront of my mind during ethnographic observations and interviews.

However, I had not conceptualized incorporating *mystory* (Pelias, 2013; Ulmer, 1989) in the research until JanCarlos turned the interview around and dared to ask me, the researcher/interviewer, about my school experiences. When he asked me how I felt about April 16, 2007, my initial response was to block him out. Shut down communication. Break contact. I desperately wanted to put up a binary researcher/ participant wall between us. After all, I was the one with the microphone and the research questions, not him. Yet, even through my resistance, I realized that the open-ended interview I had so carefully constructed to provide a space for emergent topics and questions only went "one-way" (Anderson & Glass-Coffin, 2013, p. 70). I had asked the students to share their worlds and vulnerable moments with me, but I had not reciprocated. In that moment, I felt deep shame at the unfairness, the unnaturalness, the absence of co-sharing. I realized that I had counted on, perhaps even hidden behind, the students' hazy and incomplete knowledge of my world. I had unknowingly edited and selected what I had shared about myself and about Virginia Tech. I had mostly stuck to the facts—showing the geographic location of the university, defining a dissertation, describing my program, telling them where I lived and that I had nieces and nephews their age—rather than share personal stories. JanCarlos recognized this and called me out.

JanCarlos subverted the hierarchical researcher-participant relationship and reductionist framing that I had denounced in theory/principle, but enacted in practice. I suddenly felt hypocritical for espousing the power of narrative and story to understand immigrant students' experiences, but negating to share the complexity of my stories with them. The research that I had designed with its use of narrative inquiry and positioning theory was far from positivist, but I had likely enacted it as more rigid, objective, and contained than I should have. I had unwittingly enacted research as a "transitive-relative verb, that is, a verb that requires a direct object (something) and an indirect object (to someone)" (Freire, 1998, p. 31). But Freire's rejection of teaching and learning as a transitive-relative verb also holds true for research. Just as teachers and students are intricately bound and interconnected, so too are researchers and participants: "One requires the other" (Freire, 1998, p. 31). JanCarlos' question ruptured my stance and led me to envision a reflexivity: "guided by a desire to better understand both self and others through examining one's actions and perceptions in reference to and dialogue with those of others" (Anderson & Glass-Coffin, 2013, p. 73). My soul, my intuition, and my heart increasingly called me to treat my research experience as a "text ...to be constantly read, interpreted, written, and rewritten" (Freire, 1998, p. 89).

My (Re)Search for Renewal

In what should have been my writing/defending/graduating year, I began my doctoral studies anew. My doctoral advisor/mentor/friend, Kris Tilley-Lubbs guided me towards autoethnography: "It will help you make sense of it all," she said. "Write as inquiry," she added (Richardson & St. Pierre, 2005; Richardson, 2000). I was familiar with autoethnography, but only peripherally. We had discussed and read about autoethnography in the ethnographic methods course mentioned in the introduction. I had nearly stayed up all night reading *Fields of Play: Constructing an Academic Life* (Richardson, 1997). I had read *Writing the New Ethnography* (Goodall, 2000) and cited from it in my research proposal. These and other sources had spoken to me personally and academically, but I did not intentionally pursue autoethnography, mostly because I assumed that I had encountered it too late. Due to changing my doctoral concentration from second language education to ESL and Multicultural Education, I had already added time to my doctoral studies. Doctoral students that had started their programs a year or two later than I had were defending dissertations and graduating before me. Concerns and conversations about "time to degree" and graduation rates were building up in the School of Education, and I felt anxiety about adding any more time. I worried about funding. I felt that the larger institutional message was, "Get it done and move on." But deep down I knew that transformative education does not operate on any timetable, so I allowed myself, with support from Kris, committee members, and others to abandon my fears about time. I embarked on a renewal of my doctoral studies.

I spent nearly two academic years devouring the works of Carolyn Ellis, Laurel Richardson, Elizabeth St. Pierre, Art Bochner, H.L. "Bud" Goodall, Chris Poulos, Kris Tilley-Lubbs, Norm Denzin, and others. I read *Qualitative Inquiry* as effortlessly and joyfully as bedtime reading. I attended a workshop on autoethnography with Chris Poulos at the Ninth Annual Qualitative Research Summer Intensive where I drafted the opening vignette. I took two autoethnographic methods courses. I learned about *bricolage* (Kincheloe, n.d.; Kincheloe, McLaren, & Steinberg, 2012) and a weight I didn't know was on my shoulders lifted. I suddenly felt relieved to allow the research space to evolve. I felt free to incorporate autoethnography into the mosaic of narrative inquiry, ethnography, and positioning theory that already guided the study. I realized how those prior methods and theories, fluid and emergent, were compatible; autoethnography was the natural next step in the research process (Poulos, 2009). I read and wrote until my eyes blurred. I learned that emotion IS data (St. Pierre, 1997). I read Paulo Freire and learned that my/our "ontological vocation is humanization" (Freire, 1970, p. 75). I learned what I had always intuited, but never had a language for, which is research ethics go far beyond "procedural" concerns, such as the IRB, informed consent, and maintaining the anonymity of research participants (Ellis, 2007, p. 4). Instead, when research ethics are defined in "relational" terms (Ellis, 2007, p. 4), the researcher is able to move from an *objective* stance to stand in solidarity with participants and even intervene in the world for truth, love, and justice (Freire, 1998). I learned:

> [T]hat *narrative conscience* is the primary ethical call of the human spirit, that we must invoke narrative conscience in our human dialogue and in our scholarship, and that we must, if we are to thrive as a species, develop new ways of engaging our dialogue, especially in challenging moral conversations. (Poulos, 2009, p. 48)

JanCarlos' question spoke straight to my heart where past grief and trauma resided. I needed to awaken my narrative conscience and story my way out of darkness. I needed to explore why it was so difficult to engage in authentic dialogue with JanCarlos. I needed to develop critical consciousness about my resistance to discuss the event with him and my concerns about his motivations in asking me about it. These were all ethical calls.

My journey to autoethnography was "accidental" (Poulos, 2009), emergent, and necessary. In order to be authentic, I had to "employ" autoethnography to "the unfolding context of the research situation" (Kincheloe, McLaren, & Steinberg, 2012, p. 21). I wrote an IRB continuation request to include autoethnography in my data analysis. It was approved. I successfully finished and defended my dissertation, which incorporated autoethnography in analysis and writing. I had observed and experienced other interactions with JanCarlos that necessitated autoethnography, but the very experience that initiated my autoethnographic journey did not make it into the final dissertation.

I told myself that I needed more time to reflect on and write about my April 16 conversation with JanCarlos. That was true in part. The full truth is I was not willing to be vulnerable about April 16 in my dissertation. Kris, my committee chair, had written and published an autoethnographic poem about April 16, critically examining the intersections between public and personal tragedy (Tilley-Lubbs, 2011). I knew of one other faculty member who had written a "memoir-critique" (Roy, 2009, p. 6) of the tragedy. In it Roy cautioned against personal and institutional silence about violence, mental illness, and race, especially in educational contexts. Yet I remained silent about my April 16 conversation with JanCarlos due to reasons that ranged from rational to irrational. I did not know how my committee would receive it. Nearly six years after the tragedy, I still could not talk about it without crying. I would become too emotional and lose focus during the defence when I needed to be articulate and lucid. Defending a dissertation is anxiety-producing enough. The dissertation, a university level final examination, carries tremendous weight towards degree completion. Since the university administration had been in litigation over April 16, I had paranoid thoughts that the university would overly scrutinize or reject a dissertation that referenced April 16, even though I had no evidence to support that fear. I cut the conversation from the final drafts.

But it is time to continue my open-ended and on-going journey (Ellis, 2004; Anderson & Glass-Coffin, 2013) of making meaning of my April 16 conversation with JanCarlos. I need to confront the complexity of his questions, as well as confront my researcher self. Here I recreate my conversation with JanCarlos to explore researcher/participant relationships, especially relationships that are developed in the context of schools and that represent a diverse intersection of age, power, ethnicity, culture, class, and language. In exploring this relationship, more specifically, the relationship constructed in our halting dialogue, I share "personal experience to explore cultural practices" (Pelias, 2013, p. 384). Thus, I stumble into questions about school violence, school policies, and about how we position students in actual school contexts, as well as in research about students in schools.

I recreate our dialogue in regular typeface and my meta-dialogue in italics. In the meta-dialogue I reflect on my memories of April 16 and examine my resistance to JanCarlos' questions. Portions of the reflection in the meta-dialogue also represent what I wish I had said to JanCarlos, but didn't. Therefore, I move from the past to the present and back again as I layer memory and present day reflection with analysis, critical examination, and problem-posing (Tilley-Lubbs, 2009, p. 70). I strive to represent a telling of events in the dialogue and the meta-dialogue that is authentic in purpose and in spirit. The conversation that I had with JanCarlos took place after I turned off and unplugged the microphone. Therefore, I reconstruct the dialogue from memory and notes written after the fact. I represent the verbatim accuracy of that dialogue as best I can. My memory of April 16 is murky and disjointed due to the traumatic nature of the event; therefore, the information that I provide is incomplete and interpreted through the lens of my own personal experience on that day. I also turn to Tilley-Lubbs (2011) and Roy (2009) to make sense of that day. Somehow the memories of those present on April 16, 2007 represent how-it-happened, even if specific details and experiences differ. I write to represent an ethical "verisimilitude" of dialogue and events (Ellis, 2004, p. 124). I write to develop a "critical ontology" (Kincheloe, 2003) that "involves the process of reconnecting human beings on a variety of levels and in numerous ways to a living social and physical web of reality, to a living cosmos …where new ways of being and new ways of being *connected* reshape all people" (p. 50). The answers I gave JanCarlos were imperfect and "once told, [or thought] [they] cannot be retracted" (Pelias, 2013, p. 388). But I write now to understand and honour his questions. I write to understand myself.

"WERE YOU THERE?"

I finally break the silence and answer JanCarlos' question. "Yes, I was there. I was very scared."

"Did you cry?"

"Yes." I pause and take a deep breath. I exhale. Tears well up now. They're on the brink of spilling over and running down my check. I suspect he notices. I add, "It still makes me cry." I want to break eye contact again and look out the window or look down at the designs on the waxed linoleum floor or the fine dust on the desk. I want to look anywhere but at JanCarlos. Somehow I manage to maintain eye contact. But my inner-dialogue shouts: *"I have answered your question now. Let's move on.* Simultaneously: "*Is this what it feels like to be interviewed about your life; your feelings?"*

"Yeah, my teacher cried when it happened," JanCarlos says.

"What teacher? Did you see the teacher cry? It happened several years ago. You were in middle school then, right?" I ask. My questions come out in a disorderly staccato rhythm. Still swept up in re-lived emotion and trauma, my voice sounds accusatory and shrill. *Why am I so shocked to hear that he has personal knowledge of this? Why am I demanding evidence of his knowledge? Am I questioning him to hear his story and engage in dialogue or to reclaim my stance as the interviewer?*

"Yeah, I was in middle school. Some teachers were like talking about it in the hallway. Ms. Humphrey turned on the TV to see what was going on. I saw it on TV. She was crying." He pauses and adds, "I heard she went to school there or knew somebody there or something."

"Oh," I say with sudden recognition. *I had grown accustomed to JanCarlos' use of "I heard" to talk about school and community gossip, but I settle into the acknowledgement that April 16 was not just something that he had heard about. He too had experienced it.*

That morning, local and national news outlets interrupted the daily television broadcast to report the unfolding events at Virginia Tech. Kinetic images had filled the news screen: First responders running to receive the wounded and police running with guns drawn towards Norris Hall, the site of the classroom shootings. One striking image of a wounded male student with a bloody tourniquet around his thigh being carried somewhat haphazardly by first-responders as they ran away from the building replayed frequently. Intense news coverage had lasted throughout the day as reporters broadcast news conferences with hospital staff and police and provided hour-by-hour updates.

I imagine a middle school classroom, though not on lockdown, altered and ruptured by the images of a violent act occurring miles away. Business as usual and daily instruction halted as a room full of young people, barely of adolescent age, stood or sat around a television set and watched frightening images and events unfold, perhaps in real time, as their teacher cried.

"Did you feel scared when you saw it on the news? Did it scare you to see your teacher cry?" I ask. *My breathing has slowed a bit; my voice is calmer.*

"I guess so, yeah." He seems to be searching for a way to describe how he felt. He says, "I just felt really bad." He adds, "Some kids were crying too."

"You mean the kids in your class?"

"Yeah."

"Did any of the kids say if they knew people at Virginia Tech?" I ask.

"I don't know."

I nod. "Did a lot of teachers talk about what was happening?"

"I heard a lot of teachers talking about it, yeah."

I am struck by the fact that JanCarlos might have seen images or learned information about the event before I had. I had spent the morning in a building across from Norris Hall in a windowless classroom. We were in the middle of a conversation about fieldnotes when a faculty member knocked on the door. She opened it and said: "I don't know if you have heard the news, but there has been a shooting on campus. We're supposed to stay put. I wasn't even sure if there was a class in here, but I saw the door shut and thought I would check." She was right: We had not heard the news. We immediately tried to get as much information as possible, but only a couple of us had computers with us. My memory is that circuits were so busy it was difficult to make phone or internet connection. My classmate was finally able to access the VT website and saw the emails that had informed us of the events. A 9:50am email read: "A gunman is loose on campus. Stay in buildings until further notice. Stay away from all windows" (Tilley-Lubbs, 2011, p. 144). A later email alert told us about the early morning shootings in West Ambler Johnson, a dormitory, and multiple shootings in Norris Hall. My memories of those hours are blurred. I cannot even be certain about the amount of time spent in that room and building. I do remember watching my friend and classmate cry with worry that her parents in Mexico City would see it on the news and think that she had been a victim of the shooting. We all shared this fear and wanted to make contact with our friends and family. I also needed to make contact with Jonathan. He had talked about going to the campus gym, but I still wasn't sure where he was. Some of us decided to go downstairs to use a landline in the large office space reserved for Graduate Assistants. I did not know Kris very well at the time, but I remember passing her in the hallway as we walked to the stairway. Her office was just steps away from my classroom. Since I was on my way downstairs, I did not know that my friend had made cell phone contact with her family in Mexico in the hallway outside of the classroom until I read Kris's poem years later (Tilley-Lubbs, 2011, p. 145). It strikes me how we all experienced this tragedy collectively, yet individually. At the same time, the stories that many of us who were there that day tell, in writing or in spoken conversations, resonate with one another, despite those individual experiences. The stories of others fill in the gaps in memory and perspective. JanCarlos' memories of that day broaden and fill in more of the story.

On my way downstairs to use the phone, I stopped in the stairwell and looked out through the antique windows towards Norris Hall. As I looked out across the wide oval-shaped green space that symbolizes the academic campus, I heard sirens and saw police cars and ambulances. The green space that students use as a pedestrian thoroughfare to get to classes during the day and use as a site for touch football, soccer, and even Quidditch games in the evening felt like a battlefield. Suddenly its name, the Drillfield, seemed eerily appropriate. The Drillfield, named as a space for the Virginia Tech Corp of Cadets to practice marching drills, became more relevant than ever before. Indeed, the name of the building in which I stood, War Memorial Hall, took on new significance. As a pacifist, I had struggled with both the historical and present military influence on campus. Did I struggle with that military tradition on April 16? Would I have been relieved to see a Corps of men and women marching across the Drillfield to save and protect us? Probably. I don't know.

I do know that I was afraid to linger too long at the window, so I had little knowledge of what was really going on. It wasn't until I was finally at home, reunited with Jonathan and huddled together on our well-worn blue couch, that we watched the news in a stunned daze and learned the gravity of the tragedy. Like Roy (2009), who watched the newscast on her sofa, we "gasped" (p. 14) when we watched the replay of Police Chief Flinchum's announcement that the number killed was "more than twenty" (p. 14). Complete numbness settled in our muscles and bones and anchored us to the couch. At the same time, we wanted to force our limbs to move and join Roy in her desire to "hurry up the wide stone steps of Burruss Hall and find Chief Flinchum to demand that he return those words back *to where they came from because how would we bear it if he didn't" (p. 14, emphasis hers)? Instead, we sat painfully still and listened to the rising tally of deceased and injured over the next several hours. We desperately tried to pray it all away.*

I bring myself back to the present and ask JanCarlos: "Did the principal make an announcement? Did he come around and talk about what was happening or anything?"

"I don't remember if the principal said anything."

"Did you go home early? Did school close early?" I ask.

"No. But I heard that some kids did," he replies.

I nod. *I envision terrified parents coming to pick up their children from school just because they want to hold them close. See their faces. Get them out of a classroom after hearing horrible descriptions of how classrooms miles away had been terrorized. I wonder if any of JanCarlos' classmates or teachers then had relatives there and whether they had spent hours in agony waiting for them to call and say, "I'm all right." I also think about JanCarlos' current classmates. Some of them had told me that older brothers and fathers had worked on construction projects at Virginia Tech.*

I wonder if any of those workers were on campus that day. Especially when hired out by sub-contractors, undocumented immigrant workers are intentionally rendered invisible due to the possibility of employer sanctions (Chomsky, 2014). Given this possibility, I wonder how and when those workers' families would have been notified if they had been victims. I wonder if any of his current classmates had also heard about the event that day and had worried over family members potentially working there. I wonder all of these things, but I do not say them out-loud.

We sit in silence for a few seconds.

"Why did he do it?" he asks.

I sigh deeply. "That's such a good question. I don't know. I don't think anyone really knows."

"I heard he didn't have any friends. I heard he was crazy. Was he?" he asks.

My doubt and resistance resurface. *How do I talk about mental illness with JanCarlos? How do I talk about Cho, who by anecdotal accounts was primarily a loner and did not have many (any?) friends, to JanCarlos who struggles with bullying from peers? How do I talk about the fact that Cho had depression and had not received adequate mental care services (Roy, 2009) to a kid who has also suffered with depression? JanCarlos' ESL teacher, Ms. Esperanza, had talked with his mom and school officials regarding her concerns about JanCarlos and depression. At one point, she even worried that he might be suicidal. To my knowledge, JanCarlos was never officially diagnosed. I knew all of this from conversations with Ms. Esperanza, but JanCarlos never shared any of that with me. He had shared with me that students, especially male students, bullied him in the cafeteria and "other places," including the trailer park where he lives. Some mock his small size. They make fun of him for mostly hanging out with girls with whom he has no romantic or sexual involvement. Others call him "gay" or "fag." Still others make fun of him for being Honduran. He is bullied for reasons that I cannot fathom. For this reason, he routinely ate lunch with two female friends in Ms. Esperanza's classroom. Ms. Esperanza suspected that he had once eaten lunch in a stall in the bathroom to avoid the cafeteria, so she opened up her classroom as a safe place.*

However, despite Ms. Esperanza's best efforts, JanCarlos had decided to transfer to a neighbouring school district. In addition to bullying, he had experienced increasing problems with failing grades. He had regularly put his head down on classroom desks and slept during class. Absences had increased. The culminating events that led to his decision to transfer included an argument with Ms. Esperanza about his blatant act of leaving the classroom without permission and having and taking prescription medication on school grounds. Just days after that event, he skipped class with another student and wrote graffiti, including gang symbols, on a bathroom wall. I had interviewed him about those events. He had claimed no gang affiliation. I had believed him. So had Ms. Esperanza. Ms. Esperanza had also suspected that he had felt pressure to join the other student for fear of judgment or torment, especially since that student had called him names in the past. Nevertheless, JanCarlos knew that he was spiralling out of control and his solution was to transfer

79

and start over somewhere new (McCloud, 2013; McCloud, 2015). I often reflect on his words in that interview:

> Whenever I'm in trouble, I just start like not caring about myself. That's when I tend to get in more trouble. (McCloud, 2013)

I later wrote a reflection about these words:

Trouble. Back talking and prescription pills. Trouble. Too-big-for him hoodie and gang graffiti on school bathroom walls. Trouble. Failing grades. Trouble. JanCarlos resigns himself to trouble. Trapped within "institutional workings that reduce and erase" (Ayers, 2004, p. 138). But what about the need to trouble what confines him? Oppresses him? What about the need to trouble the intersections of race, class, and language that oppress him in a dominantly white and English-speaking school setting? What is my position in all of this troubling?

Now I can't help but worry if he will ever stop caring about himself to the point where he wants to end it all. I can't help but worry if JanCarlos has ever had the desire to seek revenge on those who bully him, even though I know that there is a great leap between fantasy and action.

I recall supposed experts on school shooters and school violence who were interviewed on television after the Virginia Tech and other school shootings. I remember their declarations that there is no real profile of a school shooter. They warned against using mental illness as a deterministic predictor for school violence. They warned about drawing causal links between bullying and school violence. The truth is that I do not know anything about school shooters. However, I do believe that we need to examine the sociocultural factors and discourses that contribute to bullying (Bansel, Davies, Laws, & Linnell, 2009). I believe that we need to interrogate the cultural/political/economic systems, norms, and practices that glorify violence (Giroux, 2013). When we do that we just might begin to ask the right questions about what leads an individual to violence and understand that:

> *[T]he roots of such violence are not merely personal, lying in the realm of some unfathomable emotional disturbance. They are also part and parcel of those varied educational and cultural conditions that give meaning to such behaviour, suggesting that such violence is a normal and acceptable way to relieve anxiety, tension, and resolve problems. (Giroux, 2013, para. 3)*

Since April 16, I have fought against succumbing to the "assumption that schools were dealing with a new breed of student – violent, amoral and apathetic" (Giroux, 2009, para. 3). Many P-12 schools responded to school violence concerns by creating zero-tolerance policies. Early iterations of zero-tolerance policies were largely employed to address guns in schools (Giroux, 2009). However, these policies "now include a range of behavioural infractions that encompass everything from possessing drugs or weapons to threatening other students—all broadly conceived. Under zero tolerance policies, forms of punishments that were once applied to adults now apply to first graders" (Giroux, 2009, para. 3). Many of these policies do not differentiate, at least not initially, between knives meant to kill and knives brought to school to cut a birthday cake (Stam, 2009). As a result, zero tolerance has largely perpetuated a "culture of fear" and control in schools (Giroux, 2009, para. 12). Under these policies, students are suspended or expelled for not following dress codes, bringing scissors to school, and "engaging in a school yard fight" (Giroux, 2009, para. 8). A disproportionate number of students punished are students of colour, and they experience limited rights to due process and face harsh punishments, including time in jail and detention centres (Giroux, 2009; Nicholson, 2013; Zweifler, 2009). JanCarlos is lucky that he does not attend a school with zero-tolerance policies. His prescription pills and gang graffiti might have landed him in a detention centre or jail in a zero-tolerance school.

I am dismayed at the class, cultural, and racial injustices of zero-tolerance responses to school violence, so I try not to enact zero-tolerance in my own perceptions and judgments of students. I try not to overly scrutinize their behaviour or look at them with suspicion. But April 16 changed the classroom landscape for me. I read student behaviour differently now. I have wondered what's in backpacks; I have watched students with big or bulging pockets; I have kept an eye on students who keep their hands under desks; I have over-analysed students who look angry or sad; and I have jumped at sudden noises. An argumentative student evokes a different response in me now. I watch for violent escalation. I have learned that the stereotypical image of the school shooter as a bullied, antisocial, and/or mentally ill kid is difficult to resist. But I continuously work to decipher between irrational fear and healthy intuition and reason. I am aware that racism, classism, and ableism invade our thoughts and behaviours when we are most vulnerable and most afraid. So I am determined not to read a hoodie as suspicious. I am determined not to read brown and black students as dangerous. I am determined not to read mental illnesses as a threat.

All of these assertions and contradictions blur and mingle in the rawness of this moment. I still wonder: Does JanCarlos worry that he might experience the world as Cho had experienced it? Is that why he's asking why Cho did it? And/Or does he worry about someday being a victim? At the same time that I ask myself these questions, I am aware of the limitations of these either-or identities. I realize that I have fallen into the trap—perpetuated in schools through punitive practices and policies—of viewing students as either "potential criminals" or "infantilized potential victims of crime" (Giroux, 2009, para 1). How do I/we reject and transform these limited identities ascribed to students in schools?

I finally answer JanCarlos' question. "Was he crazy? Well, he was sick. I mean mentally sick. He suffered from depression and possibly other mental illnesses. I really don't know about the specifics of that. I do think that it's sad that he didn't get help to deal with it. Who knows how things might have been different if he had? But just because a person is depressed doesn't mean that he or she will do what he did. People with depression can get help and learn to deal with it." *Is this my awkward euphemistic attempt to tell him that just because he might be depressed that does not mean that he will end up like Cho? If so, why am I not being more intelligent and caring about it?* "As far as whether he had friends; no, I don't think he really did. That's my understanding anyway...." My voice trails off.

"Did you know him?" he asks.

"No, I didn't."

"Did you know anybody that died?" he asks.

"Yes." *I swallow hard. My eyes fill with tears again. A heaviness returns to my legs. My throat constricts. I envision the time Jocelyne brought me a box of green tea when doctors suspected I had an ulcer and told me to stop drinking coffee. I remember a shared lunch at Gillies, a favourite vegetarian restaurant near the university. I remember long conversations about teaching.* I say, "Yes, I did. She taught French. She was a wonderful person. I think about her family a lot and hope that they are doing ok. I can't even imagine how difficult it has been for them." I pause, not sure of what else to say.

"That sucks," JanCarlos says. "I would feel really bad if that happened to one of my friends."

I usually hear "that sucks" as flippant or even disrespectful, but I don't in this moment. Maybe it is the sincerity in his voice or the way he looks me in the eye when he says it, but I hear compassion and empathy in these words. The conciseness of the phrase captures it all.

I look him in the eye. All I can think to say back is, "Yes, it does."

POSTSCRIPT

This was the last conversation I had with JanCarlos. I left this conversation wanting to have the opportunity to do it all over again. I reflected back on his questions and was preoccupied by the "should haves" and "why didn't I?" moments. My answers were too brief, too selective. We arranged for another follow-up meeting, but he did not make it. We talked a couple more times with Ms. Esperanza as the intermediary, but it never worked out to meet again.

So I never thanked him for caring about my experiences on April 16, 2007. I never told him how sorry I am that schools are challenging, conflicting, and sometimes scary places to be. I never told him that adults should do better and figure out ways to establish opportunities for real dialogue about bullying, mental illness, societal glorification of violence, sexism/heteronormativity, and racism. I never told him that he is worthy simply for being human. I never told him how his honest questioning led me to critically investigate my own story and my practices as a researcher and teacher. I never told him how his willingness to engage in authentic dialogue directed me towards a transformative journey.

NOTES

[1] JanCarlos and Ms. Esperanza, the English as a Second Language (ESL) teacher mentioned in this chapter, are pseudonyms.

[2] I use the term lockdown because that is what it felt like. To this day, I do not know if that is the term officially used by Virginia Tech on that day.

REFERENCES/BIBLIOGRAPHY

Anderson, L., & Glass-Coffin, B. (2013). I learn by going: Autoethnographic modes of inquiry. In S. H. Jones, T. E. Adams, & C. Ellis (Eds.), *Handbook of autoethnography* (pp. 57–83). Walnut Creek, CA: Left Coast.

Ayers, W. (2004). *Teaching toward freedom: Moral commitment and ethical action in the classroom.* Boston, MA: Beacon.

Bansel, P., Davies, B., Laws, C., & Linnell, S. (2009). Bullies, bullying, and power in the contexts of schooling. *British Journal of Sociology of Education, 30*(1), 59–69.

Carger, C. (1996). *Of borders and dreams: A Mexican-American experience of urban education.* New York, NY: Teacher's College.

Chomsky, A. (2014). *Undocumented: How immigration became illegal.* Boston, MA: Beacon.

Clandinin, D. J., & Connelly, F. M. (1994). Personal experience methods. In N. K. Denzin & Y. Lincoln (Eds.), *Handbook of qualitative research* (pp. 413–427). Thousand Oaks, CA: Sage.

Clandinin, D. J., & Connelly, F. M. (2000). *Narrative inquiry: Experience and story in qualitative research.* San Francisco, CA: Jossey-Bass.

Connelly, F., & Clandinin, D.J. (1990). Stories of experience and narrative inquiry. *Educational Researcher, 19*(5), 2–14.

Davies, B. (2000). *A body of writing: 1990–1999.* Walnut Creek, CA: AltaMira.

Davies, B., Browne, J., Gannon, S., Honan, E., Laws, C., Mueller-Rockstroh, B., & Bendix Petersen, E. (2004). The ambivalent practices of reflexivity. *Qualitative Inquiry, 10,* 360–389. doi:10.1177/1077800403257638

Ellis, C. (2004). *The ethnographic I: A methodological novel about autoethnography.* Walnut Creek, CA: AltaMira

Ellis, C. (2007). Telling secrets, revealing lives: Relational ethics in research with intimate others. *Qualitative Inquiry, 13*(1), 3–29.

Freire, P. (1970). *Pedagogy of the oppressed* (M. Bergman Ramos, Trans.). New York, NY: Continuum. (Original work published 1968)

Freire, P. (1998). *Pedagogy of freedom: Ethics, democracy, and civic courage.* New York, NY: Rowman & Littlefield.

Giroux, H. (2009, October 20). Schools and the pedagogy of punishment. *truthout.* Retrieved from truth-out.org

Giroux, H. (2013, December 17). Radical democracy against cultures of violence. *truthout.* Retrived from truth-out.org

Goodall, H. L. (2000). *Writing the new ethnography.* Lanham, MD: AltaMira.

Harré, R., & van Langenhove, L. (1999). *Positioning theory.* Malden, MA: Blackwell.

Kincheloe, J. (2003). Critical ontology: Visions of selfhood and curriculum. *JCT: Journal of Curriculum Theorizing, 19*(1), 47–64.

Kincheloe, J. L. (n.d.). *Beyond reductionism: Difference, criticality and multilogicality in bricolage and postformalism.* Retrieved from http://132.206.28.151/ja/articles-joe-l-kincheloe

Kincheloe, J. L., McLaren, P., & Steinberg, S. R. (2012). Critical pedagogy and qualitative research: Moving to the bricolage. In S. R. Steinberg & G. S. Cannella (Eds.), *Critical qualitative research reader* (pp. 14–32). New York, NY: Peter Lang.

McCloud, J. (2013, May). *"I'm NOT stupid!": The trouble with JanCarlos.* Paper presented at the Ninth International Congress of Qualitative Inquiry, Urbana-Champaign, IL.

McCloud, J. (2015). "Just like me": How immigrant students experience a U.S. high school. *The High School Journal 8*(3), 262–282. doi:10.1353/hsj.2015.0008

Moinian, F. (2006). I can tell it as it is! Exploring how children write and talk about themselves in school. *Ethnography and Education, 1*, 231–246.

Nicholson, H. (2013). Voices of zero tolerance. *PowerPlay, 5*(2), 752–769.

Noddings N. (1984). *Caring: A feminine approach to ethics and moral education.* Berkeley, CA: University of California.

Pelias, R. (2013). Writing autoethnography: The personal, poetic, and performative as compositional strategies. In S. H. Jones, T. E. Adams, & C. Ellis (Eds.), *Handbook of autoethnography* (pp. 384–405). Walnut Creek, CA: Left Coast.

Poulos, C. (2009). *Accidental ethnography: An inquiry into family secrecy.* Walnut Creek, CA: Left Coast.

Richardson, L. (1997). *Fields of play: Constructing an academic life.* New Brunswick, NJ: Rutgers.

Richardson, L. (2000). Writing: A method of inquiry. In N. K. Denzin & Y. S. Lincoln (Eds.), *Handbook of qualitative research* (2nd ed., pp. 923–948). Thousand Oaks, CA: Sage.

Richardson, L., & St. Pierre, E. A. (2005). Writing: A method of inquiry. In N. K. Denzin & Y. S. Lincoln (Eds.), *The sage handbook of qualitative research* (3rd ed., pp. 959–978). Thousand Oaks, CA: Sage.

Roy, L. (2009). *No right to remain silent: What we've learned from the tragedy at Virginia Tech.* New York, NY: Three Rivers.

St. Pierre, E. A. (1997). Methodology in the fold and the irruption of transgressive data. *Qualitative Studies in Education, 10*(2), 175–189.

Stam, D. (2009, April 3). *Campaign cake knife gets 5th grader suspended.* Retrieved from http://www.nbcmiami.com

Thorne, B. (2004). *Gender play: Girls and boys in school.* New Brunswick, NJ: Rutgers.

Tilley-Lubbs, G. (2009). Troubling the tide: The perils and paradoxes of service-learning in immigrant communities. *International Journal of Critical Pedagogy. 2*(1), 67–87.

Tilley-Lubbs, G. (2011). 4/16: Public tragedy collides with personal trauma. *Qualitative Inquiry, 17*(2), 144–147. doi:10.1177/1077800410392334

Ulmer, G. (1989). *Teletheory: Grammatology in the age of video.* New York, NY: Routledge.

Zwiefler, R. (2009). Silenced students: Education's absent voices. *PowerPlay, 1*(1), 42–48.

Jennifer Sink McCloud
Transylvania University
Lexington, Kentucky, USA

GRESILDA A. TILLEY-LUBBS

6. THE INQUISITION/TORTURE
OF THE TENURE TRACK[1]

ABSTRACT

This autoethnographic narrative addresses the mental anguish and chaos that were the author's constant companions during the year of waiting for the results of her tenure decision at a Research I university. Having chosen a non-traditional path to tenure, she found that autoethnography and critical pedagogy could be acceptable forms of scholarship despite their creating numerous questions and consternations on the part of all involved in the process. She uses autoethnography to make sense of the process of moving through self-questioning and doubt into a place of renewed and revitalized strength and belief in her Self and her writing. She concludes with further questions about the tenure and promotion process and the devastating effect it can produce on faculty who covet the assurance of a permanent position in a university.

***

A huge cardboard envelope protruding from my mailbox cubbyhole.
Curious.
Cold fingers.
Thumping heart.

Carefully extracting it
From the middle of all other campus mail detritus
Stuffed in the box.

Confidential/Personal/Confidential/Personal ….

Words in alternating red and blue trace a diagonal path
On the large cardboard mailer
From the Provost's Office.

Hands trembling, I open the mailer and take out the letter inside.

Dear Dr. Tilly-Lubbs:
(Paranoia kicks in—was the misspelling of my name intentional?)

G. A. Tilley-Lubbs & S. B. Calva (Eds.), Re-Telling Our Stories, 85–101.

At its meeting on June 4, 2012, the University Board of Visitors reviewed the promotion, tenure, and continued appointment recommendations brought by President ...

Quickened breath.
How can I go on to read this news without anyone here to catch me if I faint from ... from what?
Anger?
Disappointment?
... Joy?

I read on, skipping to the dreaded words:

I am pleased to inform you that the Board approved your tenure with promotion to associate professor ...a deserved acknowledgment of your exemplary achievements on behalf of your students, your profession, and the university ....

There must be some mistake.

After a year of interrogation and grief about everything I do
How did I receive a letter that acknowledged my
"Exemplary achievement."

Will this news restore my life?
Will it help me to reclaim my pre-tenure-decision-year-priorities?
Will I ever be able to *fully* reclaim the Self that matters...?

Wife/Mother/Grandmother/Mother-in-law
Friend/confidante
Advisor/teacher/friend
Activist in the Spanish-speaking community
Member of a pacifist denomination based on the servanthood of radical love
Critical pedagogue
Writer/thinker?

Will I ever lose the sense
That the tenure process
Robbed me of some of the most important aspects of my life
For seven long years?

Will I ever lose the regret I feel
For messing up my family's life,
For being distant/distracted/preoccupied/
Short-tempered/lacking in patience
During those seven years plus the six before
In pursuit of a Ph.D. as a non-traditional woman

Who had taught Spanish and piano and voice
For more years than most of her students
Had been alive?

Who had continued to love and treasure
Her husband
Her three children
Who grew up,
Married,
Lived their lives;

Her mother
Who aged and died in the process of the Ph.D./tenure gerbil wheel
Of late nights
Skipped meals prepared by that same mother
Who lived across the street and
Also took care of those children while they
Grew up,
Married,
Lived their lives?

The questions slap me in the face.

The guilt and remorse about my mom
Still sit stagnant in a painful memory.

Why as a fifty-one-year old mother did I decide
To leave my position of respect and tenure
As Department Head of Foreign Languages
In a high school where my students and their families
Not only respected me, but also demonstrated deep affection?
Why did I decide to start a doctoral program?

In the alien world of the academy....

Where competition and criticism
Define the climate and culture....

Not the ivy-covered tower
Of higher learning
And intellectual discussions
And collegiality
That I remembered
From my years as a graduate student
In Spanish literature
At a major mid-western university.

That Self receded for all those years…

And almost completely disappeared

During The Year.

The Year of
GOING UP FOR TENURE.

Peers going up at the same time
Seemed to feel some tension….

But not the grinding anxiety,
The reality of the years of
Refusing to play the game,
But knowing it existed.
Denying that the hoops existed,
Much less jumping through them.

Spending an entire year
Thinking about retiring,
Withdrawing my dossier.

Fantasizing about
Refusing to go through the academic process
Of criticism and judgment.

Yet continuing to persevere.

Becoming decimated in
Body
Mind
Spirit
Self.

June 2011.
The deadline for submitting my papers for tenure and promotion

Beginning in November of that year
A black cloud of negativity over my head,
Matching the bleakness of the late autumn days outside my window,
Following me from place to place,
Occasionally raining on me with more interrogation
About my right to call myself a scholar, a writer, a poet.

Every ring of my office phone
Sped up heartbeat.
Freezing cold hands.

The unwelcome tremor in my voice …

If I decided to answer the phone.

Harder to get up every morning
An hour-long drive to my office
So bothered I couldn't even pay attention to the audiobook mysteries
Keeping me company as I drove.

So distracted I received a reckless driving ticket
Zipping along in the little red Beetle at 65 mph

Total obsession with retirement,
Escaping,
Moving on,
Thumbing my nose at the university and the entire academic system.

Joseph Roach's words resonate:
Memory serving as both "quotation and invention,
An improvisation on borrowed themes,
With claims on the future as well as the past." (1996, p. 33)

A conversation with my husband Dan
After an interrogating phone call from the Promotion and Tenure Committee.
Anger contorting my face,
Rage colouring my voice red:
"I am so sick of all of them,
So fed up with the system.
I just want to retire.
But as my choice, not theirs."

Such an oppressive belittling burden
Going through this process…
Leading me to question myself
As critically as they were questioning me.

And now this letter,
This affirmation
This blessing of my work.

Now part of the sacred fraternity
Of survivors of the process
The President of the university later calls
"The longest job interview you'll ever have."

Remembering
Early April 2012.

A letter from the Provost's Office.

I have passed through
The department,
The college,
The university committees.

Now I wait for
The formal vote by the Board of Visitors in June.

Am I really on a terrorists list
For signing a petition
Stating that Bill Ayers' involvement
With the Underground Weathermen
Was irrelevant to Obama's election campaign?

New worries set in.
Is the person who wrote the hate letter
Offering to pay my way to Europe
To live with the other Socialists
On the Board of Visitors?

Could that be used against me?

In the conservative environment of the academy,
Will someone look at my Facebook page and realize
How radical love (Freire, 2000/1970)
And radical teaching (Kincheloe, 2006/2003; Freire, 2005/1997)
And radical thought
Shape my world
My scholarship
My teaching
My outreach—
The triad that defines my academic persona?

Years of bravado about living the academic life
That allows me to live with myself,
Following my dad's advice
To look in the mirror in the morning
As a measuring stick for integrity....

Was it all going to come back and haunt me?

September 2012.
This official letter.

Does this letter erase months of agony and anger
Roiling in my gut,

Transforming my way of regarding the world?
Of regarding my work?

Sapping my energy,
Leaving me apathetic and lethargic,
Affecting not only my career,
But also my personal life.

A year of considering retirement,
Applying for Social Security—
Eligible on June 7,
Two days after the vote by the Board of Visitors
Three months before my official notification.

Summer 2012.
Plotting my retirement

No book order for my classes.
No preparation of syllabi.

Plotting how to send a letter of resignation.

Setting up my choice to leave, not theirs.

Move to Mexico.

My escape pod from this hell was ready.

Through the years, colleagues had escaped
Rather than endure the process.

Should I follow the lemmings?

Two things kept my fingers off the keyboard to write the resignation letter—
The thought of leaving my grandsons
Gavin and Isaac....

And the fact that I had not yet received an official letter.

My dad's words kept me going.
"You don't ever give up."

I had to see it through.

Summer 2011.
Phone calls and conversations about my dossier,
About the committee
Constantly recycling through my head.

December 2011.
My doctoral student/friend/co-author Jennifer and me

At my house
Sitting on the leather couch
In front of the fire,
Writing furiously
Sipping French press coffee with milk and sugar.

Ring. Ring. Ring.
"Hi Kris. Sharon[2] here.
Sorry to bother you at home,
But I have a few questions.
As you know,
Your dossier is with the Department Promotion and Tenure Committee."

As I know!
I know little else these days!

"There are a few points they would like for you to clarify."

Chest constricts,
Breath chokes my voice,
No breath.

"You apparently submitted to the committee two articles in which you used the same paragraph."

Taken aback.

"What articles?
What paragraph?"

Racing through my mind,
"What in the world are you talking about?"

"I believe they were about your service-learning.
Does that ring a bell?"

"Well, I submitted two articles about service-learning (2009a; 2009b)
To provide evidence of the excellence of my
Scholarship, teaching, and outreach.

To match my Candidate's Statement
My focus on critical pedagogy and autoethnography
My line of inquiry."

Even in a state of panic and mounting hysteria,
Academic language and robot thinking prevail.

Well indoctrinated, no?

"Talk to me about how the same paragraph appeared in both?
One external reviewer commented on that.

There is a concern about self-plagiarism."

Hands cold, trembling,
White face
Drained of all blood
Or maybe red due to
Heart thudding against my ribcage.

What if I have a stroke right now?
Then at least I could end this awful conversation.

Sudden clear mind.
Words tumbling out
Filling the need to chronologically order
At least some of the craziness of the years leading up to this moment:

June 2008,
Submission of an article to Norman Denzin.
Invitation to revise and resubmit.
Too many discourses:

Critical pedagogy
Service-learning
Mystory.

Suggestion:
Submit to a critical pedagogy journal
Or a service-learning journal.
Norman writes,
"I am only interested in the mystory."

Total revision.

September 2008.
Submission to a critical pedagogy journal.

Mid-December 2008.
Journal editor Joe Kincheloe's death.
Journal on hiatus.

What about my article?

Late December 2008.
A call for proposals for a service-learning article
Return to the original article
To extract the service-learning piece.

Expression of concern to a trusted colleague
Two articles that dealt with the same teaching practice,

But one informed by critical pedagogy,
One by service-learning.

He tells me,
"That's really not a problem, Kris.
That establishes your line of inquiry."

Both articles coming from the same source.
Both significantly, totally, revised.
Both accepted at the same time.
Both published at the same time.

My ethics questioned.
But not my senior memory.
Self-plagiarism:
Not a privilege for senior professors?

"Well, as I said one reviewer raised a question
About ownership of your words,
But this explanation makes good sense.
Can you provide documentation for all this?"

Sure.
I can provide documentation
That my words that fell onto the computer page
Fell out of my own mind.

But that's not enough.

The hard copy of Norman's letter.
All my email correspondence from the editors.

"Will that be sufficient?"

"That will be fine.
I can cite those when I write your letter of support."

...

"There *IS* one more question from another reviewer:

Why weren't your major articles about teaching ESL?"

Visions of the Inquisitor floating through my mind
Pointed hat puncturing my soul.

Phone still in my hand,
Attempting to get my voice out of my mouth.
Anger at the system strangling my words.

I remind my interrogator that
At every pre-tenure review since 2005,
I was asked the same question:

"Do you have any concerns?"

At every review
I gave the same answer:

"I don't write about teaching ESL.
I write about immigrant students and their communities.
I write about preparing a bunch of white middle class pre-service teachers
To understand the issues these kids face."

"Talk to me some more about that."

Breathing slows.
Heart still races,
But more slowly.

"The Coal Miner's Daughter Gets a Ph.D." (2011)
The impact of social class in the academy.
Using autoethnography to talk about working class kids
Outsiders due to social class
Navigating the school system,
Then the academy.

"Border Crossing: (Auto)Ethnography that Transcends Immigration/Imagination"
(2012)
The perspectives of the families who immigrate to the US
The perspectives of their families who stayed behind.

Always a focus on the stories people tell,
Not on statistics about a group.
Not about linguistics or language learning.
Always issues of social class, gender, ethnicity, nationality
About teaching marginalized kids."

"Okay.
That's all I need to write the letter."

Breathing space until January.
Then more academic game-playing.

Questions continuing.
Sporadic intervals.
Dossier traveling through the rest of the hierarchy.

Why weren't my reviewers from peer institutions?

They were.

Why did I submit articles that weren't really articles ...?
They were just poems?

Did they read them?

Under the cloak of rigor and academic rhetoric, meritocratic hierarchies are encouraged; we, as academics look upon our own, and each other's scholarship with suspicion, rather than healthy scepticism. Who's producing, who is worthy? (Spooner, 2010)

But it's more complex than that.

Or is it?

My tenure committee.

Basically good people trying to follow
Bureaucratic university guidelines.

Basically people who especially respect my extensive, authentic work
In the local immigrant and refugee community.

So why the questions?
I had the requirements.
The requisite number of articles in top-tier peer-reviewed journals.
Over a half million dollars in grant funding.
A good teaching record.
Numerous programs in the community.
Countless hours of university service.

So why the questions?
Why the red flags?

Why the resistance to a line of inquiry
That did not fit into the expected mould?

The strict and stringent expectations for
An "Assistant Professor of Second Language Education"
To write about second language acquisition.

The expectations for "scientific inquiry" as defined by the academy.
The (lack of) rhythm of
Introduction
Lit review
Methodology

Findings
Discussion.

Poems!
Critical pedagogy!
Autoethnography!

The torn veil of secrecy
That allowed me to be privy to information I shouldn't have known
About the goings-on of the secret inquisition team
Known as
The Promotion and Tenure Committee.

Walking down the hall in my building
Paranoid
Wondering who knows about my interrogation....
Who is tearing my work and me to shreds behind closed doors?

Good I didn't find out about
One negative vote from a colleague on the department committee
Until after I received the final letter.

And that I didn't know that one negative vote
Often rings the death knell for a tenure case
As it moves up through the hierarchy....
Department...
College...
University...
Provost...
Board of Visitors.

Interrogation.
Inquisition.
Torture.

Where's the research!
Where's the meaning in those
Meaningless poems?

Are those the same poems that people read
And send me emails thanking me
For being brave enough to write about the unspoken?

Voices playing through my head
Stuck on play and repeat.

Moving through the first year with tenure.

Moving from deep anger
To a sense of sadness.

How many assistant professors share these experiences?
How many have mostly good people on their committees?

How many people have colleagues who fight for them
As they slog through the hierarchy
As mine did for me?

Couldn't there could be a more humane way to work through the tenure process,
Especially for those of us who choose to follow a less common path?

I chose my path.

I knew my world would be there even if I was denied tenure.

I would still have my husband.
My kids and their families.
My world outside the academy.

I knew that my roles of
Wife
Mother
Grandmother
Would still be waiting for me
At the end of the endless road.

I had the luxury of knowing that I could retire
And my life would continue as usual....

Except for the remembered pain of failure in the tenure process.

Once again I write as inquiry (Richardson, 1994)
To understand my pain.
But also to heal
Mind
Spirit
Body
Intellect
Self.

The monkey of anxiety
No longer perched on my shoulder
Slobbering
Dripping his stinking saliva on all my thoughts
And making them incomprehensible.

Gone.

Free.

I had the courage to transgress and follow the call to autoethography
And I won the fight. (Poulos, 2010)

Ron Pelias' (2011) words speak to me,
Reminding me that I now have
Time to sit with friends
And to be pleased by their presence
And needing their presence
But yet feeling disconnected
Wanting more,
Wanting the words that might penetrate.

And so I continue to write my poems
And to sit in the presence of family and friends,
To seek the words that heal my
Mind
Spirit
Body
Intellect
Self.

"Writing out helps me heal...
[My poems] come out like a baby,
Cutting out the words that don't belong." (Mary Weems at ICQI, May 17, 2013)

The ethical questions.

Not wanting to hurt my colleagues
Who did the best they knew how to do,
But wanting to find healing
And closure
And the path to peace.

My friend Silvia Bénard tells me
That I am not narrating what happened,
But rather how I lived what happened.
Now I try to understand what happened and
To share my experience. (Bénard, 2013)

Silvia even shares Anne Lamott's (1994) words with me:
We all have the right to tell our own story.

And I have tried to do so =
In the most honest way possible,
Knowing that what I tell is

What I perceive today
About what happened almost three years ago
During one of the most emotion-laden times
Of my entire life....

Trying to process and understand.

I am following a dear colleague's advice to "refocus on [myself]"
And "to not let anyone pull [me] away from my passionate centre."
He tells me that I have found my "spiritual centre" and
I "can look forward to doing the things that really matter to [me]
And those [I] care about."

My struggle has yielded my [S]elf and my art. (Oates, 2003)

NOTES

[1] First published: Tilley-Lubbs, G. A. (2014b). The inquisition/torture of the tenure track. *Creative Approaches to Research, 7*(2). Reprinted with permission.

[2] All the names of the guilty/innocent/guilty have been changed to protect their identity. I'm not sure if it's due to fear for my job, or if it's because I know that good intentions were the underlying force for all the events/situations/circumstances that made my year such a tortured inquisition.

REFERENCES

Bénard, S. M. (2012). From impressionism to realism: Painting a conservative Mexican city. *Cultural Studies ⇔ Critical Methodologies, 13*(5), 427–431.

Freire, P. (2000/1970). *Pedagogy of the oppressed* (30th anniversary ed.). New York, NY: Continuum.

Freire, P. (2005/1997). *Teachers as cultural workers: Letters to those who dare to teach.* New York, NY: Continuum.

Kincheloe, J. L. (2006/2003). *Teachers as researchers: Qualitative inquiry as a path to empowerment.* New York, NY: Routledge.

Lamott, A. (1994). *Bird by bird: Some instructions on writing and life.* New York, NY: Pantheon.

Oates, J. C. (2003). *The faith of the writer: Life, craft, art.* New York, NY: HarperCollins.

Pelias, R. J. (2011). *Leaning: A poetics of personal relations.* Walnut Creek, CA: Left Coast Press.

Poulos, C. (2010). Transgressions. *International Review of Qualitative Research, 3*(1), 67–88.

Richardson, L. (1994). Writing: A method of inquiry. In N. K. Denzin & Y. S. Lincoln (Eds.), *Handbook of qualitative research* (pp. 516–529). Thousand Oaks, CA: Sage.

Roach, J. (1996). *Cities of the dead.* New York, NY: Columbia University.

Tilley-Lubbs, G. A. (2009a). Good intentions pave the way to hierarchy: A retrospective autoethnographic approach. *Michigan Journal of Community Service Learning, 16*(1), 59–68.

Tilley-Lubbs, G. A. (2009b). Troubling the tide: The perils and paradoxes of service-learning in immigrant communities. *International Journal of Critical Pedagogy, 2*(1), 67–87.

Tilley-Lubbs, G. A. (2011). The coal miner's daughter gets a Ph.D. *Qualitative Inquiry, 17*(9). doi:10.1177/1077800411420669

Tilley-Lubbs, G. A. (2012). Border crossing: (Auto)Ethnography that transcends imagination/immigration. *International Review of Qualitative Research, 4*(4).

Gresilda A. Tilley-Lubbs
Faculty of Teaching and Learning
School of Education
Virginia Tech
Blacksburg, Virginia, USA

SECTION 3

OBSERVING THE SELF AS VULNERABLE OTHER

KELLY MUNLY, GRESILDA A. TILLEY-LUBBS
AND CARL SHEUSI

7. HENRY AND SNEAKY

Finding Resolution to My Ontological Question about Service

ABSTRACT

This chapter presents Kelly Munly's reflexive exploration of service experience in two settings: Adult Foster Care, and cleaning. She reflects on how the latter provided a pivotal moment that informs her understanding of her motivation for caregiving. She incorporates moments of dialogue to clearly illustrate the life experiences that inform her ontology. Introspectively, she considers life experiences, academic literature, and relational contexts that further contribute to her broader understanding. Visual models and scripting provide tools for arriving at a new point of connection with populations served through caregiving professions. This work has implications for professional caregivers and other social service providers who seek ways to feel more connected with those they serve, as well as supporting those professionals to be honest with themselves about their own internal processes and social positions.

Henry Helping Me

"Hey Sneaky. How'd you get here? Do you have your car?"

I smile at Henry's use of his nickname for me. He likes to shake his finger at me and accuse me with a smile of "sneaking" into the Adult Foster Care home every time I'm there.

"No, Henry, I took the bus."

"Did you drive?"

"No, I took the bus."

"You got a ride?"

"Yep."

"Mmm, hmmm." Henry smiles and pats me on the shoulder.

BACKGROUND

In this conversation, Henry, an 82-year-old Adult Foster Care[1] resident, was caring for me in a reversal of our roles. I study adult development and aging as part of my doctoral work, and I had decided to work with Carl,[2] an Adult Foster Care provider,

G. A. Tilley-Lubbs & S. B. Calva (Eds.), Re-Telling Our Stories, 105–122.

to fulfil a gerontology practicum requirement. He provides care for multiple residents, including Henry.

Carl has a background in philosophy, psychology, and holistic health studies, as well as years of experience providing intensive community-based family counselling. He heard about the opportunity to provide Adult Foster Care from a friend, and appreciated it as a way to separate from the corporate, billing-driven therapeutic contexts that he had previously experienced. He also relished the opportunity to create a person-centred environment that would truly be a home for individuals.

Documentation and structure are inherently part of the services funded by Medicaid, but through Adult Foster Care, Carl has greater opportunity to create for his residents a meaningful environment that goes far beyond the billable hour. His Adult Foster Care home is his own home, and he lives in the same town with his parents and siblings, providing an opportunity for extended family interactions for his residents as well. Carl is one of my best friends. We met in 1996 and reconnected when I returned to graduate school closer to his home in 2009. He has become one of my most valued confidantes. Through our ability to have deep and honest conversations about life, I really began to understand the rich experience he was facilitating for his residents—and for himself—through Adult Foster Care.

I was drawn to the humanitarian possibilities of Adult Foster Care because of strong relationships with my grandparents, and because I have been shocked to see what they and their friends have endured in terms of ageist attitudes and sometimes abusive or neglectful care. I also once worked at a health care centre that the local Emergency Medical Teams jokingly called the "Death Care Centre," because people came in but never left. I have memories of Alzheimer's patients not getting their diapers changed out of a care provider's spite and distorted way of channelling her own stress. However, in the midst of this sometimes neglectful and abusive environment, I found human beings, rich with endearing and vibrant qualities. For example, my friend Lilly, a resident of the "Death Care Centre," with waved and artfully sprayed red hair and a flirtatious nature, attempted to seduce and play with all that came through the door there, not inhibited by the fact that she was confined to a wheelchair and needed help to go to the bathroom. She was seen as a troublemaker at the "Death Care Centre."

I have been inspired by Adult Foster Care as a small setting that can provide a context for embracing the unique personas of its residents, whether they are Medicaid dependent or have private funds, whether they have been destitute and suffering from disabilities their whole lives, or whether they are recently ill. The small setting and home-like nature of Adult Foster Care provides an opportunity for more time spent between the care provider and care recipient, which fosters deeper relationships that have an opportunity to be reciprocal (Foucault, 1977).

I structure my autoethnography by presenting non-sequential content, including current reflections on my research in the context of interviews with an elderly woman and the author's memories or flashbacks of visiting his own grandmother, which provides a compelling way to bring in the richness of experience that might be fundamental to a research project. Furthermore, Evans' (2006) incorporation of historical background on issues related to health care for women, with marked implications for elder women, brings context and power to the piece. In my autoethnography, I present my perspectives on Adult Foster Care in the context of service work, similar in some content to Evans' work on elder female health and institutional care.

I intermix descriptions of Adult Foster Care settings with flashbacks on experiences I have had working in nursing homes and other care settings with older adults, and with my own older family members. I provide some historical and research context (see Note 1) for the care setting to underline the social relevance of this piece. Thinking of autoethnography in general, and the aims of my piece in particular, I refer to Clews and Furlong's (2006) statement that narrative inquiry, including autoethnography, provides a "means to understand and express the tacit knowledge from human experience that shaped professional practices" (p. 200).

I incorporate writing tactics, such as narrative snapshots that bolster the evocative force of the piece, including snapshots of myself in the context of the story I present. I include artefacts such as related documents that embody meaning related to the piece, metaphor, and an idea of the journeys in my life (Muncy, 2005). I implement narrative snapshots of the individuals I present in this autoethnography, though with some caution out of respect for their identities and vulnerability. I hope that the narrative snapshots are vivid enough to support an understanding of the equity between care providers and clients, the deconstruction of the binary in this relationship, and the personal freedom experienced by care recipients.

The distinction of "analytic autoethnography" from "evocative autoethnography" informs this piece, since it serves to solidify autoethnography as work that contributes to "developing theoretical understandings of broader social phenomena" (Anderson, 2006, pp. 373–375). I am "a full member of the research group or setting" and I reference others, not just myself, as participants or voices in that context (p. 378). I strive to present the social and theoretical relevance of this topic, so I have included others' observations and dialogues, including informal conversations with Adult Foster Care clients and providers. Although these conversations have not been explicitly stated in my piece, they have helped to shape my text.

I assert that, "A distinction between analysis and creative or evocative first-person writing styles is unnecessary and counterproductive" and that the "intensive self-immersion and the discoveries" are some of the strengths of analytic autoethnography that contribute to its relevance and subsequent social power (Vryan, 2006, p. 407). My goal is for this piece to help readers "better understand or explain other people, experience[s], and/or context[s]" (p. 408). I keep this in mind as I seek to portray my own experience as one care provider, alongside my experiences with Adult Foster Care clients and providers having their own unique experiences in the system in which they live and work.

DISCUSSION: REFLECTION ON HENRY IN THE LARGER
CONTEXT OF ADULT FOSTER CARE

Henry smiles a little, giving me the feeling that he knows we are sharing a joking moment that is special to each of us. He scratches his head through his white hair and stoops over to open the refrigerator to get his water bottle. It is interesting to me how taken care of I feel in these interactions with Henry, even though I am supposed to be caring for him. I don't know why I am surprised, as this sense of reciprocity is in fact an aim of this Adult Foster Care agency. Wall Residences does not believe in a caregiver-client binary in which the client is a receiver of care, without reciprocity in the relationship. Wall Residences recognizes the importance of acknowledging the reciprocity that certainly exists in some form between all care providers and care recipients. But my feeling surprises me every time. I feel like I gain more than I give. I provide a presence for Henry. Along with Carl, I do my best to create opportunities for Henry to have experiences that he would not have had in an institution. He provides me with a sense that all is well in the world. He provides me with jokes and smiles and caring.

Me Helping Henry

I smile at Henry and watch as he brings his dishes to the counter.
   "Do you want me to do these?" he asks.
   "Sure." Henry cannot hear me well, so I pat him on the back and smile.
   "Okay." He methodically washes his dishes.
   "I think I'm going to go out for a smoke," he says.
   I nod my head. "Okay."
   I keep an eye on Henry as he proceeds to smoke his pipe outside to make sure he does not fall. I provide a presence for Henry.

Orchestration of Opportunities

In family-oriented Adult Foster Care settings, person-centred care does not model strict recreational structure, but rather the orchestration of opportunities in which individual clients have the space and time to express their individuality and power of choice. The care provider thereby has the opportunity to behold and appreciate the resident as an integral part of a family and community.

   When I first started working with Carl and his clients, I brainstormed about activities I could implement to foster the development and community integration of Carl's residents. For example, I understood that Carl's resident Henry enjoyed socializing with friends and people at church, and that he often took to spontaneous singing of tunes and hymns. It thus seemed natural to think that engaging Henry to socialize with others in a nursing home setting, giving him an opportunity to share those tunes and hymns, would be a meaningful form of community integration.

However, I quickly understood that as a provider or back-up worker, the nuances of designing such activities frequently lose meaning with shifting circumstances and understandably fluctuating wishes and needs of residents. Often all that is required is to offer open opportunities in benign settings, and residents will discover their natural and preferred way to meaningfully engage with their surroundings. Realizing this fuller understanding of person-centred planning in an Adult Foster Care context came to full fruition after the following pivotal moment with Carl and Henry.

I went with Carl and his residents on an excursion to the Village Garden nursery in Appomattox, Virginia. It was a beautiful autumn day. The sun felt warming. There were barns and rows and rows of potted chrysanthemums. A woman in overalls came out of a barn to meet us. Her mood was forthright; she seemed tired but open and welcoming. Henry looked toward her with a smile and as she came very close to us, began talking with her about a song. I felt some apprehension, knowing that Henry had the habit of monologue conversations that could continue for long periods of time. I looked at Carl, who, perhaps out of habitually finding himself in unexpected situations, looked neutrally ahead from beneath his baseball cap, with a small smile and supportive presence. Without waiting for her interest, Henry puffed up his chest and smiled at the woman as he began to sing all the verses of the tune *I Wish I Was Single Again*, which he called *The Devil's Grandmother*:

I wish I was single again
I wish I was single again
For when I was single, my pockets did jingle,
O, I wish I was single again.

Henry straightened his wiry frame as he sang, his shirt coming untucked, with a handkerchief stuffed midway down his torso in a gap between his shirt's buttons. Tobacco stains dotted his shirt and hands, and the tell-tale pipe emerged from his front pocket. He smiled as he sang, in usual friendly performance, affirming those around him with nods, but unable to hear or process responses from those around him. I looked to Carl's model of allowing Henry and his other residents to have their own experiences.

Well, I married me another, O then
I married me another,
O then I married me another,
She's th' devils grandmother.
O, I wish I was single again.

Seemingly as a reward for Henry's song, the woman in overalls offered us a complete tour of the nursery in a compact garden truck, from fish ponds to pumpkin patch. I laughed to myself as the woman, Henry, and Carl sat in the front, and another resident and I sat in the back enjoying an unexpected moment of traversing rough terrain. The outing concluded with the selection of a gigantic pumpkin, and

I reflected on how it would offer Carl's residents and me a chance to practice another one of our hobbies of cooking, preparing, and sampling pumpkin bread and pies. Henry would contribute through joyful eating. This beautiful autumn day gave me an opportunity to understand that appropriate person-centred lifestyle strategies in Adult Foster Care settings are not about finite activities or strict structure, but about offering Adult Foster Care residents similar lifestyle opportunities that anyone would desire—opportunities for engaging with life and experiences according to spontaneous preferences and whims.

Just like we all have hobbies and preferences, Henry enjoys a variety of activities: calling friends that he has known most of his life, with the help of amplified sound on the house telephone; singing folk tunes and hymns and expressing himself to the site supervisor or to me; searching for and organizing items in his room; and smoking his pipe and drinking coffee outside. I too like to listen to music, cook, read good books, sing to myself, drink coffee, and talk to good friends. I appreciate opportunities for these activities on my own time, and not on a schedule. After my liminal moment at the nursery, I now suspect that Henry feels much the same.

Ongoing Discussion: Inner Conflict Regarding Roles

Sometimes when working with Henry, I have felt like a peer, especially during moments of realization when I discover that we have hobbies in common, such as listening to music and drinking coffee. I have also felt this way during the times when I realize he is taking care of me, just as I am of him. However, at other times, I have felt like the objective practitioner or scientist, distant from Henry and analysing him according to the categories of his problems. I may also sometimes feel like a peer because, inspired by my close relationships with my grandparents, I have always had friends of all ages and diverse health conditions. I am also a social scientist, so sometimes my career mind-set dominates in my interactions with populations that need service and interest me.

I find myself fluctuating between these two interpretations of experiences. Henry is sensitive to how others see him, sometimes seemingly intuitive about what others think and feel about him. I remember sitting with Carl across the room from Henry and talking about Henry's tendency to monologue. Henry could not hear us, but his countenance changed from enjoyment to something that appeared like quiet anxiety and shame. I became quite sure that Henry had perceived our conversation, either by reading our lips or by intuiting the feeling of our conversation. I felt terrible when I realized that this might have happened. It seemed to me that Henry's mood swung from happy to pensive and anxious when I was in a more relationally distant mode as an objective and insensitive observer, rather than an equal peer. I recognize the practitioner and scientist in me and try to use intellectual means to grapple with this conflict.

Carl has described similar ongoing efforts, day in and day out as the primary, full-time care provider. The graphics depicted below in Appendices A and B, titled

"Care Recipient" and "Care Provider" have helped me to intellectually see and strive to embrace that providers like Carl and me are very much the same as Henry and Carl's other residents, with the potential to be objectified (indicated by the outer circle) and the potential to be appreciated for the warm people that we are (indicated by the direct quote in the inner circle). I present graphics specifically illustrating Henry and myself according to these layers of possible perception by others. Henry and I simply find ourselves in different life circumstances due to cumulative intersections of advantage or disadvantage. For example, Henry has not experienced the benefits of being with family (biological or adoptive) since infancy, and this lifelong experience of lacking familial belonging intersects with an experience of intellectual disability across his lifespan, as well as intersecting with dementia in old age. On the positive side, Henry's evolving resilience, his love of people, the opportunity to live independently between several decades of institutionalization and his time with Carl in Adult Foster Care, and his strong thirty-year relationship with his church community have all contributed to his positive memories, reflections, and continued enjoyment in life. I have experienced a strong biological family network since birth, I am fortunate to have reasonably good health, and I have been given or found opportunities to pursue education through the doctoral

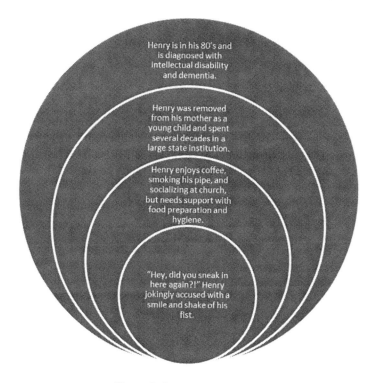

Figure 1. Care recipient Henry

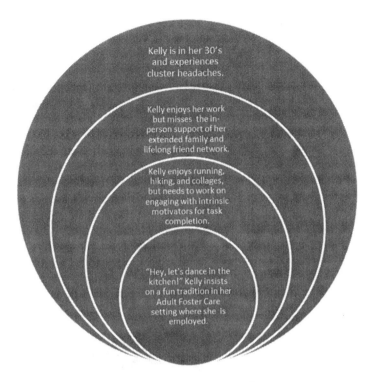

Kelly is in her 30's and experiences cluster headaches.

Kelly enjoys her work but misses the in-person support of her extended family and lifelong friend network.

Kelly enjoys running, hiking, and collages, but needs to work on engaging with intrinsic motivators for task completion.

"Hey, let's dance in the kitchen!" Kelly insists on a fun tradition in her Adult Foster Care setting where she is employed.

Figure 2. Care provider Kelly

level. On the negative side, I sometimes struggled with navigating life as a child of divorced parents and two very different family cultures, I have had moments of isolation as a doctoral student, and my optimism in life has sometimes waned as a result of these experiences intersecting. I still realize my privilege, however, and that my struggle has been largely temporary.

Epilogue (the Rumination Continues): Henry and Sneaky

I watch Carl, fatigued and writing his notes for the documentation required by the public agencies that regulate Adult Foster Care. Henry moves from the living room to the kitchen, looking at me, and he gives me one of his little smiles. I am tired too and almost don't smile back, not because I don't care, but because I am processing my own thoughts. I catch myself neglecting my role and give an encouraging smile back. Is it part of my role to simply be myself? To provide an opportunity for Henry and the other residents to experience me as part of the human dynamics of their home, imperfect? I later realize this is another liminal moment.

"Carl, I'm going to rest for a moment."

I go into a side room to sit and close my eyes. Carl continues to work on his notes and greets another back-up worker entering the living room to take the day shift.

"I'm thinking of taking the guys to the day centre, they have some good activities this week," she shares.

Carl smiles quietly, his cap pulled down over his early morning face. "Okay."

I can envision the guys moving into the living room, having bathed, eaten, and dressed, ready for their daily routine. They are objects of this routine, with some plans they like, and probably some plans they don't like. In this routine they will have some opportunities for their jokes, dissatisfaction, grumbles, and praise. Carl and his workers, including me, try to make the opportunities a reality. We all function within a structure, and sometimes we are more successful than others.

I hear a knock on the door. I get up from the comfortable chair where I am resting and see Henry's smiling face.

"Are you going to be here tonight?" he asks tenderly, holding his walker in one hand. He bunches up his face and I know a joke is coming. "Don't you sneak off without saying good-bye!" He laughs and shakes my hand roughly.

I realize that I feel energized and warmed by this interaction. "Bye, Henry! I will see you later!" I give a smile that I intend to be reassuring and watch him as he follows his morning routine, walking carefully out to the back-up worker's minivan, surrendering to the day.

ONTOLOGY AND EPISTEMOLOGY

So, why do I care about caregiving? Why am I drawn to it when it is fatiguing? Is it caring or is it a compulsion? Why do I do it, and why do I explore it?

I grew up in a household that practiced meditation stemming from ancient India, and I too practiced this and eventually took traditional training to become a meditation teacher. The understanding accompanying this teaching and practice is that all of reality—all that we see around us, static, dynamic, and down to the quantum level of existence—manifests from a field of "pure Being" or "pure consciousness." This understanding was absolutely enmeshed in my world view as I grew up. Intellectually, I can grasp that there may be a different "reality," but I believe it would take a dramatic life event to shake this vision or understanding of things from my cognitive-perceptual experience. However, this understanding of reality and existence, which ultimately posits all things as equal, all rooted in unbounded pure Being, a field of consciousness, feels compatible with a driving service orientation that was especially prominent with my maternal grandparents. Even from a selfish perspective, if at the level of Being, as the Upanishads say, "I am That," "Thou art that," and "All this is That," why would you not join hands with other human beings to achieve a better quality of life for all? This was compatible with the Methodist Christian service orientation of my maternal grandfather, who was a minister, and my grandmother, a minister's wife on fire with advocacy for whomever had a need. We lived with them during my early childhood, so these influences were primary for my initial orientation in life.

However, there may also be a disconnect between my root influence of Eastern philosophy and practice and the "Love thy neighbour" maxim of Christianity. Under the hat of Eastern philosophy, meditation is the means to transform manifest reality from the level of Being or unbounded consciousness; hands-on social work is considered a healthy behaviour, but otherwise a band-aide and not significant transformative work. With these different understandings of reality combined within myself, my epistemology or perspective on knowledge and meaning in life is naturally influenced. For example, finding it difficult to separate from my rootedness in Eastern philosophy, I largely accept my social service orientation as something I love, but not as necessarily transformative on a large or profound scale. I realize that I love social service because I feel that I bring meaning to others' life experiences, and perhaps more than that, they create meaning for me. I admit that there is this selfish component, especially in light of ambivalence that can arise due to the difficult nature of social service work, such as care work, compounding the potential for ambivalence inspired by my spiritual orientation. The epilogue above effectively conveys my experience of ambivalence in Adult Foster Care work, primarily due to fatigue, perhaps couched in an unspoken spiritual ambivalence. However, this ambivalence also transforms into interpersonal meaning for me as I realize the meaning that I bring to Henry's experience, the meaning that he brings into mine, and that we are all human in our efforts to create good experience.

Privilege

My ontology brings together or is an expression of different moments or levels of my experience. This ontology naturally influences my epistemology, or how I value diverse forms of knowledge. Both of the formative influences in my ontology reflect privilege and subsequent power in my beginnings, although at times mixed with some moments of disparity. The fact that my parents had an opportunity to take an Eastern meditation course, and beyond this, to spend several months becoming teachers themselves, reflects a location of finances and time. They were both in college, surrounded by education and educated peers, when they learned about such an opportunity. They both had jobs to pay for their costs, but were able to live with parents who supported them before and after their meditation teacher training courses in Europe. Our capacity to practice this technique indicates that we all had a moment in the morning and in afternoons, before and after work or school, when we could practice. We did not work three jobs. They each worked only one job, and in my case, I attended school. We all had more than our basic needs taken care of, allowing us to enjoy and appreciate the benefits of a spiritual technique that has contributed to an ontology that includes a unified field underlying all manifest particles in everything around us, creating a sense of human equality and unity in that common source.

My maternal grandparents' service orientation stemmed largely from my grandfather's privilege to take training in seminary, and my grandmother's capacity to be a full-time minister's wife and mother at home. However, they were temporarily poor at different parts of their life—they relied on Social Security, without retirement, after my grandfather had a stroke. My grandfather was often hungry through seminary, on the weekends eating only crackers that he had managed to take from the restaurant where he worked during the week. However, he had the opportunity to be at the university as a student, despite hardships, although his ongoing hunger and stress may have been the foundation for later health problems. My grandmother shopped at thrift shops. Nonetheless, there was a sense of having profited from education and of having enough. My great-grandmother was there and lent money to my grandparents once. I would say their privilege was that of education and knowledge, and land to live on, but not always money, nor new things.

In my current state of dissertation research design, I realize I am privileged and empowered as a researcher to ask questions of Adult Foster Care providers who may be working at such a job because that is simply a job available to them—a job that is all encompassing, not always allowing opportunity or time for such intellectual pursuits, self-reflection and hobbies. They may feel caught by my questions, just as I feel caught by "Why aren't you married?" and "How is it going with your dissertation?" These questions trigger feelings of vulnerability for me, and a questioning of my own adequacy in relationships and professional life. If they asked me such questions, I would need to feel a surge of inner strength to combat the simultaneously rising vulnerability; I may momentarily not feel the privilege of being the researcher, or, if I choose, I can posture with this researcher identity. However, having this choice to posture is a privilege.

Motivation to Serve

My spiritual upbringing—in one sense influenced by Eastern, Vedic ideas of relative non-attachment (i.e., freedom from feeling bound or attached to relative existence, or all that we see or otherwise perceive around us), and in another sense influenced by a Christian service orientation, has created a complex mix of ambivalence and a desire to serve. The presence of ambivalence in my experience may also contribute to my curiosity about the ambivalence experienced by others in the service professions, including Adult Foster Care providers. Perhaps even if initially motivated by a service orientation, does this drive fade into a greater ambivalence? Freire's (1970) *Pedagogy of the Oppressed* is a helpful resource to reflect on this question, and on the value of encouraging constant reflection to connect with those to whom we owe service due to prior inequity and injustice. I may also need to go more deeply into Eastern texts to explore motivations for *karma yoga*, or unity with others through action. Eastern philosophy is diverse and multifaceted. Possibly my ambivalence could be resolved through greater exploration of how Eastern thinkers have managed to negotiate the contrast between meditation for individual and societal transformation, or on a more relative level of existence, action to alleviate immediate suffering and struggle in relative life. For me, understanding and fully integrating the meaning of social service into my being and consciousness may involve the "hermeneutical bridge-building" between Western and Eastern philosophies (Steinberg, 2012, p. 193), as well acknowledging that there is a "cultural conceptual context of knowledge" (Easton-Brooks, 2012, p. 39) including the epistemologies that inform who I am, what is important, and even what is profound and transformative. Resolving my ambivalence in this way and consequently gaining clarity about and comfort with who I am and what is important to me would assist me with going forward professionally with greater confidence about the compatibility of my personal and professional selves, and with the belief that I am sharing knowledge worth having with students. As I have intended for social service to be an integral part of my research and teaching in a university setting, clarifying this ambivalence will help me to gain professional clarity.

Resolution of the role of social service within an ontology and epistemology influenced by Eastern influence may also be resolved by embracing tenets of care theory that emphasize the reciprocity in caregiving relationships. I have reviewed this reciprocity as a major part of my dissertation theoretical framework, forming the basis of opportunity in which care recipients can experience being valued participants in relationships and communities (Noddings, 2010; Tronto, 1998). Embracing this care theory perspective places emphasis on the relational value that I receive as a caregiver, and the motivation for my service as essentially self-serving.

I am aware that this reciprocity in caregiving relationships with elders has been continuous from my close relationships with grandparents as a little girl, and related awareness of myself as the recipient of relational richness from these intergenerational connections, as can be evidenced by this childhood memory:

Childhood Memory of Intergenerational Reciprocity

My grandpa smiled at me, his eyes glimmering with some mischief. We both liked to eat. We were going to McDonald's, *where old lonely people in the country go to be near others,* my grandma would later say, after my grandpa died. We drove down Route 4 quietly, and I kept looking at my grandpa. *What if he would have a heart attack right now,* I thought to myself. *What would I do?* I casually opened the glove compartment and surveyed the tools, as if looking for one that might save a life. I closed the compartment and looked at my grandpa again. I smiled and savoured the moment with a little bit of nervousness about the unknown losses ahead.

Are my relationships with care recipients in my adulthood simply efforts to sustain these warm relational connections that were extinguished with the death of my grandparents? This may be partly true, although I also have a separate impulse to care for individuals who are more vulnerable, even when it is not convenient for me, as illustrated by my flashbacks with Henry. However, this impulse to care for a more vulnerable person again often leads to relationally rich experiences. Is it thus my long-term memory of this richness that sustains this behaviour for self-serving purposes, or is my caregiving impulse truly intended for the care recipient's benefit? Continuing to reflect on my relationship with more vulnerable individuals and my motivations to provide care may simply be good Freirean practice to sustain clarity of intention and momentum toward social justice for individuals needing care (Freire 1970). Individuals experiencing disability and who need care experience social injustice across multiple intersections, often experiencing lower income, especially as disability intersects with age, gender, and race (Carey, 2009; Redfood and Houser, 2010; Stoller and Gibson, 2000a, 2000b). Without resolution of my perspective on the meaning and impact of social service action along with transcendental, transformative action through meditation, I choose to pursue both paths with the intention of bringing transformation to contexts and experiences that call for social justice action and change.

ONTOLOGICAL RESOLUTION THROUGH THE KARMA YOGA OF CLEANING

Life has provided an experience of *karma yoga,* an experience of unity with others through action, though which action I am achieving both self-preservation and overcoming a sense of class separation. This experience has moved me past the recognition of reciprocity that I find in caregiving to one closer to sameness that can only be achieved through sharing actual lived experience. This experience came about through an opportunity to clean.

Opportunity Knocks

"I'm doing some caregiving work to tie me over until I finish school," I said. "I wish I had more hours though." *My budget was tight.* My apartment manager Sharon's manner made me comfortable to confide in her. I felt I was living with a subtle, but steady, nervousness about making things work as I began my last year of graduate work, and I reflected on my numerous efforts to apply for other jobs.

"Well, we got cleaning jobs." Sharon said. "I work in the office five days a week, clean in the evening, and do caregiving for a woman on weekend nights. I've been doing that for a few years now. I get uneasy if I take off more than a few days. I've only taken off a few weekends in the past few years. I'm doing okay, but I want to have enough to be there for my kids." She walked along side of me as she talked, looking at me and smiling steadily.

Wow, that's a work ethic, and it sounds pretty good. I wish I were that kind of busy. What was I going to do? Say I was too good to clean? I had just said to a

friend earlier in the summer, "At least I'm not cleaning toilets." Murphy's Law.
I couldn't delay my answer too long, because that would reveal my reluctance,
my inner snob. "As needed" cleaning would be a perfect supplement to my
assisted living work, convenient and something I could do when not working
on my dissertation. I could clean in the middle of the night if I wanted.

"Yeah" I said with a smile and enthusiasm that I tried to make genuine, "I would like that."

Sharon was waiting for my response, and yet was momentarily startled when I responded. "We have more than 100 apartments to clean this summer. I just didn't think you...." She stopped. "I can always get people to work" she smiled maternally.

"I am not a very good cleaner," I said. "I have never done it professionally." I had thoughts of one of my best friends, a prior roommate, who had sometimes become upset with me because I was such a poorly skilled housekeeper. I had learned to keep my mess in my own room. I was getting better though.

"Why don't you start by helping me? I'm cleaning Apartment M5 tonight."

"Okay great. Just text me when you would like me to stop by."

"Sounds good. It will be sometime between 7:00 and 9:00." Sharon radiated assurance.

Circumstances forced me into this karma yoga that contrasts with the Christian service orientation that surrounded my childhood, but which still perpetuated a sense of separation between my family and myself and others. Kris Tilley-Lubbs (2011) discusses a similar liminal experience of separateness of identity in the context of doing research with families experiencing the struggles of immigration; while sharing their cultural background through family ties of marriage, she realizes that her privilege and separateness remain. Similarly, my financial circumstances compelled me to work at a job that I knew would be temporary, and not something I would do as a lifelong occupation.

Separateness

I was four, and I watched Pat vacuum in my grandmother's house. Her head was bent over and her face was not visible as she focused on the bright blue rug in my mother's bedroom. Pat's dark brown hair cloaked any glimpse of her face. She pushed the vacuum back and forth, conveying a sense of resignation to her plight. Pat was 40, she had six kids and her mom, and she had moved the family to southern Maryland from what my grandma said was Appalachia, maybe West Virginia or North Carolina, to escape an abusive husband. My grandparents lived on Social Security and had health problems, but when she could afford it, my grandma would hire Pat to give her some needed income. My grandma was always collecting clothes and household items from yard sales and thrift shops to give to Pat and her family, or to send to a charity in Appalachia.

The family lived in a house back in the woods in the working class bay community where we lived. It was almost like a hollow, without the mountain. I didn't go there back in the woods. The kids that lived there got into trouble and were older than I. But they weren't intimidating anymore when they were in our house. Sometimes two of the older girls would babysit me. *What did they actually feel about me? Was I the privileged little girl to them, spoiled in their working class context?*

Closer, But Still Separate and Different

Now I am going to clean, to be given an opportunity to make things work. I'm not looking for hand-outs from family. I have exhausted my opportunities for departmental funding, and I need to be in this small university town with limited job opportunities to be close to my advising. Sharon is moving fast around the apartment, showing me the processes of using *Dawn Power Soak* on the blinds and the kitchen cabinet handles, using the *Magic Eraser* to clean off shower scum, and prepping the kitchen cabinets with degreaser.

I feel slow in comparison as I lie down on the floor to reach into the back of the lower cabinets, my t-shirt and jeans becoming soaked with degreaser. My skin is a little irritated. I should use gloves, but sometimes it's faster not to. My hands will feel it the next day. I clumsily mop the stripper onto the kitchen tiles for the second time. The first time I waited too long to scrape it off with the razor blade, and the tiles were still dingy. This one bedroom apartment has taken me 13 hours. I feel a sense of satisfaction and even elation as I am close to completion in scraping the second round of stripper. I see the clean white tiles. Sharon kindly helps me with mopping on the wax. I am awkward.

Not the Same

The experience of unity through the action of cleaning is not perfect. I am still separate, having the possibility for privilege in my future, a future of one well-paid job, not several underpaid jobs. But, I am closer through life experience, and it has been a real moment, compelled by life experiences, not contrived and not theoretical. This has given me a taste of unity in experience that moves beyond the reciprocal relational value that I discovered when first working with Henry in the Adult Foster Care setting. Here I find greater union through economically forced experience. This has been more powerful for me than a fabricated simulation to experience what it is like to be poor, living with a disability, or old, for example. There are both online and seminar resources and trainings to try to simulate these experiences; however, we do not seek out forced or compelled life experiences to help us relate better to others. Therefore, in efforts to create better understanding and relationship, it is necessary to foster simulations.

With that in mind, during a conference paper presentation titled "Autoethnography: Care Settings and Medicalized Models of Caregivers," Kris and I implemented performance methodology of scripting and reading the types of graphics presented in Figure 1 and Figure 2 as a further means of living the experience of care providers and recipients. Using this methodology, we were able to cast a critical eye on what happens in different care settings, and specifically how care receivers are seen by their caregivers and the surrounding care contexts. I asked conference volunteers to read brief scripts with us, representing individuals receiving care in Adult Foster Care and Nursing Home settings, as well as representing myself as a caregiver. I also asked the audience to reflect with me as each script was read, reflecting on the experiences of each setting and individual. The scripting included alternation between more objective observations and more subjective, personal reflections on each person being described, whether care receiver or caregiver. The following script is about another Adult Foster Care resident than Henry.

Tom

Guest Reader: This is about Tom, who lives in an Adult Foster Care setting, funded by Medicaid ID.

Guest Reader: Tom is in his 50's and experiences mental illness and intellectual disability.

Kelly Comments: This is Tom's description in his care plan. I'm glad that in the Adult Foster Care home, I have had the chance to really know him, and he has the chance to feel known.

Guest Reader: Tom has lost his most emotionally supportive kin, his grandmother, and is abandoned by other family.

Kelly Comments: Tom and I sometimes talk about our love for our grandmothers, and how we miss them, and what they used to cook.

Guest Reader: Tom enjoys comics, mythology, and cooking but needs support to follow through on tasks.

Kelly Comments: Tom's intellect and capacity to remember facts about his comic characters and mythology amaze me. Sometimes I have trouble following through on tasks too.

Guest Reader: "You're the bomb and the bee's knees!" Tom exclaimed with usual affection. "Will you help me make fried apples?"

Kelly Comments: As always with Tom, I'm aware of the reciprocity in our relationship—I gain at least as much as I give. I leave the Adult Foster Care feeling warm from these interactions. Tom is a devoted friend, as much as he can be, and really more of a friend to me than I am to him.

Kris and I found that the conference presentation participants and listeners were engaged with and enthusiastic about the content. They expressed being moved by the issues conveyed through the scripting, relating to an area that was not previously dominant for them in their life experiences. We would like to continue to use scripting and performance methodology to bring crucial issues to the community, whether issues related to caregiving, long-term care, service-learning, or immigration. The scripting we create is based on authoethnographic reflection, field observations, and interviews. We hope to evoke individual and community interest in issues important to us, including creating integrated and relational care settings for individuals in our community—individuals that could be us at any time.

NOTES

[1] Adult Foster Care responds to the 1999 Supreme Court Olmstead Decision to provide community-integrated alternatives for long term care for adults with disabilities (Virginia Department of Social Services, Division of Family Services, Adult Services Programs, 2010). Adults with intellectual disabilities need ongoing care and, among the older adult population, are at greatest risk for comorbidity with additional disability and mental illness (Phillips, Ajrouch, & Hillcoat-Nallétamby, 2010). In addition to a need for ongoing care, it is the right of individuals with intellectual disabilities to live as independently as possible, with choices available for friendship and chosen activities within the surrounding community (Brooker, 2004; Kitwood, 1997; Wall Residences, 2010b). Adult Foster Care is structured uniquely in every state, in regulatory guidelines, number of residents, and funding mechanisms (Mollica, Simms-Kastelein, Cheek, Baldwin, Farnham, Reinhard, & Accius, 2009). Adult Foster Care offers a community-integrated long-term care option that has the potential to both provide medical care and to support person-centred choices among residents (Sherman & Newman, 1988; Virginia Department of Social Services, Division of Family Services, Adult Services Programs, 2010; Wall Residences, 2010a; Wall Residences, 2010b).

[2] I make an effort to partially mask Carl's care context to better protect the anonymity of his residents.

REFERENCES/BIBLIOGRAPHY

Anderson, L. (2006). Analytic autoethnography. *Journal of Contemporary Ethnography, 35*(4), 373–395.
Brooker, D. (2004). What is person-centered care in dementia? *Reviews in Clinical Gerontology, 13*(1), 215–222.
Carey, A. (2009). *On the margins of citizenship: Intellectual disability and civil rights in twentieth-century America.* Philadelphia, PA: Temple University.
Clews, R., & Furlong, D. (2006). Family caring for older adults: Teaching and learning from our own stories. *Teaching Showcase Proceedings, 2006. Acadia University, Canada.* 197–204. Retrieved from http://ojs.acadiau.ca/index.php/AAU/article/view/76
Easton-Brooks, D. (2012). The conceptual context of knowledge. In S. R. Steinberg & G. S. Cannella (Eds.), *Critical qualitative research reader* (pp. 33–42). Thousand Oaks, CA: Sage.
Evans, K. D. (2006). Welcome to Ruth's world: An autoethnography concerning the interview of an elderly woman. *Qualitative Inquiry, 13*(2), 282–291.
Foucault, M. (1977). *Discipline and punish.* London, UK: Tavistock.
Freire, P. (1970). *Pedagogy of the oppressed* (30th anniversary ed.). New York, NY: Continuum.

Kitwood, T. (1997). *Dementia reconsidered: The person comes first.* Buckingham, UK: Open University.

Mollica, R., Simms-Kastelein, K., Cheek, M., Baldwin, C., Farnham, J., Reinhard, S., & Accius, J. (2009). *AARP Public Policy Institute research report. Building adult foster care: What states can do.* Washington, DC: AARP Public Policy Institute. Retrieved from http://assets.aarp.org/rgcenter/ppi/ltc/2009_13_building_adult_foster_care.pdf

Muncey, T. (2005). Doing autoethnography. *International Journal of Qualitative Methods, 4*(1), 1–12.

Noddings, N. (2010). *The maternal factor: Two paths to morality.* Berkeley, CA: University of California.

Phillips, J., Ajrouch, K., & Hillcoat-Nallétamby, S. (2010). *Key concepts in social gerontology.* Thousand Oaks, CA: Sage.

Redfoot, D. L., & Houser, A. (2010). *AARP Public Policy Institute research report. More older people living with disabilities in the community: Trends from the National long-term care survey, 1984–2004.* Washington, DC: AARP.

Sherman, S. R., & Newman, E. S. (1988). *Foster families for adults: A community alternative in long-term care.* New York, NY: Columbia University.

Steinberg, S. R. (2012). Critical cultural studies research: Bricolage in action. In S. R. Steinberg & G. S. Cannella (Eds.), *Critical qualitative research reader* (pp. 182–197). Thousand Oaks, CA: Sage.

Stoller, E., & Gibson, R. (2000a). Advantages of using the life course framework in studying aging. In E. P. Stoller & R. C. Gibson (Eds.), *Worlds of difference* (pp. 19–28). Thousand Oaks. CA: Sage.

Stoller, E., & Gibson, R. (2000b). Inequalities in health and mortality: Gender, race, and class. In E. P. Stoller & R. C. Gibson (Eds.), *Worlds of difference* (pp. 269–283). Thousand Oaks, CA: Sage.

Tilley-Lubbs, G. A. (2011). Border crossing: (Auto)Ethnography that transcends immigration/imagination. *International Review of Qualitative Research, 4*(4), 385–401.

Tronto, J. C. (1998). *An ethic of care. Generations, 22*(3), 15–20.

Virginia Department of Social Services, Division of Family Services, Adult Services Programs. (2010). *Adult foster care program manual.* Retrieved from http://www.dss.virginia.gov/files/division/dfs/as/as_intro_page/manuals/adult_fc/adultfostercareguide_1_2010.pdf

Vryan, K. D. (2006). Expanding analytic autoethnography and enhancing its potential. *Journal of Contemporary Ethnography, 35,* 405–409.

Wall Residences. (2010a). *About us.* Retrieved from http://www.wallresidences.com

Wall Residences. (2010b). *Policy 2.10- Mission Statement. Unpublished back-up worker training document.* Floyd, VA: Wall Residences.

Kelly Munly
Department of Human Development
Virginia Tech
Blacksburg, Virginia, USA

Gresilda A. Tilley-Lubbs
Faculty of Teaching and Learning
School of Education
Virginia Tech
Blacksburg, Virginia, USA

Carl Sheusi
Wall Residences
Lynchburg, Virginia, USA

SILVIA BÉNARD CALVA

8. FROM IMPRESSIONISM TO REALISM[1]

Painting a Conservative Mexican City

ABSTRACT

This chapter explores the difficulties I have experienced moving from Mexico City, the largest metropolitan area in Mexico, to a provincial capital in the centre part of the country, the city of Aguascalientes. In order to do that, I present a short narrative of certain incidents that show how I have sorted out the journey in a search of developing a sense of belonging. This is an autoethnography exercise where I follow what Ellis (2004) calls narrative analysis, which "assumes that a good story we itself is theoretical.... When people tell their stories, they employ analytic techniques to interpret their worlds" (pp. 195–196). I have also realized that, like Richardson and St. Pierre argue (2005), writing is a way of knowing because it was due to the introspection process I experienced as I was writing that I came to understand how much my story was mostly related to gender issues.

Sparkling Lights

Before definitely deciding to move to Aguascalientes in 1992, I had constructed an idea about the people who lived there. My perception was like a painting with very luminous sparkles, barely any varying hues of colour, even fewer shadows, and lots of empty spaces.

For example, something that caught my attention was the statement from my partner, who was born there and whose family lived there when we moved a few years later, everybody lived in harmony, and his brothers and sisters had a lot of fun being all together. Furthermore, he assured me, they were very close but at the same time they were very respectful of one another. Those were my first impressions.

Two events come to my mind that exemplify those luminous sparkles I dotted onto my painting as I followed my partner's optimistic view, which at that time I believed was right. The first occasion was a simple conversation when I commented: "Have you noticed how divorce is more and more common?" and he said, "That is in Mexico City, not in Aguascalientes, where people get along much better." And I believed him.

The other glitter I stippled onto my canvas occurred at Christmas. After we spent our first Christmas Eve with my family, he told me that with his family

G. A. Tilley-Lubbs & S. B. Calva (Eds.), Re-Telling Our Stories, 123–131.

Christmas celebrations were really fun, that with them we were in fact going to have a good time. Mentally, I embellished his comment with how I imagined a wonderful Christmas ought to be. I did it mostly by myself and with no further information about what he meant: there everybody gets along well and have so much fun that their Christmas together has to be far better than at my parents'. My family tends to be serious and I knew that there were tensions among us. A popular version of our families' differences can be observed in the movie My Big Fat Greek Wedding. His family is similar to that of the bride and mine is more like the groom's. My attitude was very much like the groom's: feeling seduced by that festive, joyful, and fun family, I was eager to merge into it.

But I had many more paint colours available to complete that canvas than those I made use of before I decided to permanently move to Aguascalientes. And they were certainly not all that glamorous.

Brushstrokes of Colour: Tones and Shadows

I got married in Austin, a month after my partner got there and three years after I started attending graduate school at the University of Texas. A few months after his arrival, he went to a friend's house to help them move because they were going back to Mexico. I stayed in the apartment to study for my rapidly approaching comprehensive exams. I had to read mountains of texts about formal organizations and the family, which were my specialty areas.

There I was, in that tiny but cosy apartment, sitting at my big desk and reading about the family, when all of a sudden I heard voices calling my name from the outside. The efficiency apartment was on a third floor, but with a balcony facing the street. I did not want to pay too much attention to the voices because I knew anybody looking for me would never shout like that. They would come upstairs and knock at the door. Besides, everybody knew that although that kind of communication was common in Mexico, it was not welcomed in the United States, especially in that apartment complex where members of the Episcopalian Church seminary used to live. Although available for anybody by that time, the apartments were close to the library and the teaching spaces that were still being used to educate the future ministers of that church.

But the screaming did not stop, so somewhat convinced that they could be calling me and a little worried that the neighbours would feel irritated and complain, I leaned out from the balcony and found two mature women, very well dressed, standing on the street like two girls, looking up as if anxiously hoping to get an answer. Yes, it was for me—one of those women was my mother-in-law! I knew that because of their age, and the way they were dressed, but I had seen those two women only once before in my whole life. I thought: "Which one is she? Will I be able to distinguish her? And, well, what are they doing here?"

I went downstairs to receive them. There were so many things going through my head while I was walking down the stairs: "I'm not dressed correctly, the apartment is too small, everything is visible, even the bed, the air conditioning is not on and it is very hot, my partner is not home ...." Before I could finish my train of thought, I found myself standing in front of them, saying hello and thinking, "I don't know how, but I can tell which one is my mother-in-law." We climbed the stairs together to the apartment, studio, efficiency, or however else it could be called, but the fact was that it was too small as compared to their standards. After inviting them to come in, they realized there was not much to see, so they sat down. As soon as I could, I called my partner to let him know his mother was with me and to ask him to get there ASAP. Meanwhile I offered them coffee.

I have warm memories of that time we spent together in the apartment, each of us sitting with a coffee cup and a small plate underneath. I was seated on a woollen cloth sofa, and they on a worn-out plastic vinyl one. Those pieces of furniture were very hot, but I had turned on the air conditioning before I went downstairs to meet them. We talked about everything and nothing, I remember them complaining about "Americans," and also that they had come because the other woman's son was marrying a *gringa* from San Antonio, so they had come with him by car to San Antonio and then to Austin. Up to that point things seemed to be holding up all right.

My partner got home about 45 min later. To me, that was supposed to be the one most positive event. That was why my mother-in-law was there, to see her son, and he showed up, doing well and very happy. That was what I thought. But she met an untidy man, about 10 kilos thinner, and with a few burns on his arms. Yes, he had lost a lot of weight during those months. She had not known it and we had for-gotten all about it because he was overweight and the loss was due to not having the kind of food he liked in Mexico. He was often homesick for a cheap restaurant close to his place in Mexico City, where he had tripe tacos several times a week. The burns on his arms had become a reason for teasing between us. Now that I was busy preparing my comprehensive exams and he still had no regular school activities, we had agreed that he was going to do the cooking. He really did not know how to cook, and he was quite clumsy, so the stove or the oven would burn him. Nonetheless, we did not consider any of that to be very serious. On the contrary, it was part of the joy of learning how to live together. I had thought his mother was going to be very happy to see her son, but instead she was shocked. All he could do at that point to improve his mother's opinion was to take a good shower. Once he had showered, we went out for supper to the Fonda San Miguel, a restaurant different from other Mexican restaurants in Austin in the mid-80s. The place looked like a very elegant but traditional Mexican house, *the casco de una hacienda*, restored with materials brought from different regions of Mexico: the doors, the chairs, the tables, the lamps, they were all "authentic Mexican." And the menu was not Tex-Mex—not tortillas with cheddar cheese, burritos, and fajitas. The menu was full of elaborate Mexican dishes with recipes from different regions of the country. Of them all, the one I remember best was *chiles en nogada*.

Once at the restaurant I felt a lot better. We had reached a land closer to what I imagined those two women understood as adequate for their comfort and satisfaction. I could sense this, from the little information I had from them. I positioned them in the category of upper middle class Mexicans in small cities. They preferred to be in a in a fancy restaurant that served the kind of food they were familiar with, not in one that served the kind of Mexican food popular among Chicanos and served in common restaurants. We had a good time eating and drinking, and we talked about one thing and another, not very serious. The tension of the reencounter of my now mother-in-law with her son seemed to have loosened up and everything flowed more naturally.

On the way out, my mother-in-law and I were seated together on a typical Mexican cement bench. I believe we were waiting for the car to be brought to us. I don't know where the rest of the group had gone. Catching me off guard, she let out a phrase that I have not been able to forget: "You must not be a slut because otherwise my son wouldn't have fallen in love with you." What did she say after that? I don't know, I have not been able to remember it during all these years. I think she mentioned something about her desire for us to have a Catholic wedding. I only remember her statement as an introduction to something else. Reflecting back, I can tell for certain that she was serious about her religious beliefs. Catholics do get married by the Church and they stay married no matter what, "until death do us part."

"Why would she label me like that? What can guarantee a man won't end up with a slut? Am I a slut? What does she mean by that?" There I had strong evidence, a short but clear-cut phrase that condensed her beliefs about women and marriage. If I had stopped to think about it, I would have been able to give my painting many brushstrokes, providing nuances to the sparkles, and I could have filled in some of the empty spaces in my canvas. But what did I do? I ignored it. I did not talk about it to my partner. I did not ask my mother-in-law what she meant. I did not tell her I was not a slut. No, I just went on with their visit, as if nothing had happened. At that point I did not even understand that according to her beliefs, being a slut was connected to not being married by the Catholic Church. I came to realize that as I had thought about it while writing this text.

And why had my mother-in-law visited us months later instead of going to our wedding? Why hadn't she been present that day? Her son decided not to invite either his mother or his father because he did not want them to be together. They were not divorced. They never were, but they spent all the years I knew them until he died, fighting, arguing, always distant from each other. They were a good example of those married couples in Aguascalientes who do not get divorced, as my partner said, not because they were happy as I had been led to believe. When he told me about the low divorce rate in Aguascalientes, I jumped to the conclusion that it was because people got along better there than in Mexico City, but I learned it was because they did not see divorce as a legitimate option to solve unsustainable situations.

But I let it go. I probably thought that marriages like my partner's parents belonged to a different generation and so I went on with my busy life. I visited my in-laws once or twice a year and when we were there, we had big family suppers, played cards, ate big breakfasts and suppers, and had long fun talks. Those were the kind of activities that I also used to do with my family. I very much enjoyed those activities, which reminded me of my own family many years before, when all six sisters and two brothers lived together with my parents. Besides, Aguascalientes was always sunny, the sky was very blue, and the city looked always well organized and clean. At that time, everything seemed so good and simple, not like my life in Mexico City, where I had grown apart from my family, and where the city was chaotic and polluted.

On one of our visits, about 3 years after we got married, a group of my partner's closest old friends appeared on the scene and they offered me the opportunity to add more colours to give depth, shape, and clarity to my painting. My partner's closest old friend and his wife invited us over for supper with two more couples, all of whom had grown up together in my partner's neighbourhood. All but my partner had continued being in touch with each other because they were related as a family.

It may be unfair of me to remember only the negative moments I spent in that place, but as years have gone by, those are the ones I remember when I try to understand how I could decide to settle in a city like Aguascalientes, thinking that I would not be touched by its people's mores and norms. There were two dialogs at that dinner that let me voiceless. The closest of my partner's friends and his wife argued:

He: I like our little female dog because she is always happy to see me. At night when I get home she always moves her tail for me to say hello.

She: I always move my tail for you too, but you don't treat me as well as you treat her. And you don't treat the *gata* (derogatory word for the domestic servant) that well either. Do whatever you want, if you wish I would put her in bed with you, but treat her well because what am I going to do if she quits?

He: You are going to go shopping in McAllen to spend our money. That's what you'll do.

She: Yes but you already went wild with your friends the other night, didn't you?

After that, one of the other couples was talking about how many kids they were willing to have. The wife was 6 or 7 months pregnant and started complaining that her husband wanted to have more than two kids: "I have already told him, with me only two kids." Then, moving her head to talk to him, she said disgustingly: "If you want more, go look for them somewhere else."

As soon as we left I told my partner:

- Hey, those are trade relationships not love relationships! "You go wild with your friend and I go shopping to McAllen!" And what about the vulgar comment about

127

moving her tail, what is that? And the other one with her comments that if he wants more kids he can fool around, did she really mean it? Was she serious? That's really something. Boy, I can't believe it!

- Ay, Benard, that's the way they are. No big deal.

Then I narrated the incident to one of my sisters'-in-law. She didn't say, "No big deal," but she laughed. And the same as my partner, she then told me things she knew about had happened to them, and just like him, she implicitly expressed her appreciation for those people about whom I had being making awful comments. Her empathy with those I had criticized made me feel very ashamed of myself so I decided to shut up and keep it all to myself.

Finishing Touches

Once again, I went back to Mexico City, where I lived at that time, and I buried the incidents under my big city busy life. There I had to deal with contamination, heavy traffic, the neighbours, rats, and so many things I hated, that when I had the opportunity to move to Aguascalientes, I just naively packed my partially sketched canvas and ventured to my new hometown.

Now that I think about it, and I have been writing a long piece on my autoethnography of which this is only a small piece, I realize that this kind of fragmented knowledge, based on few flashes and intuitions, is very often the source of my everyday knowledge from which I draw the routes of my actions.

Many years had to pass before a strong desire to reconstruct my sense of self allowed me to elaborate the painting, including many more colours to give nuances, shades, and depths to the whole painting, but it has certainly turned out to be much darker than that first sparkly draft.

Clues for Drawing the Whole Picture

My partner: a key word. I first wrote this article in Spanish and I had a hard time finding the right word in my mother tongue to refer to him: *Esposo* and *marido*, which could be translated as spouse and husband, were too traditional words for what I knew they meant in my Mexican background. Then I thought about *compañero*, but that word, as used by academics since the 1960s, is very loaded with meanings, part of which I share. Nevertheless, I was very critical of how my university professors —most of whom had participated in the 1968 students' movement— used it so familiarly, but when it came to their personal comments and their specific love relationships, they were quite traditional and often chauvinistic.

So, in my Spanish draft I made a note making reference to the fact that I did not understand my relationship as that of husband and wife, that I wished I could refer to him as my *compañero* as I understood what that meant to be, and it was that my marital relationship did not develop according to those ideals. But I as I thought about my options, I decided not to use his name, which at first I thought would allow me to get rid of all those implicit meanings and try to convey them on the text, as I described the tensions between my expectations and my everyday life. Thus, I decided to call him *Él* (He). Then a Colleague, who read my Spanish draft, a man, said I should use the word husband because the word *Él* would lead the reader to a misunderstanding of *Él* as a synonymous of God. I still don't know whether to take the comment as hilarious or accept my feelings of frustration and disappointment.

Then, I translated the text to English, and when I faced the dilemma of which word to use to refer to him, I was very pleased to find the one I wanted: partner. I kept telling myself it was great there had been a sexual revolution in the United States and women could talk about their love relationships in terms of a partnership. My dilemma, translated into another language, easily appeared to be taken care of. I wrote the article and presented a draft at the International Congress of Qualitative Inquiry in May of 2012. Nobody made comments about the word I used. But I kept working on my drafts and when I sent a final copy to Kris Tilley-Lubbs, my friend and colleague in the United States, she wrote the following comment next to the first appearance of the word partner:

Why partner here? Isn't the fact he was your husband a big part of the social construction of identity and also part of the tension in the scene with your mother-in-law? Granted, there would have been awful tension, but for an entirely different reason. Maybe I am thinking of Mexico of many years ago, but partner seems more US academic.

There it was: I had travelled alone through the social construction of marriage, from my family in Mexico City, through Austin, Texas, and until I landed in Aguascalientes. In my individual journey, I constructed my own meaning of a couple relationship, chose the person I thought would follow with it, and moved around the geography of those cities assuming it was possible to live according to my own definitions, regardless of the place where I lived and assuming He (my husband, my spouse, my partner), would be willing to come along so that together we could figure out how to live in a fair and equitable relationship.

Why on earth could I assume all that, especially considering that I am a sociologist and had taken my qualitative exams in my PhD program in the area of family? At this point, having spent a lot of time writing an autoethnography about my difficult process of learning to live in Aguascalientes, I wonder why I assumed so many things. I go from an awful feeling of failure as a sociologist to providing some explanations that can help me make sense of my own process. Instead of talking about what I learned (or did not learn) in graduate school, I will refer to my personal life history to contribute a possible explanation.

Despite having been raised in a traditional Mexican family, with my mother being very Catholic, my father gave me space to escape the mandates of that church. I clearly remember the Christmas I went to Mexico City on vacation and talked to my father about the possibility of my boy-friend moving to Austin the following semester:

- What do you think would happen if I don't get married?
- You Know it is the same to me, you know what I think about marriage. But Mom, well, she would not want you to do that. You know I had to get married by the Church because of your mother ....

My father had been raised with no religion. His mother, a German Protestant, and his father, a French Catholic, had at first agreed that when they had kids, the males would be Catholic and the females would be Protestant. But by the time their children were born, they really did not do anything about religious affiliations and my father and his three sisters grew up with no religious affiliation. When my father proposed marriage to my mother, and asked my grandmother for her hand in marriage, she, a very traditional Catholic, agreed, with the condition of my father's acceptance of a Catholic wedding. He did and, therefore, in 1949, he had not only to marry within the Catholic Church, but he also had to go through all the preparatory rituals required by the Church: Baptism, First Communion, and Confirmation.

I had been living in Austin for 4 years when I talked to my father, and I had seen people from very different and varied backgrounds at the university, where whatever your beliefs and thoughts were, you had to be respectful of others. Of course it was not that simple, but it was far more open and respectful than what I had seen in Mexico before I moved to the United States. So, when my mother-in-law visited us in Austin, and made her comments about my morals, and then when I later witnessed those younger people from Aguascalientes being so cold and practical about their marital relationships, although I was shocked and in disapproval, I never envisioned that they could have an impact on my personal life, or moreover, that those were part of my partner's worldview as well. And to make things worse, when I had to phase those socially constructed conceptions of marriage once living in Aguascalientes, they ended up shaking my own worldview. It was as if I had opened an old cabinet stocked with out-dated mores and norms and they just knocked me down.

Writing autoethnography has taught me the lesson I did not forgive my undergraduate professors in Mexico City not to have learned themselves when I observed their inconsistencies with regard to their use of the word *compañero*. I had to spend many years living in an intimate relationship before I could come about to realize certain understanding of its complexity and the relevance different social settings play on it. This has been a hazardous sociological adventure.

Coda

Laurel Richardson has very well analysed the process such as the one I travelled through in writing this text. She refers to it as CAP (Creative Analytical Process) and argues that writing can be a way of knowing, that is, through that process of writing, without knowing exactly which direction we are going to, or what the outcome will be, we write as if we were trying to understand and give meaning to our own experience. Once we finish a text, it "cannot be separated from the producer, the mode of production, or the method of knowing" (Richardson & St. Pierre, 2005, p. 962).

Through my years as a social researcher, I have experienced CAP, but I had not either made it explicit or shared it with my colleagues because it is not considered to be a legitimate way to produce knowledge. If this is true still in other countries, it is more so in Mexico, where I can count with my fingers texts from academia acknowledging that the process of writing itself has any relevance in the process of producing knowledge or, even more, that researchers' personal experience has anything to say about understanding a sociological problem.

I came across the Richardson and St. Pierre article last July as I was reviewing qualitative methodology texts, particularly those on autoethnography, at Virginia Tech during the 4 months I spent there as a visiting scholar invited by the Department of Teaching and Learning, School of Education during my sabbatical year.

Writing this text has proved myself what Richardson and St. Pierre (2005) so clearly state:

Language is how social organization and power are defined and contested and the place where one's sense of self—one's subjectivity—is constructed. Understanding language as competing discourses—competing ways of giving meaning and of organizing the world—makes language a site for exploration and struggle. (p. 961)

And, drawing from my experience, I could add: The use of different languages to define and contest one's sense of self makes that construction far more complex.

NOTE

First published: Bénard, S. M. (2013). From impressionism to realism: Painting a conservative Mexican city. *Cultural Studies ⇔ Critical Methodologies*. doi:10.1177/1532708613495801. Reprinted with permission.

REFERENCES/BIBLIOGRAPHY

Ellis, C. (2004). *The ethnographic I: A methodological novel about teaching and doing autoethnography.* Walnut Creek, CA: AltaMira.

Richardson, L., & St. Pierre, E. A. (2005). Writing: A method of inquiry. In N. Denzin & Y. Lincoln (Eds.), *Handbook of qualitative research* (pp. 959–978). Thousand Oaks, CA: Sage.

Silvia Bénard Calva
Departamento de Sociología y Antropología
Universidad Autónoma de Aguascalientes, México

DYANIS POPOVA

9. METAMORPHOSIS

A Journey through Grief

ABSTRACT

In an introductory experience of accidental ethnography (Poulos, 2010), a doctoral student and recent divorcee, exposes her journey through personal trauma, and coming out on the other side. This autoethnographic exploration documents the failures and triumphs that shaped her life experiences, and placed her on the path to who she would become personally and professionally. Extracting meaning from lived experiences, the author hopes to add her own narrative to available cultural resources, helping others on their own journeys of self-understanding.

***

Chest to chest
Nose to nose
Palm to palm
We were always just that close.
Wrist to wrist
Toe to toe
Lips that felt just like the inside of a rose.
So how come when I reach out my finger
It feels like more than distance between us.
In this California king bed
We're 10,000 miles apart.[1]

THE END OF AN ERA

"I can't have dinner with you."

The statement was perfunctory, and devoid of all emotion. I turned slowly and looked toward my husband, who was perched on the edge of our wooden dining table amidst an assortment of wine and water glasses, fancy silverware, and decoratively folded blue and white napkins. "What do you mean? Do you have plans?" It was our wedding anniversary and I had taken the day off to clean our large apartment and prepare an elaborate meal. We had been arguing more in recent months, and

I had hoped that this dinner would allow us the chance to bond, away from the heavy drudgery of bills and daily responsibilities.

"I can't have dinner with you. I can't do this anymore. I'm leaving." Again that tone, detached and indifferent, emitting a crisp note in the air like a breath of frost. As our eyes met, I could feel his intent, and for the first time I truly understood poetic recitations of hearts rendered from chests. The room began to spin, the beige apartment walls blending with matching carpets, with decorations slowly swirling into a breath-taking display of lights. The only things holding me upright were shock, horror, and maybe a little pride.

I kept my shoulders straight and looked about the room, shaking my head for clarity. Thirteen years of framed memories stared back at me accusingly, laughing and pointing, their ridicule audible and their grins caustic. The ceiling fan spun slowly above, mirroring both the flickering light of the tapered candles and Alexander's seeming indifference. A combination of foods, from both my Caribbean island and his former Soviet republic, sat in matching serving dishes on the kitchen counter, and as I watched the serving spoon drip slowly in my hand I became aware of the smell of the stew starting to burn on the stove behind me.

I approached him gingerly, blindsided by this notification, the spoon unknowingly depositing globules of brown sauce on the carpet next to my bare feet. As I reached my hand toward his, his body tightened almost imperceptibly and his eyes …his eyes closed, the green flecks almost blackened by the emotion, or lack thereof, that his body fought to hide. He slid slowly to my right, just beyond my grasp, and sighed, a sound long and slow, like the closing of an old rusted gate. I stood frozen, afraid to make eye-contact, staring resolutely at the wall. "For a bit …you need some time to think?" I hoped. My heart swelled in my chest with the anticipation of possibility, then crashed into the deepest canyons of my soul as his head moved slowly from side to side, "No, for good. I …." His voice trailed off as he stood, back rigid and face turned, moving toward the door. "Where are you going to go?" I asked in bewilderment and with a considerable amount of disbelief. I barely heard his response indicating he had places to go, my brain muddied and cloudy, the sauce now dripping on my painted toes. He turned to face me in the open doorway and paused, his eyes softening for a moment, reminiscent of the man I loved, urging me forward. As I moved, they hardened again, and with a brief "I still care about you," he turned, the soft click of the door echoing like a scream in the centre of my soul.

I slowly glanced around the room at the shadows on the walls cast by the light of my special anniversary candles. My head thundered with silence as I walked toward the front door of my third-floor apartment, past the now silent pictures. With every remaining ounce of strength, I placed my left palm on the closed door and stared longingly at my wedding ring as my body slid to the floor in a dazed heap. I curled my body into a tight ball, no longer aware of the location of the spoon, not smelling the now ruined pot, hoping that I would wake, wishing it were a dream. Nothing changed. The door didn't open and the phone didn't ring. My silent screams to the universe, to my ancestors, and to my husband went unanswered. I lay and I wept.

The following night found me in the same position, but this time I lay on a soft bed over 700 miles north in my father's spare bedroom. The foggy call to my father the previous night when I realized my husband was unlikely to return had resulted in a plane ticket and a long weekend. I had survived a crowded plane and four hours in two cars, all the while fighting the huge tears that had taken siege of my pride. My tears had streamed down my face, causing visible discomfort on the faces of those around me. Now, in this safe place of love and family, my tears had turned to silent sobs racking my frame unrepentantly with each memory. We were soul mates. What had gone wrong? What had I done? How could I fix it? I had done all I could do, more than most would have done. I had been emotionally, physically, and financially supportive, and I had been both a best friend and a lover. Wasn't that supposed to be enough?

My father and step-mother blessedly stayed away during my visit but periodically the concerned pre-pubescent face of my brother would peek around the bedroom door, silent and yearning to help. As I wept, humiliation, disappointment, rage, depression, and love all roared ferociously through me, threating to lend voice to my soundless cries. Plans for buying houses and having babies swirled through my brain accusingly, adding to the ongoing racket as I lay alone on the bed where for years I had lain with Alexander. My father, rarely emotionally flamboyant, hugged me feverishly with his eyes each time we sat together. His concern and his love were palpable, and an important stabilizer for my diminishing clarity. He talked to me, without expecting a reply, about good relationships and bad relationships, love and hate, disappointment and regret. I felt broken into a million pieces but his words splinted me together, allowing me to return to work and a reality I now wanted no part of.

SORTING THROUGH THE ASHES

The summer had passed. My smiles and attempts at positive greetings at work were always replaced by the darkness of my apartment with its closed blinds, drawn curtains, and silence. Upon my return from my father's, I had moved some clothing and toiletries into the living room and there I stayed, wrapped in blankets and tears. The coloured piles, sorted by worn once and too dirty to wear again were a constant reminder of my failure as a wife and a woman, and they would soon need to be sorted by number of wearings in my efforts to avoid my bedroom door. The hallway bathroom allowed me to bypass going through our bedroom to the shower, so the bedroom door sat closed, relegated to the world of what could have been. A small spider's web, whose tenant I never saw, grew larger as the days passed and as the moon made its cyclical journeys across the sky. The rancour in the air slowly permeated all it touched, until everything was infused with a brackish sorrow that coloured the world a slate grey.

This period of mourning went deeper than even I noticed at the time. I showered, dressed, ate, and went to work automatically, repeating my routine as I had countless times before, trying to be strong for my parents, less concerned for myself. My 5'3" frame dwindled to under 100 lbs, unnoticed and uninterrupted. Each day as I dressed, I pinned my waistbands a little tighter, poufed my cheeks out a little farther, and convinced myself that the hummingbird rhythm of my heart was normal and not a contributor to my sallow skin or protruding cheekbones. How do you mourn your one true love? How do you accept the death of a dream?

Night after night as I returned to this dreary dungeon, safe from the prying eyes of friends and family, I sought refuge in my overstuffed sage linen couch, hugging the memories from the cushions and grateful for their comfort as they held my increasingly secret tears. The questions never stopped and the voices in my head mirrored my anguish, often keeping me awake often until dawn. The slightest sound, look or gesture would often send me retreating to a restroom to swipe at my face in the hope that no one would notice the red blotches almost obscured by my dark skin. The voices, my constant companions, would pause periodically only to be replaced with wails that would probably have been quieter if given voice. What's going to become of me? How can I live without him? What will people think? Is what I felt real? How will I face my friends? The humiliation and uncertainty inferred by these questions weighed heavily, but the loudest voice issued a solitary statement that stood strong and fierce, YOU HAVE FAILED! There was no reasoning with this voice, no making it understand that I had tried, that I had loved, that I had given more of myself than I knew existed. I was a failure, plain and simple. Who and what I was simply just wasn't good enough.

One night as I lay in my refuge watching the rising of the moon and sun, I contemplated my pasts, present, and futures. My tears spun the silver wedding ring on my hand as it hung limply over a pile of unopened bills, its hematite centrepiece that had grabbed my eye at a music festival whirling mockingly. I could no longer watch TV or listen to the radio, for fear of being overcome with agonizing sorrow, so I sat always in silence, the internal wails and whimpers of my inner thoughts the only background to my pain. My future lay demolished at my feet, the scarred landscape a grim reminder of the beauty that came before. I formulated and reformulated strategies to save my marriage, to prove that I was the one, to make him come home.

I had assumed that time, time to think and time to remember, would be enough. The lack of warning and the feeling of being blindsided had left me disoriented, sure that this was all just some crazy mistake. I believed that the love we shared was so profound and so unique that providing Alexander with the time he needed would make us stronger once we were reunited. But the months passed. Friends and family urged me to move forward but I waited …and waited. My mind fluctuated between memories of lingering, love-filled Sundays and more painful memories of ending my 12-hour workdays with an empty kitchen and a mound of dirty dishes left by his friends. It moved between stories of undying commitment and pre-destiny to emptied bank accounts and his all night online poker binges. How could my life have become such a paltry collection of memories? The months turned into years and the hope began to fade. There were visits to pick up personal items but we remained distant, separated by a wall of personal anguish. Phone calls were tinged with frustrated longing and ended in angst and raised voices, each of us tired of the arguing, tired of hearing about past mistakes.

A FLASH OF CLARITY

Almost Two Years Later

The sound of birds filled the air as I stood on the banks of the river fighting my memories. The slight resentment I felt at being herded away from the sanctity of my apartment soon started to fade, replaced by calm and a resoundingly hushed awe that always overcame me in the presence of bodies of water. As I surveyed the scene, I revelled at the sound of the river lapping against rocks, the tickle of honeysuckle in the air, and the soft hum of unseen insects against the breeze.

My two good friends and co-workers, Brian and Jonathon, had appeared at my door near sunrise laden with fishing poles, tackle boxes, and a truckload of sunblock. My repeated refusal to participate in the world of the living had been disregarded, and there they were, eager to bring light into my life. They rushed through the open door and started tossing clothes from my burgeoning living room collection into my arms. In all the chaos I started to laugh. It started as a soft chuckle and grew into an alien-sounding hearty guffaw. When last had I laughed? When last had I allowed myself to experience joy?

"C'mon suck it up. You've got to get out of this house!"
"Ugh" I grunted as I my eyes rolled upwards.
"You're just gonna waste away!"

I had heard this so many times. Everyone was so concerned, but this time was different. I had no way out and they would not leave until I stepped outside of my apartment. I mischievously contemplated exiting and then retreating to lock the doors when they were halfway down the stairs, but Brian and Jonathon were cunning. They would have found another way in. Then, they asked the question that changed the rest of my summer, and maybe my life: *Why not?* Perfect in its simplicity, this phrase left me speechless, and just for a moment, it silenced the voices. *Why not?* My hands fell limply to my sides and something clicked. *Why not?* What did I have to lose? Anything could be better than this. In reply, I methodically dressed and let them guide me out the door.

Our three colourful kayaks glided seamlessly down the river. Local horror stories of hidden whirlpools and man-sized Muskie with razor sharp teeth filled my brain as I watched my reflection in the glassy surface. But why not? I had nothing to fear. What more could go wrong? I dismissed the stories and instead concentrated on keeping both my paddle and fishing pole securely in the kayak. We floated aimlessly, occasionally paddling in circles to stay close to a prime fishing spot, revelling in the sunshine and the rhythmic sound of the paddle blades parting the surface of the water.

The world slowed that day and my pain was muted. I cannot describe the sense of serenity and purpose that overcame me during those ten amazing hours. Getting stuck on rocks and navigating Class 1 rapids may be commonplace for the average kayaker, but for me it was a championship belt that represented by ability to overcome adversity and the unknown. I held my paddle above my head in triumph as we coasted toward the dock, imagining its gold-coloured plating glinting in the sunshine and the roar of the crowd echoing against the cliff walls.

DEEPER INTO THE MIRE

Alexander was coming over today, another chance to remind him of how special we were and how devoted I was. A long shower filled with tears of hope preceded a set of rituals in which I rarely participated. I blow-dried and oiled my long hair, and used layers of powders on my face to look as if I had done none of it at all. The subtle peach on my eyelids matched the shimmering hues of my toenails and my skin glistened under heavy doses of jasmine-scented lotion. I wore my favourite sweatpants, the ones that accentuated my now muscular body, and a light pink Casper t-shirt that he'd always liked. I sat in silence on that sage linen couch, my frame reminiscent of those long services in the church choir: back straight, hands clasped in my lap, feet flat on the floor, knees together.

My heart leapt at the light knock on the door and soared at the sight of Alexander's wavy obsidian mane and those piercing hazel eyes.

"Hi." My smile faltered lightly and his face softened.

"I'll only be a minute."

"Take as long as you need." I muttered as I tried to muster an alluring smile.

I remembered to release my death grip on the doorknob to allow him access to the strange apartment. The tiny space was a jumble of our belongings, as I had kept everything he hadn't taken. I no longer remember what he was looking for but I remember his face with its olive skin and a hint of pain in his eyes. The herniated disks in his neck that had precipitated this entire debacle had caused a slight limp on his right side, and I ached to hold him and tell him it was all going to be okay. As he completed his search through a pile of boxes, my trembling hand extended a glass of cold water already sweating in the mid-summer heat.

"Thanks," he murmured as he sat looking around my new place. "This is nice, small, but nice." My nervously clenching fists, fighting my subconscious request to remain at my side, had begun to ache and my heart felt as if it would seize from exhaustion.

My brain lost the fight and my hands rushed forward, taking Alexander's large, rough hands in mine. "Please" I urged as tears spilled from my eyes "Come back. This is special. We can get through this. We've survived worse. Thirteen years, Baby! I can be here for you."

My rushed statements met nothing but silence. His face remained unmoved except for the throbbing of his jaw muscle. After seeming eons had passed, his mouth opened. "I can't. It's not fair to you. I need time to myself to figure out where I want to go in life. I can't be a husband right now. I need to be selfish and think about myself. I've become too dependent on you."

In desperation, my knees dropped to the floor and my hands clasped his even tighter. "Please" I begged, "PLEASE. Tell me what to do, how to help, how you could stay!" My tears had become languishing sobs, echoing from the very centre of my soul. I begged like I had never begged before. My life was on the line and my very existence would end without him.

His face became pained and he pried my fingers open, removing his hands. "I can't." In my recollection, the words sound so finite, but I also remember my brain scrambling, seeking other ideas, seeking new pleas.

I stayed there on my knees, too afraid to look up as he rose, too afraid to turn around as he walked away, hoping that if I stayed still time itself would sympathize and give me a few last moments of hope, love, and life. The click of the door as it closed behind him shattered every last hope, and his final tremulous "I will always love you," burned like acid on the open wound.

INTROSPECTION

These painful recollections do not in any way encompass all my and Alexander's efforts, all our pain, and all our loss. They are however some of my most powerful and life-shaping memories as I reflect on life's journey. This experiment in autoethnography (Ellis, 2004) began as a class assignment to write an episodic account. In retrospect, had I known this piece would eventually be submitted for publication, I would probably not have selected a topic that provided such a personal window into my deepest emotions. Accepting the challenge of why not, I wrote on, hoping that my words would lend some direction, and the words indeed took on a life on their own as I wrote and shared through the tears. This class activity precipitated a foray into accidental ethnography as a method, attitude, and process, constantly improvising and shifting, and seeking knowing-in-action (Poulos, 2010). I would often sit staring at the blank screen and sob, awash with emotions that I had long buried. Sometimes after an hour, my fingers would begin to move of their own accord, flying over the keys with purpose and determination. My eyes rarely read the words on the screen until I needed a break and a moment of sanctity in the world of the living. Sometimes the clarity of my thoughts and feelings would amaze me and I would wonder where all that pent up energy had been ensconced. Almost three years later I was over him, right?

I tossed and turned contemplating how to present this personal retrospective in an academically valid format. How would this type of writing affect my life as a doctoral student and a qualitative researcher? Would colleagues and mentors think me unable to produce sound, academic writing? I was concerned that others might deem this writing useless unless these experiences were related to traditional research, theory, and analysis (Bochner 2001), and view it as nothing more than self-absorbed "navel-gazing" (Ellis et al., 2008, p. 324). My exploration of this type of autoethnographic inquiry was hindered by my struggle to entwine my personal and academic worlds, but as I read more I realized that these experiences could not be theorized and neatly boxed into categories and data sets. This is a story of personal struggle and triumph-in-process as I endeavour to transform adversity into positive energy and personal success. In one such example, Lee (2006) spins a moving tale of surviving her daughter's suicide, and without being hampered by theory, the reader is transported into Lee's personal story as she leaps back and forth in time, exploring and transcending her grief.

I was also concerned with exposing my inner self to faceless colleagues and critics, and becoming vulnerable and emotionally naked (Ellis, 1995). How would I feel if strangers knew of my weaknesses? How would I feel if Alexander were to read this piece? Am I betraying years of trust by exposing his weaknesses? This narrative is by no means objective and reminds me of my grandmother's repeated utterance that for every story there are three sides: his side, her side, and the truth. Is this story a correct representation of the truth? How much of the bad did I even want to include? In all reality, I didn't want to make him sound horrible. I still want him to like me. My eyes roll at the irony of such a thought. What we had was great and wonderful while it lasted, but a series of misunderstandings, missteps and misattributions led to the erosion of what once had been so pure. Unlike Tillman (2010) in her story of divorce, my claims cannot be substantiated by court documents, and I am left to hope that maybe he won't hate me for exposing him as well.

I spent considerable time wavering on how much of him to include. I admit, I am still angry at Alexander, and I feel disillusioned, dismayed, and betrayed. I will not, however, let this take control as I will always love him in some way. With these selected vignettes, I have endeavoured to showcase my experiences and coping mechanisms without painting Alexander with an overly critical brush. I force myself to remember the most beautiful times; our wedding invitations had simply stated: "Today, I marry my best friend," with no illustration other than a young couple holding hands, walking toward the future. Now, that was no more than a memory, and a shadow of the past. I realize now that "[T]here is no way of seeing, hearing, or representing the world of others that is absolutely, universally, valid or correct" (Van Maanen, 1988, p. 35). It is obvious that I cannot have presented every aspect of a thirteen-year relationship within this piece. Some things had to be left out for time, and out of respect for the parties involved, resulting in a presentation of selective memories (Giorgio, 2009). I tell the truth as I remember it, and as I felt it.

It is only in retrospect, through narrative, that one is in a position to survey the whole that is one's life, and it is only through such a survey that there exists the possibility of obtaining the truth about that life, indefinite and ungraspable though it may be (Freeman, 1997). I feel some guilt at not sharing this piece with Alexander before I shared it with others, but a story of his lived experiences would add another layer of introspection for which I am not mentally prepared. I write this burdened by a fear of the unknown, not knowing how he would react and not wanting my words to cause pain (Ellis, 2007). I have toyed with the idea of hiding behind a pen name and hoping for the best, but I have come a long way. As hurtful as my experience may have been, I am proud of what I have accomplished and I embrace the knowledge that without this trauma, I might not have blossomed into the person I am today.

This story is my voice, through snapshots of a lifetime, on a journey of self-understanding. I am attempting to extract meaning from my lived experiences, rather than trying to present an exact chronological depiction of events (Bochner, 2001). I am sharing these experiences not as an act of personal catharsis, but rather to connect to and feel connected with survivors of similar trauma (Giorgio, 2009). This hopefully relatable story of loss and grief (Ellis, 2009) is a journey from who I was a lifetime ago to who I am now, and who I hope to be. The presence of this grief reminds me that life is often unexpected, and as clichéd as it may sound, even the best laid plans simply don't work out. It reminds me that love is what we make it, and it reprimands my naivete in believing in one true soul mate. Some may see this as cynicism or perhaps bitterness, and maybe those are factors, but the skipping, smiling optimist who always saw the best in everyone has been replaced by a brisk realist who is always prepared for the worst.

This writing has allowed me the opportunity to document the balance I seek as I move forward into the terrifying unknown. My story is still incomplete as I have not yet exorcised my grief and am still often overcome with frustration and a profound sense of loss. Toward the end of our time together, there were far more dark days than not on a roller coaster ride with increasingly fewer highs than lows. Though I have by no means mastered the art of self-reflection I have faced my worst fear: being 33, single, and childless, and although the taste of this reality is sour in my mouth, I have come out stronger on the other side. Like Smith (1999), I hope to add my own narrative to available cultural resources, helping others on their own journeys of self-understanding and community empathy.

A NEW BEGINNING?

This piece documents a series of critical incidents that changed me philosophically, physically, emotionally, and professionally. My support of Alexander meant putting plans to complete my master's degree on hold and to work at a job I disliked. In retrospect, Alexander's decision gave me the freedom and resolve to return to school and pursue a doctorate about which I am passionate. *Why not?* Time for daily reflection had always been an ideal to which I could only aspire. It is a way of life now. Reflection, about the big picture and the little things, has shaped everything from my relationships and my eating habits to my teaching practices and research interests. It is much harder to anger or frustrate me, and I try to find and appreciate joy and life in everything I do. This practice has allowed me to take ownership of my words and actions, and the way in which they can affect those around me. I still feel a bit burdened by this freedom, like a convict released after a lifetime and fearing life on the outside, but in many ways I feel like that proverbial butterfly, slowly unfurling my newfound wings.

Life has changed quite a bit since that last humiliating day, and over one year later I sit on the same linen couch, in front of the same block wood coffee table, this time in a house surrounded by countryside. To my left sits a man, tall and slender, the opposite of Alexander in every way that matters. His eyes are never cold and his heart is always warm, and he has been a friend through months of continuing turmoil and doubt. Yet I still weep. The pain has not lessened, but I have learned to manage, no longer sinking into my depression but rising above it. I have survived recommendations of religions, strategies, changes in locations, and even medications, and still I hold my head high, barely above water though it may be. This man, my friend and my lover, has professed his love even knowing that I cannot yet verbalize the same. I care for him deeply but my heart is still rent with wonderings of what could have been, what should have been. I feel for him what I would describe as love but using the word itself seems a little trite. How can one believe in soul mates one year and then believe in finding new love the next? Will loving this man devalue what came before? Can you truly love more than one person in a lifetime? What if he comes back and I'm not available?

My face twitches lightly in a smile as I write this last question. Almost three years have passed and I am still questioning the finality of a marriage to someone who almost broke me completely. Or did I almost break myself? As this man at my side smiles sweetly, fading into the blessed sleep I so often still seek, I recall the advice of elders, reminding me that this past love will not disappear, but only fade. I hear the voice of my father crack with emotion as he talked about the love he had for the woman from whom he has been divorced almost thirty years, and the pain he endured in his journey through his new life. I want the pain to end and I sometimes wish I could forget it all. I need to remove the last of this cracking shell and allow myself to feel vulnerable again. I still gaze at the empty place on my hand and ache, but increasingly, the cold hazel eyes in my memories are replaced by happy blue smiles and a southern twang that sets my heart at ease. I want to take the hand of this man at my side and offer him all that I am without fear that one day, he too will leave; without fear that the warmth in his heart and in his eyes will inevitably become icy and cold. I sit on this couch and I yearn, my heart unsure but my will strong. The weeping, like time, will pass and I will be better for it.

NOTE

[1]   From Rihanna's 'California King Bed' (2010).

REFERENCES/BIBLIOGRAPHY

Bochner, A. P. (2001). Narrative's virtues. *Qualitative Inquiry, 7*(2), 131–157.

Ellis, C. E. (1995). *Final negotiations: A story of loss, love, and chronic illness.* Philadelphia, PA: Temple University Press.

Ellis, C. E. (2004). *The ethnographic I: A methodological novel about autoethnography.* Walnut Creek, CA: AltaMira Press.

Ellis, C. E. (2007). Telling secrets, revealing lives: Relational ethics in research with intimate others. *Qualitative Inquiry, 13*(1), 3–29.

Ellis, C. E. (2009). *Revision: Autoethnographic reflections on life and work.* Walnut Creek, CA: Left Coast.

Ellis, C. E., Bochner, A. P., Denzin, N. K., Goodall, H. L., Pelias, R. & Richardson, L. (2008). Let's get personal: First-generation autoethnographers reflect on writing personal narratives. In N. K. Denzin & M. D. Giardina (Eds.), *Qualitative inquiry and the politics of evidence* (pp. 309–333). Walnut Creek, CA: Left Coast.

Freeman, M. (1997). Death, narrative integrity, and the radical challenge of self-understanding: A reading of Tolstoy's *Death of Ivan Ilych. Ageing and Society, 17*(4), 373–397.

Giorgio, G. (2009). Traumatic truths and the gift of telling. *Qualitative Inquiry, 15*(1), 149–167.

Harr, A., Jackson, J., Renea, P. & Delicata, A. (2010). *Title of song* [Recorded by Rihanna]. On *Loud* [CD]. New York, NY: Def Jam.

Lee, K. V. (2006). A fugue about grief. *Qualitative Inquiry, 12*(6), 1154–1159.

Poulos, C. N. (2010). Spirited accidents: An autoethnography of possibility. *Qualitative Inquiry, 16*(1), 49–56.

Smith, B. (1999). The abyss: Exploring depression through a narrative of the self. *Qualitative Inquiry, 5*(2), 264–279.

Tillman L. M. (2010). Deadline: Ethics and ethnographic divorce. *Qualitative Inquiry, 17*(7), 596–598.

Van Maanen, J. (1988). *Tales of the field.* Chicago, IL: University of Chicago.

Dyanis Popova
Faculty of Teaching and Learning
School of Education
Virginia Tech
Blacksburg, Virginia, USA

JEN HENDERSON

10. WHAT REMAINS

ABSTRACT

In this poem, the author explores feelings of loss and commitment in light of her visit to Joplin, Missouri, in 2011 after an EF-5 tornado levelled much of the town, killing 161 people. She draws on autoethnographic methods and a critical pedagogy lens to re-envision her role as a social scientist trying to understand the complexity of weather disasters.

***

The sun, a white disk in a blue sky, over
Missouri. Jackhammers pulse the air
like mechanical cicadas. Brown dirt flecked
with fragments of wood and cement,
glossy shards of Joplin.

Homes ripped open to reveal dollhouse lives,
empty now, the frayed remnants of blue siding peeled
back from the walls like skin from a wound.
I'm detached, caught off guard, just as they were
when warnings sounded two months ago in May.

Tornado warning fatigue, meteorologists
declare, kept residents from retreating with the sirens.
I have taken shelter from these storms.

"Are they coming our way, honey?" Sally asks months before.
She presses her lips together and sees
red and green clusters on radar
that night. Dane and I are thrilled at the possibility of
severe weather in Virginia. My mother-in-law
forgotten and terrified, lugging her suitcase, repacked,
down the stairs. "Just in case," she says.

We hide in the basement to reassure her.

G. A. Tilley-Lubbs & S. B. Calva (Eds.), Re-Telling Our Stories, 145–147.

Now, the sycamore trees broken, stripped of bark from
winds blown 300-miles-per-hour. How fragile we are,
our bodies.

In the blistering heat I stand in the streets
waiting. How to lose everything?

A lone man fixes a home near the damage path, sleeveless
t-shirt, jeans, faded ball cap. His olive skin suggests Hispanic;
Georgia drawls thick from his lips. "I came here to volunteer," he says.
"I had to do something." After Katrina, he lost everything. I see sweat
bead up on his forehead and feel it drip down my own back.

The home he repairs is nearly done, the roof patched like the paint.
He narrates a family who didn't escape. The father, he says, ran back
inside for his two small children, his wife. They died together.
"You have to pay it forward."
He returns to his work and I to my search for answers.

Eight-foot high debris lines what used to be sidewalks, bone-white
corpses, trees and empty foundations,
stairs ending in thin air.

Yeats. World War I. Dread and chaos unrecognizable
to everyday experience.

  "Turning and turning in the widening gyre …

  Things fall apart …

  …Mere anarchy is loosed upon the world."

I see the piles of remains, detritus of lives left behind, thousands of tons
shipped across the country to become another disaster.

How did this happen? The heat of the day falls heavy on my skin.

Then, carefully organized,
a simple wooden desk holds several small trinkets: a toy ambulance,
stapler, orange-handled scissors. My eye falls to the larger item on the table,
BELIEVE, all caps, in burnished metal. Against the backdrop of tragedy, irony.
My eyes drift down to hand-crocheted blankets
pale green, pink and tan. I think of the ones my mom used to make for me and my
sister each Christmas. To the right sits torn black luggage,
in the centre, a red Coca-Cola sign, a collector's item broken in two.

A stuffed bear holds a small football, yearbooks, at the forefront
nearest to me, a cluster of fake red flowers
woven into a wooden cross.

I stand silent in front of a memorial. A shrine.

Imagine the family gathering these small traces of their child,
collecting what remains.

I search for clues to who this person might have been.
I feel desperate to know, to erase anonymity.

There. On the shorn remnants of a tree inscribed, "See you in Heaven."
Small hearts scratched into the grey wood. "Love, Rochaelle and Buddha."

I return to the cluster of items to find what I've missed. To the left
of the Coca-Cola sign, a graveyard on the foundation of this home. In letters
inscribed in a half circle, as the name might appear on a head stone:
"Rachel P. Markham." Below this, "I love Yew!"
A heart-breaking goodbye: "See you soon."

I crouch on the ground, annoyed by the sound of life
moving on around me. Traffic. A low chatter across the street
where workmen install new power poles.

I wipe tears from my face. *What good can I do?*

Across the street, another house
untouched.
A blue tarp stretched over a roof. Spray-painted on its side are three short phrases,
"2430 Murphy" and "State Farm."
Declarations of place and possession. Closest to the front door
"God Bless Joplin + USA."

As someone who hasn't been to church in decades, these words
echo of what I—what we all—hope for this community,
the one they'll rebuild on this spot. Blessings.
Love. Recovery.
Resilience.

Under an unfeeling blue sky.

Amen, I say under my breath. *Amen.*

REFERENCE/BIBLIOGRAPHY

Yeats, W. B. (1919). The second coming. In R. Finneran (Ed.), *The collected works of W. B. Yeats, Vol. 1: The poems.* New York, NY: Scribner.

Jen Henderson
Science and Technology Studies
Virginia Tech
Blacksburg, Virginia, USA

SECTION 4

MULTICULTURALISM CRITICAL AUTOETHNOGRAPHY

PAMELA C. SMART-SMITH

11. AN INVISIBLE IMMIGRANT MADE VISIBLE

ABSTRACT

Liminal spaces, hyphenated spaces, intercultural, (in)between-ness, transnational, global, multi-ethnic, multiracial, multicultural, third culture, Cross Cultural Kids.

These are some terms that describe those of us who are not easily categorized culturally, showing the complexity of the situation for children who grow up (in) between and outside of just one culture. In this autoethnographic poem, the author explores these cultural interstitial spaces that mirror the physical and philosophical border crossings these children experience. She tries to make sense of growing up as a military child within the confines of the social, political, and cultural influences of the Cold War.

She also attempts to write herself out of limbo (Bell-Villada, Sichel, Eidse, Orr, & Neil) into a space of greater knowing of Self and the context of the time. She uses writing as a "method of inquiry" and as a way of "knowing—a method of discovery and analysis" (Richardson, 1998), because the "ethnographic experience is not separable from the Self" (Richardson & St. Pierre, 2008). She also seeks to offer insight into the countless children who grow up in what can often be contradictory hyphenated or liminal cultural spaces. She frames her work within the context of critical pedagogy, which as Giroux (2011) argues, "[I]lluminates [the] struggle over assigned meaning, modes of expression, and directions of desire, particularly as these bear on the formation of the multiple and ever-contradictory versions of the 'self' and its relationship to the larger society (p. 4)."

KINDERGARTEN

A multicultural parade.
Some children reach back
Trying to connect to the past
Grasping tenuous ties to the old world
While others attempt to release their chains.
I follow the leader, blissfully unaware,
Never knowing how much I must follow.

We circle the Quonset huts,
Metallic, prefabricated shells of buildings

G. A. Tilley-Lubbs & S. B. Calva (Eds.), Re-Telling Our Stories, 151–161.

Dotting the military landscape,
Holding the elementary school overflows.
Pine trees towering over head.
Fighter jet noise drowning out the teacher's voice.

Mama Dolores,
My grandmother,
Bought my shoes.
Dark red with white polka dots.
Clicking to the beat of my castanets.
Head held high in a white with red polka dot flamenco dress.

I am Spanish!

An adult asks, "Do you know how to dance?"
I show her my best flamenco moves.
"¡Olé!"
My accent flawless.
My whiteness stands out.
My blue eyes stand out.
My Shirley Temple blonde curls
Hang midway down my back.

I know who I am.

Or at least that's what I told myself then.

Duck and cover
Your flimsy school desk will save you
From the dropping radiation bombs.
Better dead than red.
There is no time for self-reflection
"We've a common enemy to fight."

Home with my Mama Dolores.
Eating her *sopa de ajo.*
Just a little garlic soup to cure what ails us.
She tells me stories about little *pajaritos*
I no longer recall.
The birds and their stories long forgotten.
The tears I shed over them,
Still close to the surface.
I think she loves me.

Mother works nights at the commissary.
Father is often gone TDY
Temporary Duty Assignments

That don't feel so temporary.

Playing outside
Walking to the candy store
Through towering pines
On a dusty dirt path
Worn by thousands of feet over many years.

Walking without adults.
Hands clutching Deutschmarks
The German money we use to buy everything off the base.
Buying gummies,
Coca Cola bottles are my favourite.

Ramstein-Meisenbach.
The United States air base in Germany
Where we still duck and cover in school
With Cold War fear.

Better dead than Red!

No gate,
No armed men,
No concertina wire to block our path.
Those come later.
Right now
There is freedom.
Though maybe it's just the freedom of youth.

Mama Dolores goes home to her hamlet of fewer than 1000
In the Pyrenees
She will return with *chorizo* sausage and cured ham and sausages
Sewn into the lining of her coat.

So they don't seize them at the border.

She knows food in Germany isn't as good.
In the United States, it is worse.

She always remembers the days of hunger,
Of war,
Of brother against brother.
Sister against sister.
Family against family.
She remembers her world ripped apart.
Husband disappeared like a puff of smoke out the prison bars.
One day allowed to hug his children, then next day gone.

Ephemera of Spanish Civil War.
Human detritus.

Splintered Republican factions fighting the
Militaristic Nationalists.
All those opposing the national identity,
Painted red by a wide stroke of the propagandas brush,
Communists.

Red.
Now dead?

My Republican grandfather
Refuses to flee.
He is captured and jailed.
Lies gathered to hold him.
They said he escaped.
They lie.
He just disappears.

Un desaparecido ....

The Guardia Civil arrives and barricades the windows of their house.
Nationalistic army green outfits,
Hated square shiny black hats.
Symbols of oppression.

He might come back.

They lie.
They know where he is,
But they will not tell.

Neighbours arrive and carry out the furniture.
They steal what they can.
Leaving a single mother
With three children to feed.
Mama Dolores left to beg for money, food, medicine from "friends."
Her three-year-old dies from a curable disease.
No money for medicine.
My uncle, 11 years old,
Pulled from the house in the deepest night,
Pistol held to his head.
Threats, jibes, taunts flow.
"Where is your father?" they ask,
Pushing his face into the dry Andalusian dirt.
Soon the family flees

North to Catalonia.
Working in textile factories.
The price your family pays for being Red.

At least they are not dead.

DEATH AS A FIVE YEAR OLD

School nears the end.
Only a few weeks to go.
They come for me.

I am sitting,
Jostled.
Shaken and moved.
Bumpy tracks.
The rhythm of the train,
Oddly soothing.
My mother near me.
Silent,
Numb.
Only death can quiet her.

Next memory.

Adults whispering.
"She should've taken her medicine."
"She liked salt too much."
"Don't let her see her."
"She's too young."

In my grandmother's house.
On the brown leather chair.
Legs sticking to the leather.

It's warm.
She's in the room around the corner.
People come in and out.
They go behind the door.
Slam!
The wind catches it.
The sound defying the silence of death.

I am defiant.

A neighbour comes.
The door

Propped open.
Peeking through the crack.

No one sees me.

Mama Dolores
Lying there.
Sleeping.
So quiet.
Her hair
Not messed up.
Wrinkles smoothed out,
Still,
No worries to crease her brow.
No anger.
No happiness.

Lying there in her best dress.
Waiting.
Thinking she will just get up.

She doesn't.
She can't.

Staying with my cousin.
Children don't go to funerals.
We don't see dead bodies.
We don't get to say
Goodbye ....

Goodbye.

My mother leaves me
In Spain for the summer.
I learn to embroider.
Acting like Heidi,
But dancing the Sardanas.

Unified in a circle,
Dancing, little hops.
Arms held high.
Clasping those next to me.
Left then right, repeat.
Symbol of Catalán pride.

Am I Spanish?

Mother always tells me I am American.
American first.
So why do I fit here in the mountains?
In Cataluña?
With my cousins?
Walking to the Catarineta fountain
Famous for Ribes water that
My uncle swears is the best.

ON THE CUSP OF 16

White walls.
Always white.
Antiseptic and cold.
Fifteen years of moving.
Four countries later.
Second birthday spent on a plane.
Used to new places.

Used to M-16s.

Duck and cover,
Code red,
Gas masks,
F-16 Fighter jets,
Sonic booms,
Security police.

Living in a little piece of the United States on foreign soil,
Never feeling really from the United States.
Used to not understanding US popular culture.
Used to not being fashionable
Or in-tune with TV shows or fast food.
Used to reverse culture shock.
Used to leaving friends.
Used to leaving schools.
Used to leaving what family I know.
Used to leaving homes.
Used to white glove cleaning and moving inspections.

Hell.

Who am I kidding?
You never get used to it.

I am not used to it.
Having no choice.
Sending us where they want.
When they want.
Courtesy of Uncle Sam.
Courtesy of the Air Force.
No one asks if it is okay.
Daddy's job calls us.
No choice.

Make each new place home.
Postcards
Link to my past.
Bringing them to every new place.

In a new room,
Attempts to make it home.
Copious amounts of blu-tak to put
Teen Beat posters on the wall.
My teenage dreams.
1980's memorabilia.
The closets pale yellow,
Postcards cover the doors.
Odour of Kimchee,
Fermented spicy cabbage,
Permeates the drains
Of this two-storied apartment.
Bleach down the drains hasn't killed the stench of rotten cabbage.

I spend hours falling
Into and out of memories
Wishing I were somewhere else.
Looking to the past.
Writing letters to old friends.
Never sent.
Keeping up correspondence for only a few months.

Friends become disposable.
Interchangeable.
Attachment is impossible.

Losing people
As soon as you come to love them.
Best not to love.
Loving only temporarily.

Loving quickly, deeply ....

Letting go before it hurts.

Becoming best friends with my mother,
Dropping her when I find new friends.
Forgetting her
Until it's time to move again.
The cycle repeats.
New place.
No friends.
Full of teen angst.
Ready to explode.
Living with the enemy.
Living near the enemy.
Air raid drills.
Seoul City
At a standstill.
Buses and traffic abandoned mid-drive.
People streaming underground.
A city of nine million
Stopped.

On the base
Soldiers
Hit the dried out benjo ditches.
Happy they are not used for open raw sewage
Any longer.

"Code red!"
Speakers blare.
Gas masks on.
Red Commies
Ten minutes flight time away
Playing war games.
Living in fear.

What if today
Is the day
The reds make us dead?

PRESENT

Now 43 years old,
Not living on a military base,

The cold war
Over.

Red is not better than dead.

A son seven years old,
With my blue eyes.
Me, no longer the blissful little girl,
Without questions about her identity.

Still with blue eyes,
With blonde curls,
Shorter and darker,
Still framing a fair-skinned face.
I am a doctoral student,
An administrator.
A mentor.
A wife.
A daughter.
Sandwiched between generations.
Tired.
Chronically ill.
Spread thin.

Living rural southern
Among the hills and valleys
Of my father's youth.

Not international.
Who am I?
I am invisible.
Stranger in a strange land
In a land that isn't supposed to be
So strange.

US of A
Labelled:
American.
White.
Middle class.
Bilingual.

Legally:
US citizen by birth.
British by marriage.
Spanish and Catalán by soul.

160

Identifying as:
Everything and nothing
Simultaneously.
Juxtaposed and confused.

Adult Cross Cultural Kid.

REFERENCES/BIBLIOGRAPHY

Bell-Villada, G. H., & Sichel, N. (Eds.). (2011). *Writing out of limbo: International childhoods, global nomads and third culture kids*. Newcastle upon Tyne, UK: Cambridge.

Giroux, H. A. (2011). *On critical pedagogy*. New York, NY: Bloomsbury.

Pollock, D. C., Van Ruth, E. R., & Van Reken, R. E. (2009). *Third culture kids: Growing up among worlds*. Boston, MA: Nicholas Brealey.

Richardson, L. (2000). Writing: A method of inquiry. In N. K. Denzin & Y. S. Lincoln (Eds.), *Handbook of qualitative research* (pp. 923–948). Thousand Oaks, CA: Sage.

Richardson, L., & St Pierre, E. A. (2008). Writing. A method of inquiry. In N. K. Denzin & Y. S. Lincoln (Eds.), *Collecting and interpreting qualitative materials* (pp. 345–371). Thousand Oaks, CA: Sage.

Pamela Smart-Smith
Faculty of Teaching and Learning
School of Education
Virginia Tech
Blacksburg, Virginia, USA

RONG CHANG

12. NEVER FORGET CLASS STRUGGLE

An Autoethnographic Reflection

ABSTRACT

In this chapter, I use autoethnography as the method to write my lived experiences as a new immigrant from China. The purpose of this writing is to illustrate the difficulties and challenges I faced as a female immigrant. In writing, I confront and investigate these experiences in order to make sense of and find meaning in them. I also consider how these experiences are situated within the social and cultural background of the United States. The data are from my personal journal and reflections. This chapter not only portrays the difficulties and challenges immigrants can face, but also seeks to build an understanding of immigrants' life experiences in the United States and to bring their perspectives and voices into the mainstream discourse.

INTRODUCTION

In the long winter night,
I hear a lonely bird singing.

It is a quiet winter evening. Snow falls silently on the ground in the darkness. I sit in my warm bed reading. The red lampshade on the nightstand casts a crimson shadow. The rays touch a black and white photo of my mother, forming a golden red ring around it. For two thousand years, the colour red has been a symbol for happiness in China, but tonight it makes me pensive. I put the book on my comforter covered with fuchsia coloured spring flowers and green leaves. In her picture, my mother's eyes express such a serene and tender feeling. I look at her, hoping so much to hear her voice again. I wait, but she only smiles. Her eyes convey so much love, and I know that through the pure white snowflakes, she is watching me from heaven. She died twenty some years ago. I left China a year after she passed, so I have been an immigrant in the United States for twenty-three years.

This silent night, the bird's lonely song brings another image to my mind. I see a young woman in her late twenties dressed in a white shirt and a pair of black pants, with a black bowtie around her neck, a typical working outfit for a restaurant server. She looks at me through the haze of the red rays and twenty some years of memory. Her gaze is sad and lost. Tears stream down her face. She looks so lonely

G. A. Tilley-Lubbs & S. B. Calva (Eds.), Re-Telling Our Stories, 163–172.

and helpless. The image makes my heart ache. I cannot help but close my eyes, and reach out my arms to embrace that image, to embrace the memories of myself from those twenty some years ago.

Up to now, I have always avoided to deal with the complexity and depth of the emotions evoked by my past. I have always tried to block these memories. However, tonight they are like aspen trees in a spring field sprouting upward and waving back and forth, their roots spreading in the earth, breaking through layers of dirt with the force of life. No matter how I guard myself, the new sprouts still pop up in my mind. Memory has its own will. I know that facing the past is unavoidable (Poulos, 2009).

I am among the many people who have left the motherland for other countries in order to escape political, or religious persecution, or to avoid economic difficulties, and other social ordeals (Berger, 2004; Portes & Rumbaut, 2006; Zhou, 2009). I left the homeland to escape what my parents experienced in China and to search for a safer life. What I did not know was that coming to America, I would have to deal with so many issues that all immigrants face including language difficulties, culture shock, the process of assimilation into a new society, discrimination and that, I would have to face additional challenges due to being a woman, wife, a mother, and a daughter (Berger, 2004; Githens, 2013).

Up to this time, I have not been able to articulate the strong emotions associated with my early life in the United States as a new immigrant. However, my unconscious mind has its will to take me down memory lane. Here, in my bedroom, twenty-three years later, I am that young woman again.

Revisiting the past is not easy; it is like opening an unhealed wound. By doing so, I find myself in that vulnerable position again. The memories come alive, and the emotions flow. I start to write, in order to make sense of these experiences through writing. My intention is not only to relieve sorrow and regrets, but also to write as inquiry (Richardson & St. Pierre, 2005) to make connections of my personally lived experiences to a larger picture of social and cultural understanding (Ellis, 2004).

Now, where do I begin?

I AM NOT FROM THE COUNTRY CALLED PREJUDICE

What a beautiful land,
With soft rolling mountains,
Green forests,
The peaceful lakes reflect the blue sky,
The white clouds,
But, I am so lost,
Lost in this beautiful land....

It is late summer of 1990. The night is young, and the restaurant is lively and busy. The lights are dim in the dining room, and the air is a mixture of smoke, perfume, food, and alcohol. The dining room is large, easily seating 150 people. Customers in brightly coloured summer clothes are talking and laughing. There are a few large, colourful totem poles, their colourfulness reflected in the customers' drinks. The carved wooden totem poles smile with big open mouths and deep dark eyes. Several Chinese folk art paper cuttings hang on the walls; the biggest one is an angry-looking red dragon framed on the wall in the centre of the room. Red flames come from his open mouth. Soft music blends in the sounds of people's conversations. At the corners of the room, lovers in straw-covered booths surrounded by fake palm trees kiss in the shadows.

I am a new waitress in this restaurant. I understand very little of the language I hear spoken around me, and very little about the restaurant itself. The dishes on the menu are strange items I have never heard of or tasted. In fact, I only came to this mid-sized town on the East Coast from China a few weeks ago. Unable to speak English and without other marketable skills, this was the first job I could find. Walking through the dining room, hearing the waves of sounds come and go, feels like standing by the ocean, with the tides getting higher and stronger. It makes me feel weak, as if the tides could swallow me at any moment. I am overwhelmed and confused; my steps are unsteady, and my voice is small and nervous. Nevertheless, I keep taking orders, moving as fast as I can to put water, crackers, and butter on the table. I clean up dirty tables when customers leave. The drinks on the menu amaze me: Volcanos, Zombies, Scotch on Ice, Bloody Mary. I wonder what they are made of. They certainly look delicious. The orange, yellow, green, and deep red drinks in differently shaped glasses and bowls are strangely enticing. The names of the dishes sound even more exotic: Chicken with Almond, Shrimp with Lobster Sauce, steaks, and Banana Flambé. These kinds of names and descriptions for food and drinks do not exist in the Chinese language. It is impossible for me to associate them with anything I have tasted or even imagined in my entire life.

While I am struggling to start my new life in America as a waitress, across the Pacific Ocean, people in China are struggling to feed themselves. As I remember, a person who has ten thousand yuan or one thousand dollars is considered rich. After forty years of political movements, especially after the Great Cultural Revolution, China has become one of the poorest and the most populated countries in the world (Jiang, 1997). Recently arrived from China, I still recall vividly how desires to have material possessions are subjected to criticism and punishment by the government and the Communist Party. My education from China consists of Communist ideologies interpreted by party leaders. Like many other Chinese, I also was led to believe that liberating people from capitalistic oppressions is the duty of Chinese people. Now, working at this restaurant in the United States, surrounded by happy and healthy customers, I cannot help wondering why people in China have such different lives than these people in the United States.

While I am running around trying to understand what the customers are saying to me, going as fast as I can to carry food and drinks to them, I feel poor, confused, and conflicted. I never felt poor when I lived in China simply because I did not know what it meant to be rich. As I begin this new life in the United States, I feel poor in so many ways. The fluent and standard Chinese I used to speak has lost its meaning and stopped functioning in this new environment. I miss my voice, and soon I realize what it really means for me to not be able to speak the language.

One night, a young African American couple walks in and the hostess seats them in my section. On my way to get the drinks, the boss says in a hushed voice, "They can wait." It takes me a minute to comprehend her instruction. After I put water and crackers on the young couple's table, I leave them alone to wait on other customers. I do not know how much time has passed when I see the young couple waving at me. Running to their table, I realize I had almost forgotten them.

"Are you ready to order?" I ask eagerly. The young lady looks at me. She is silent.

Soon she begins to speak in a very clear voice:

"Are you prejudiced?"

"Prejudiced ...." I repeat after her, trying to think what it means, but I cannot. I have not learned this word; maybe it is a country's name. After a moment, I say to her,

"No, I am Chinese; I am from China, not from Prejudice." I answer her the best way I can.

"Is this a joke?" She is angrier with me now, but I do not know why. I am Chinese. I told her the truth. She stands up and throws the red napkin at my face, saying, "We will not come here ever again!"

The red napkin touches my face, and then slowly drops on the floor, still clean. It lies on the dark green carpet, strikingly red like blood. Obviously, I have been punished, and humiliated by something I have done, but I am oblivious as to what that could be. All of a sudden, I feel hungry and thirsty. I have been working for six hours, running and trying to meet people's requests. I have been trying to satisfy them without drinking a sip of water myself. Other customers are looking in my direction now, and one busboy walks quickly to the office. The boss rushes out wearing a polite smile on her face.

"I apologize. That waitress is new. Please come back again," she says to the young couple. But they keep walking and slam the door behind them. The busboys, a group of immigrants from Vietnam, are laughing now. They are. All are in their early twenties, but look like teenagers.

They start to sing with a heavy accent, "I am not from Prejudice," and they laugh.

The boss walks by me again and says, "You will share more tips with the others tonight."

"But why?" I can't help but ask.

"YOU made the customer mad."

"But you instructed me to let them wait!"

She does not answer and walks away. The napkin in my hand reminds me of the red scarf I wore when I was a child in China, but now, it is something that people throw in my face. What have I done? What does prejudice mean? Why are the busboys laughing? What is there to laugh about? They look so happy and amused by what has happened to me. There is no use asking them since my poor Chinese-English cannot communicate with their Vietnamese-English. Obviously, they know more than I do.

I wipe my tears and continue to work. "I am not from Prejudice" becomes a popular song that evening. I know I need to work. I have to swallow my pride, because now my income depends on happy customers, the tips they leave on the table—the crumpled green bills, mixed among the cigarette butts, unfinished drinks, dirty utensils, and used napkins. Late that night, I look up the word prejudice in my Chinese-English dictionary and find the word's real meaning. My heart aches with anger, astonishment, and shame. I want to tell that young lady if I ever have a chance to see her again that I too have experienced prejudice. I do not know that in the United States people with a different skin colour get different treatment. I only followed instructions from the boss. Now I realize that I am not only poor in English language ability, but also I am poor in social-cultural understanding (Berger, 2004; Githens, 2013). I realize that I have lost "the way of framing ideas, communication, and self-expression" (Berger, 2004, p. 6). My English ability only allows me to translate computer programs, since I am an electronic engineer from China. While in this new world, I need a different set of language skills to understand the new social and linguistic surroundings. My world has turned upside down. Yet, what happens to me a few days later shows me how powerless I am.

I work four days a week. I often go to work at five in the evening and stay until whenever the boss does not need me anymore. Business usually picks up at around six. The waiters and waitresses arrive early to get ready for the night. After working there for two months, I have gained some insights about where the best tippers often sit, and which areas are the second best, and so on and so forth. I find that two white girls usually have the best stations. One man from Taiwan often has the most tables. A woman from Taiwan does not have to share her tips with the busboys, and a girl from a Middle Eastern country often has the not-so-good stations. My stations are often the leftover ones. Sometimes, I get to help the waiter who is too busy to take care of all his customers. There are also two hosts. Both are white and blonde, pretty and fashionable. I hear they are paid very well. They do not have to wear a white blouse and black pants. They are students from local colleges, not immigrants.

One lucky night, I have the opportunity to serve two tables on the stage, an area in the centre of the restaurant built to look like a bamboo pavilion. The customers I serve are in a good mood, and they have had quite a few rounds of drinks. One table favours Zombies, the other table favours Volcanoes. I push the cart that carries drinks and food up and down to the pavilion many times. I hear my customers make comments about my appearance, saying to one another,

"She is Chinese, but she does not have oriental eyes. How come her eyes are so big?"

I do not know how to react to these comments that refer to me. I want to tell them that some Chinese do have big eyes and that not all Chinese look the same. I want to tell them China has fifty-six minority groups; each has their language, culture,

167

history, and physical characteristics. But, my limited vocabulary does not allow me to do so. However, in my mind, I am shouting in Chinese. I cannot help feeling put down, because of who I am with my physical features. I receive a twenty-dollar tip that night from one table, and fifteen dollars from another. The news is spreading among the bus boys and even to the bosses. When the customers finally get up to leave, drunk in each other's arms, the female boss calls me to her office. Under the blue fluorescent light, she looks pale and thin, and her eyes are sharp.

"Take out everything from your pockets!" she says with a firm voice.

"But why, why do I have to do that?" I ask.

"The busboys said you did not share your tips with them." I can sense her anger.

"But I did! I had forty dollars total, and I gave fifteen to them!" I exclaim.

She points to each of my pockets and makes sure I empty their contents onto a dark brown table. Soon, my total meagre possessions are on the table. They consist of a set of keys, my learners' permit, one twenty-dollar and two five-dollar bills, wrinkled as if they had a long night of work like me.

"There!" she exclaims, pointing to the two five-dollar bills.

"You should only have twenty-five dollars, but you have thirty in your pocket! Why do you have five dollars extra?" She is excited. Her cold voice is like a thin knife slicing through my heart.

"I brought five dollars with me, just in case, I need to buy something. Why do you think all the money in my pockets is tips? It is not all tips!"

I answer with a trembling voice, tears welling up in my eyes. I feel as if my clothes have been forcibly stripped from me. Standing under the dim florescent light, with my pockets emptied and turned inside out, I feel naked, so naked as if my soul has been exposed to the rainy and dark night. When I leave, raindrops mix with my bitter tears as I walk through the night. I ask myself "Why am I here? What I will become?"

THE EXISTING CLASS STRUGGLE

Shouting at the top of my lungs:

> "Never forget the class struggle."
> "Never forget the class struggle."
> In my junior high English class,
> Long ago, in China.

It is summer. We sit in a classroom, hands behind our backs, bodies straight, and eyes focused on the blackboard. It is my first English class. According to the teacher, we are learning the most important sentence in Chinese and English, "Never forget the class struggle!" It is a hot day; there are about fifty children in the classroom. The heat emanates from the hard dirt floor in waves, mixing with body odour. In northwest China, water is like gold, so we do not use water to wash ourselves. It is too wasteful to do that. In the dry summer heat and the suffocating smells, I shout

out the words with the rest of my classmates. I shout more loudly. I need the teachers and the rest of the class to know that I can change, and I will change because I belong to the class that needs to be reformed. In my heart, through the loud shouting, I beg people not to abandon me. I am willing to carry the heaviest load of fertilizer to the mountaintop. I am willing to clean the outhouse as many times as they need. I am willing to do anything so I will not be an outcast. I want to belong, to belong to the people from a class other than my own. Many years later, after arriving in America, these words echo in my mind again. I am learning their meaning not as a twelve-year-old child but as a new immigrant. I find again that I belong to the lowest class, just as I did in China during the Great Cultural Revolution. However, this time it is for the opposite set of reasons. During the Great Cultural Revolution, I belonged to the lowest class because both my parents were educated and from wealthy and educated family backgrounds. They were the people that the Communist Party aimed to eliminate (Jiang, 1997; Macfarquhar & Schoenhals, 2006). As their child, I was automatically categorized into the group of children who also needed to be reformed or eliminated. In the Party's eyes, my parents had contaminated and corrupted me, so I was not fit to be a future good citizen, but rather I was a potential threat. In China, the social capital of my parents could bring death sentences to themselves and to me during the Great Cultural Revolution. In the United States, lacking that capital means no future. What shakes me is that I have to learn what the class struggle means through the relationship with my husband.

NEVER FORGET CLASS STRUGGLE

I first meet my husband during a business trip to the United States. My company in China sent seven engineers to work with a U.S. company to build oil-drilling equipment in the United States. I am the only one who speaks limited English and I am also the only female. The apartment where we stay provides rides back and forth from the hotel to the worksite. We depend on local Chinese residents to help us with transportation to do our grocery shopping. Mr. Li, my husband now, is one of those local Chinese who frequently visit us and offer to help since my group does not have a car and no one knows how to drive. We are from China, the bicycle country, where a good bicycle is the most valuable item in most households.

It is close to Christmas, which seems to be the most important holiday in the Western Hemisphere, but it means nothing to the group of Communist Party members except me, since my parents had told me so much about Christmas when I was a young child. It is cold and snows often. Christmas wreaths are hanging everywhere, in store windows, on lampposts in the streets, on top of the fireplace in the hotel lobby. Christmas music permeates the air. One day, Mr. Li sends flowers to our group. What a surprise! My colleagues wonder how much they could have cost. None of us had seen such a huge basket of brilliantly coloured flowers in China, and we do not understand the practice of giving flowers to others. Our group leader ponders over it. He makes the decision to let that basket of fresh and colourful flowers stay in my room, thinking that leaving the flowers in his room would be a sign of accepting a capitalistic way of living.

"What a waste to pay money to buy flowers! No use for it! Let Xiao Bai have them," he says, using Bai, which is my last name, and the typical way to address younger colleagues in China.

"And please call to tell Mr. Li not to send flowers anymore. It is too wasteful," he adds.

I am the translator and the contact person for our group. My standard Chinese and youthful voice has been well received by the local Chinese. I carry the flower basket to my room. It brightens my day and softens the homesick feeling I have been experiencing. I have never seen such a beautiful basketful of followers before. It is also my first time to hear the name of the flower: "Bird of Paradise." The flower has such a wonderful name! It sounds so free.

Like many people we meet in the mid-sized town, Mr. Li is well educated. He is from Taiwan and did his graduate study at a university in the United States. Later on, he went into business. He is very different from my male colleagues. He is polite, reserved, and well dressed, and speaks excellent English. When he walks by, his chewing tobacco leaves a nice fragrance, not like my colleagues; they are all heavy smokers who smoke whole day. They look like walking chimneys, smiling with their smoke stained teeth.

I have not considered the many differences between Mr. Li and myself when he asks me to marry him. I vaguely feel the vast differences between us, but I cannot pinpoint them. I walk into the marriage willingly blindfolded. Leaving China is the most important thing. What if there is another Great Cultural Revolution? What would I do if the government decided to send me to reform camps, just as they did to my parents? Could I survive that? I do not want to live in fear for the rest of my life. I take my father's advice, and I run. I run away from China but have no idea what I am running into.

Soon after my arrival in the United States, during a casual conversation, my husband mentions the need for me to have a job. We are outside, sitting on the patio. The grass is very green. It is a quiet evening. My previous experiences in the United States living in the hotel and working at the factory were so different from what I am experiencing now. I am no longer under the surveillance of the group or anyone else. I feel free until my husband's voice startles me.

"You need to start to work soon. I will find you a job," he says while drinking beer.

"What kind of work can I find?" I ask, eager to show that I am not going to be a burden.

"You have no marketable skills, and you cannot speak English. You can only work as a waitress," he replies.

"But I don't know anything about restaurants and my English is not good." I start to worry.

"I will find a menu for you, so you can start to learn it, and I will find a place for you to work." His voice is calm and determined.

Next day, I get a printed menu in English and the following week I become a restaurant worker. That conversation changes how I look at my marriage. I do not plan to stay at home; I want to go to school, and I want to become a useful person in this new life. Nevertheless, it surprises me that I have to work so soon, because he had told me how financially sound he was before I came.

This is also the first time we discuss money. Before my move to the States, he never showed any financial distress. In fact, he had said to me that whatever was his would be mine, and there was no worry. I cannot understand the reason for me to start working so soon. In my perception, Taiwanese men are more traditional and take the role of supporting a family, a very different practice than what I had experienced in China, where women are educated as men's equal partners, and expected to work alongside each other. I am used to work and want to be a productive person, but having to start working so soon takes away the time we need to get to know each other as husband and wife. And it takes away the time I need to learn English. But, things do not happen as I had wanted. Finally, I realize that even though we are married, I am on my own in so many ways.

He has put it plainly, "It is not fair for me to support you. You need to support yourself."

That sentence not only shocks me but also changes how I view our future. It puts our relationship into a state of uncertainty compounded by my need to support myself without any marketable skills. All of these put a great distance between us. I have traded one kind of insecurity for another. The difference is that no matter how difficult life was in China, I always had my family's love and support. Now in this beautiful new land, I know no one. I am alone with my grief. I feel so lonely in the spacious house that does not belong to me. With a heavy heart, I become a restaurant worker.

CONCLUSIONS

I have been thinking about my lived experiences. What do they reflect, what do they represent? What do they tell me? What can I learn from them? I remembered how things happened, but I did not know why they happened. As I approach the conclusion of this writing, I realize the struggle of power is the centre of all my lived experiences. As a female immigrant, in my early life in America, I had no power in this stratified society. The powerlessness and its results are reflected in all my lived experiences. Twenty some years later, as a doctoral student, have I gained power? Am I still that powerless? No, I have come a long way ….

As I put my pen down, I know that the young woman is walking toward me, through that rainy night twenty some years ago. She and I meet in my writing. We embrace through twenty-four years of sorrow, struggles, persistence, and hopes.

In revisiting our past, she and I realize that many things have happened, and many things have changed, but the lifelong, complex, and multidimensional resettlement immigrants' face (as cited in Burg, 2006) still is part of our life.

So I tell my younger Self, that I did not give up. She and I have both walked on a long and winding road, but together we have found a way. There is no fear of people abandoning us anymore. Steadily, she and I will continue to walk forward.

REFERENCES/BIBLIOGRAPHY

Berger, R. (2013). *Immigrant women tell their stories*. New York, NY: Routledge.

Ellis, C. (2004). *The ethnographic I: A methodological novel about autoethnography*. Walnut Creek, CA: Altamira.

Githens, M. (2013). *Contested voices: Women immigrants in today's world*. New York, NY: Palgrave Macmillan.

Jiang, J. (1997). *Red scarf girl: A memoir of the cultural revolution*. New York, NY: HarperCollins.

MacFarquhar, R. (2006). Michael Schoenhals. *Mao's last revolution*. Cambridge, MA: Belknap.

Portes, A., & Rumbaut, R. G. (2006). *Immigrant America: a portrait*. Berkeley CA: University of California.

Poulos, C. N. (2009). *Accidental ethnography: An inquiry into family secrecy*. Walnut Creek, CA: Left Coast.

Richardson, L., & St. Pierre, E. A. (2005). Writing: A method of inquiry. In N. K. Denzin & Y. S. Lincoln (Eds.), *The sage handbook of qualitative research* (3rd ed., pp. 959–978). Thousand Oaks, CA: Sage.

Zhou, M. (2009). *Contemporary Chinese America: Immigration, ethnicity, and community transformation*. Philadelphia, PA: Temple University.

Rong Chang
Faculty of Teaching and Learning
School of Education
Virginia Tech
Blacksburg, Virginia, USA

DYANIS POPOVA

13. DECOLONIZATION OF THE SELF

Reflection and Reflexivity

ABSTRACT

In this chapter, the author reflects on immigration experiences during her journey through academia and on how exposure to critical pedagogy and autoethnography contributed to her personal perspectives and overall worldview. Through vignettes and theoretical discussion, she explores the symbolic violence inherent in the process of personal decolonization.

***

As a writer, the idea of being a colonized person, and my struggle with what that represents, calls to me in part due to my academic research interests. It is a murmur just below the surface of my consciousness, a reminder of my histories, and a harbinger of future possibilities. Born and raised in the former British colony of Trinidad and Tobago, I am the child of a colonized history, always leaning forward trying to be more … more than just an (island) girl.

In the Caribbean, there is often a feeling of trying to be better than the legacy that island life dictates and infers. Hall (2001) discusses this sentiment and highlights that Caribbean feeling of being "almost about to tip over, striving to reach somewhere else" (p. 285). Since times of slavery, it has been assumed that high culture resides outside the islands, in the land of the colonizer rather than in that of the colonized. To this day, more prestige is awarded to those who have received education, training, and life experiences abroad. For my grandparents' generation, all things of value and prestige were to be found in England or potentially even Europe, but by the time I was born, much of that grandeur had also been attributed to the United States.

I recall the status awarded to classmates who had bought their new backpacks, shoes, and Trapper Keepers in England or the United States. Even if they had been able to get the exact same items locally, their foreign-bought possessions were more appealing and more valued. They were what everyone wanted. I remember also the long lines outside foreign restaurant chains like McDonalds, Pizza Hut, Subway, and Dairy Queen, even though the flavour and value of the local chains were often better. Just the name of a foreign franchise was enough to elicit ravenous consumption. It didn't matter how it tasted or how much it cost. It was all about the brand. I was in Form 3 or 4 (9th or 10th grade) when McDonald's first arrived on our shores. The lines to the entrance wrapped around the block. In the capital the restaurant was within walking distance of Burger Boys, a local chain that was cheaper and served burgers twice the size with twice the flavour. But the lines outside McDonald's kept growing ... it must be better ... it was "from foreign."

This general attitude pervaded and pervades much of our daily lives and culture in the islands and with the arrival of U.S. cable television in Trinidad around the same time period, the culture of commercialism took hold and now dominates much of what we see and believe. When I was a teenager, local music was only valued and appreciated at Carnival and Christmas times. During my last visit home in 2008, the popularity of Lean Cuisines and fur-lined winter boots astounded me. This colonization not only involves consumerism but also the ways in which people view themselves and if/how they value their home culture(s). Many local items and ideas are expected to be sub-standard and to some, even uncivilized. Though there is a growing movement to reclaim a sense of pride in all things local, we are still a people bound in a state of what Bob Marley describes as mental slavery. This neo-colonial state is often accompanied by an element of unconsciousness, in which we often fail to realize how many of our perceptions can be traced to our colonial roots. This outlook fosters a capacity of rootlessness in the West Indian (Walcott, 1999) and oftentimes a sense of inferiority that can last a lifetime.

As a young person, I saw colonization simply, as part of history. In my mind, since we were taught reverence for the tomes written from the perspective of the colonizer, we had received physical independence and we were free. I was raised to believe that life was full of possibilities and that I was the architect of my own fate. I wasn't necessarily light-skinned enough, or rich enough, or exotic enough to have a relatively effortless path to success, so I had to be smart enough. Grasping this freedom of choice and possibility, I left my homeland to seek my good fortune and pursue my studies in the land of milk and honey: the United States.

From the moment I landed, I retained an unconscious sense of being less than. This feeling slowly became part of my conscious state. I struggled for years to find and claim my place in this society. My mother had left her successful clothing design and tailoring business behind, in part motivated by her desire to support my educational efforts in person. She didn't want me, her only child, to be alone in a new country. My father and step-mother were also in the United States, albeit far away, but my mother saw her presence as a necessity for my security and success. So here we were, ready to begin anew, often referred to by more established immigrants as "fresh off the boat" newcomers. The harshness of our new reality was in many cases difficult to bear, and for years I took refuge in my studies; my books had always been my best friends. But then, years later, after a failed marriage and my subsequent return to school and books, I found Paolo (Freire), and Frantz (Fanon), and Cynthia (Dillard), and Linda (T. Smith) ... and I began to think. I began to contemplate what Oyewumi (2005) describes as our world sense, with numerous ways of knowing and learning, so different than the European notions with which I was raised. I understood my learning to be a product of my colonization and something that warranted more investigation, and perhaps even resistance. The knowledge I held about my country, my people, and essentially myself had been shaped by these colonial understandings of culture, beauty, and worth.

In making space for my body, mind, and spirit to be part of my work (Dillard, 2012), my cultural memories have helped shape who I am in all my multiplicities. My experiences as an immigrant have shaped my academic and professional journeys and have shattered the rose coloured glasses I never knew I wore. Theory has lent voice to the vexations of my spirit and has helped me find the words to express these emotions and advocate on behalf of those who follow. There is so much power in this land and just my presence here speaks to a privilege denied to many in my twin island republic. This privilege, of which I am now fully aware, has been dwarfed by my realizations of who I am related to those around me and the perceptions they hold due to the way I look and sound, and to the paths (both chosen and enforced) of my ancestors. I have come to realize how many of the voices in my head are the remnants of histories. They are the songs of my great-grandparents, the hopes of my ancestors, and even the judgements of the oppressors. These feelings stem from generations before me who told me that I had to work twice as hard, climb twice as high, and perpetually struggle against misperceptions as I strove for success.

In this piece, I explore the meaning and feelings of being a colonized person and look at power and privilege in U. S. society through the eyes of an immigrant. My arrival to this country awakened my consciousness and opened my mind to aspects of my colonial identity that were invisible to me in the land of my birth. I trace the ongoing process of my personal decolonization through vignettes that represent key moments of cognizance. These excerpts from my experiences serve as an avenue toward reflexivity (Humphreys, 2005), and trace my journey of learning to read the world and my place in it (Freire, 2000). Using writing as a method of inquiry (Richardson & St. Pierre, 2005) I bear witness to and deconstruct these experiences and their influences on my life, my interactions, and my pedagogical perspectives. Through the autoethnographic process, my stories have taken on a life of their own. Like Wright (2009), the central feelings of powerlessness during this academically driven exploration were unclear to me and this much needed contemplation helped me to better understand what these feelings meant and how they have influenced me as a daughter, scholar, and teacher. I have never been much of a journal writer, though I have tried, but the vignettes that follow arise from buried memories too powerful to remain permanently hidden.

Critical autoethnography has provided me with the space and the language to connect my experiences to the dynamics of power and privilege I encounter daily. This piece evolved from an initial deconstruction of self as the Other. Like my academic work, "[T]hese battles are almost everyday battles; having to justify and legitimate every single action of mine (with the assumption that my legitimacy is always suspect as an outsider – a questioning 'brown soul')" (Dutta & Basu, 2013, p. 150). This process of reflection and reflexivity is ongoing and essential to both my inner peace and the ways in which I endeavour to connect to those around me, both as an academic and as a sister-being on this earth. The essence of these two selves is apparent even in the way I express myself, sometimes alternately, both academically and colloquially throughout these vignettes.

REALITY STRIKES

It was one of the greatest weeks of my life. The long white envelopes continued to deliver euphoria and a sense of accomplishment through the mail slot. I had been so despondent recently, watching all my high school friends go off to college. With my middle class background, I had always expected – no assumed – that I would be with them. Reality was my cruel companion that year after high school. That middle class upbringing had been a well-crafted illusion; there was no money for school. I had ignored my knowledge of my parents' poor, working class background. I had been too caught up in the life they were trying to give me and had lost touch with the reality of my situation. Not to worry, this year had been an experience no college could give me. I had worked as a waitress and bartender, without a legal permit, between the high rises of the city, knowing that I would eventually achieve my objectives and that college was just around the corner. My mother would figure it out. She always did. All I needed to be like one of my friends was a student visa. For that to happen, I just needed one of those envelopes to say, "We are happy to inform you. ..." And then they started coming. And they all gave me happy news. Brown, UPenn, Johns Hopkins ... they had all accepted me!

The clutter of the tiny living room surrounded my mother and me as we sat amidst the accolades and paper work. As the stream of dusky light coming through the window moved across the room, the small white paper in my hand became more and more crumpled from ordering and re-ordering my options. In which state did I want to live? What classes could I take? I began to dream about future successes. I could see my future self in a classic black suit, my long (only in my reveries) legs shrouded in the finest silken hose, and my feet housed in the same exquisite Italian leather as my briefcase that contained the keys to world peace and community love. This Eurocentric notion of a successful adulthood framed all my hopes and aspirations. The next words spilling from my mother's lips knocked me out of my reverie:

"So, how much is it?"

My eyes darted to the woman next to me ... cost? There was no way to put a price on my happiness! I slid to the floor amidst the week's coloured papers searching for the price tag for my future success and happiness. I grabbed the first one I found.

"$30, 000 a year ... plus room, board, and books ... but I can work to cover that."

I reached for another, not recognizing the worry and sadness that shadowed my mother's face.

"$28,000, $32,000, $23,500."

I will never forget those numbers. They walk with me often, reminding me of who I am, from whence I came, and especially of the limitations of my reality. She placed her firm yet gentle hand on my shoulder to quiet me.

"Is there a place we can actually afford?"

I'm certain she saw the uncertainty and confusion on my face. I felt my shoulders sag as the truth became apparent. There was no money. I had no concept of the reality of this cost. At an exchange rate of about TT$6 to US$1, US$30,000 quickly surpassed what my parents could spare for my education. My future was becoming my fantasy.

UNCOMFORTABLE COMPARISONS

"In this town you have three choices. You can get drunk, get high, or get laid. There's nothing else to do."

I was greeted by these words my first semester as an undergraduate at a rural university on the East Coast of the United States. I had been accepted to this university during a trip to visit my father as he was completing his doctorate. I had not been able to accept admission to any of the costly universities mentioned above but on a whim, my dad suggested I talk to the head of the program most similar to my initial interests. Long after initial application deadlines, but based on an excellent transcript, I was granted acceptance to a more reasonably priced program.

Today was the start of the college weekend: Thursday night. For the next few days all my friends would be engaged in any combination of those pastimes. There was a part of me that wanted to be normal, that wanted to be part of traditional college debauchery, but I had too much to do. Family and friends had put their finances on the line to get me through the student visa process, and now I had the weight of their hopes and dreams on my shoulders. There was no time for partying. I had to work. If I wasn't in class or consumed by class assignments, I worked. Through short breaks and summers I worked. The twenty hours per week at minimum wage allowed by immigration law was insufficient so I found ways around it: 21 hours of credits, 40 hours a week; I worked.

"C'mon out with us! You've got to learn to have fun!"

It was a rare night off and I felt the excitement of their anticipation. My brain started doing the math. Extra money was hard to come by but surely I could afford a drink! To my left, Nicole sighed.

"I know money is tight … it is for everyone … but you can have fun one night. You never do anything fun!"

She pulled out a notebook to show me her own efforts at balancing a budget. I blinked several times as I leaned forward, sure that my eyes had made a mistake.

$3000 per month? How could she possibly make $3000 a month! She didn't even have a job! How could her parents possibly afford to send her that much money? As had become my habit, I instantly calculated the exchange rate. TT$18,000! It was almost too difficult to comprehend.

"Damn it!" Nicole lamented. "I'm sooooo broke! After rent, food, and shopping, I'll barely have $300 a week to spend!"

As I slowly turned to face my friend, my thoughts began to spiral. Her leftover spending money was more than double what I made in a six-day work week! Her overall income was more than my parents made in a month! I had always looked at Nicole's family lifestyle as being similar to mine. I knew that my family was on the lower end of middle class but I had assumed that was the norm, the majority. I didn't know any truly rich people. My parents had come from a life of almost constant financial struggle and I must have based my opinion on that comparison. I had lived in a nice house in a friendly suburban neighbourhood, I had attended a costly private elementary school, and in many cases if I wanted something, I only needed to ask and complete my chores. My mother would do whatever it took to make sure I was happy, and to maintain what I would later recognize as no more than an impression of middle class status.

I now looked at Nicole through a new set of eyes. Her tiny frame draped in a casual sweater and stretchy pants did not belie wealth. Through my new eyes I noticed for the first time the lustre of the fabrics draped over her, a softness that often indicated high quality and price. I wondered for the first time if the diamond studs in her ears and on the matching bracelet that always adorned her tanned wrists were real. It had never occurred to me before that they might be. My real jewellery, a few treasured pieces, only saw the light of day on special occasions. Wow, she was lucky.

My perspectives on life, status, struggle, and privilege began to change. Over the next few months, I realized that what I once saw as luck often had much more to do with circumstance. "Well-off" took on a new meaning and I began to recall how hard my parents had worked to provide me with a sense of financial security though they had never shared their struggles. Young men and women like Nicole abounded on this picturesque campus. It seemed that everywhere I turned I was enveloped in shrieking high-pitched voices and the popped polo collars of privilege. This was a university where I was the minority. Here, students drove cars my parents still aspired to own, and most didn't have to work. Their parents paid their bills so they could concentrate on their homework. Their middle class was different than mine. Was I, were they, even middle class at all? My friends all described themselves that way, but either I was more impoverished than I had ever before realized, or they were wealthier than they cared to admit. I began to question my understanding of wealth, where it came from, and what it meant in the grander scheme of things. In essence I realized that I did not belong with them. Our understandings of struggle and status were different. Mine was no better or worse but I knew then—I was not one of them.

BAN' YUH BELLY[1]

It broke my heart every day to know that my mother went home physically and emotionally bent. Although I was attending college in a different state, we spoke often, and I could hear the weightiness and exhaustion in her voice. Her ability to support me financially was largely dependent on her staying in the city far from the rural mountains I now called home. What had happened to our lives? Where was our American dream? Circumstances had propelled my mother from running a successful business back home to barely eking out survival in this strange land.

Those few days during my annual visit from college to the city reminded me of what I had to accomplish and what was at stake. This morning, despite her determination, her hacking cough and high fever prevented her from getting out of bed. She couldn't afford to be late for work. Her visa had expired but she had stayed, not wanting to abandon me as I left for college. The deals for work hours that she made with her boss in order to raise my tuition were tantamount to selling her soul, and I felt responsible. I was not the only reason she had left Trinidad behind but I also knew that much of it was because of me. She had given up many of her hopes and dreams to support me through college. Missing work for her could result in a call to immigration, a forced return home, and the end of my college career. Her boss had her under her complete control, often refusing to pay her as a manifestation of her power and authority over my mother's life.

Watching my mother's laboured breathing, I offered to cover for her so she would not have to risk the U.S. lady's vengeance. I took a dollar cab to the train, packed in with others like sardines, and began the hour long journey to a brownstone neighbourhood lined on both sides with shiny cars supported by polished tires. The three story home in front of me was forbidding, but if my mother did this every day, so could I. The lady circled me as I entered, her eyes directed down her sharp nose, past her tightly pressed lips, inspecting everything from my hair to my shoes. She was dressed in white and tan linen that made the rich mahogany of her short, wavy hair even more striking.

"I'm assuming you know what to do?" she questioned.

I nodded in response and found my way to the utility closet that connected the kitchen to one of the living rooms that my mom had described.

For ten hours I dusted, mopped, and scrubbed every surface of her home. The opulence was striking yet quite tastefully displayed. This was an old brownstone with almost everything made of real wood that needed to be oiled at least once a week. The furniture was the same dark stain accented with muted tones and so picturesque that it seemed to be rarely used. The bedrooms upstairs told a different story. The dark wood was draped in clothing or toys, every so often making it impossible to go more than twenty feet without acquiring an armful of items. At least the children were at their grandparents for the day, so my work load was much less than my mother usually dealt with. I did not have to tend to them as well. My mother's boss returned from her first floor office often, looking over my shoulder and touching surfaces in my wake to check for dust. How much dust could there be if my mom had just done all of this yesterday? By the end of the day my hand had curled almost into a claw-like grasp and my back was on fire. I took satisfaction only in knowing that I had spared my mother this one day of anguish. I waited for the lady to return at the end of the day and signal her approval so I could leave and make the last train home.

She sauntered up the staircase to the room where I stood waiting, not wanting to deal with the possible repercussions of sitting on one of her chairs.

"Did you have any trouble?"

"No, ma'am" I muttered politely, keeping my eyes on the ground as I knew was expected.

"Don't let me find out you stole anything! I know how you people are."

I could feel the flush beginning on my face and my blood started to roil under the skin. I fought to press my lips together, not wanting to cost my mom her job. I could taste the metallic moisture leaking from between my teeth and the inside of my lip as my body and brain fought an imperceptible battle. My eyes slowly raised to meet hers as my brain won the battle.

"Steal, why would I steal?" I asked slowly.

"Probably because it's all you know."

Her calm certainty at this statement was the last straw. I steeled my back and as eloquently as I could, I shared with her some of my family's history. We might be struggling now, but we were honest, educated, hard workers. Did she think my mother had always scrubbed toilets for people like her? I was going to a good college dammit and I had good grades. I was going to be somebody!

I took tremendous satisfaction as I watched the colours of her face progress first through shock at my cheekiness, then anger at my presumptuousness, and finally perhaps a little chagrin. I ended my tirade with a reminder that my mother wasn't the only one breaking immigration laws. I knew the penalty that she would face as well. My mother was not alone in this. *How dare this arrogant woman act like she was better than me? What made her think I would not stand up for myself? How did my mother do this every day?* I shared my appreciation for her letting me take my mother's place that day and moved quietly past her extended hand toward the now brightly lit street. My outburst had changed nothing other than my awareness of self. My mother returned to work the next day and continued to labour under the lady's wrath for another few years.

THE COLOUR INDICTMENT

"They told her when she came to the States that black people would steal from her and that she should be careful."

This was my boyfriend's justification for the disdain directed at me by his mother. I had been in the country about four years, but they had both been here for far longer.

They were used to the rhythm and flow of U.S. culture and had adopted many of its ideas and ideals. Coming from the Caribbean, race was enacted and envisioned quite differently than here in the United States. The strict black and white binaries created by the one-drop rule in the United States erects and maintains barriers among different racial groups, whereas in the Caribbean, our history of racial and ethnic blending and re-blending has forged a more flexible understanding of racial differences. Racial differences were still acknowledged but we did not have the particular history of institutionalized racism that had created this tense and oftentimes subtly segregated society. Racial and ethnic differences had never factored into my choice of friends or relationships. I had met this olive-skinned young Slav when I was a freshman and had few thoughts about our differences. Although he had lived here as a teenager, we bonded instantly over our mutual foreign-ness and we were inseparable for the following decade, and even longer.

His family had seemed friendly and welcoming until he began to explain his mother's honest yet biting words during a visit to her house from our school. She had calmly and with certainty stated,

"She's so pretty. It's a shame she's black."

These words were not muttered in quiet tones or under the assumption that I could disregard them. She was sitting right across the couch from us in a worn and comfortable armchair, almost looking through me, unaware of or uncaring about the impact of her words. This was not our first meeting, though it was the first time she had made a conscious attempt to use English in my presence.

I had thought that any coldness I had perceived stemmed from the fact that I was dating her only son and that she was being protective. That at least made sense to me. After this nonchalant statement, she resumed regular conversation with her son about school and work as if no offense were possible. I have to admit, I was stunned. Any racism I had experienced prior to that day was direct and blunt; those people would not have offered me dinner in their homes. Without any specific action on my part, she had already deemed me unworthy, just a passing interest.

My boyfriend's only response was a shrug and those words. He implored me to remember that she was not racist, just cautious because of the kind of black people she had been exposed to as a new immigrant living in a low income neighbourhood in Washington D.C. It was normal to him. She had reacted that way to all the black friends he brought home from his majority black high school. The one or two friends she liked and welcomed were deemed acceptable because they were "not really black." What did that even mean? Did blackness in some way dictate criminal intent? How did my blackness relate to criminal inclinations? Was it something specific about me like the way I behaved or the way I spoke? I was young, determined, had a high GPA, much higher than her son's actually, and worked very hard. Were my blackness and its perceived connotations enough to detract from that?

No one defended me. I did not defend myself. I sat, replaying her words in my head, the continuing conversation skipping by my awareness in a low buzz. I felt no anger or need for blame in response to her statement, only sadness and confusion. I knew race could be a disadvantage. My country was not free of inequality but I felt as if my personality and my achievements should outweigh any reservations someone might have. I was okay to look at but not to get too involved with? I know it was all in my head, but the coloured twinkles adorning the Christmas tree in the corner lost some of their shimmer. My fight or flight response kicked in and it was mostly flight. I wanted out. I wanted to seek refuge in the familiar or at least in a place where I was not assumed guilty upon sight. Unfortunately for me I was staying the night. I was trapped. So I did the only thing my brain could handle without retort or tears. I sat, spine rigid, and contemplated my chocolate skin while trying to understand the apprehension and disgust it seemed to generate.

MY HERE AND NOW: PERCEPTIONS OF/FROM MY HOMELAND

"You must be a real Yankee[2] by now eh?"

"At least your life must be good in the States ... better than if you had stayed here."

"Doh come back here nah ... it have nothing here to come back for."

"I could never live in Trini again. Dem people does seem so backward and slow moving sometimes."

"I miss the calm, contemplative nature of those cool, British summers when I lived in London."

Thanks to social media outlets that did not exist when I came to the United States, I have both maintained and developed connections with resident and ex-pat Trinbagonians[3] worldwide. I hear these sentiments echoed repeatedly in numerous contexts. These often oblique comparisons indicate the belief on both sides that life is better away from the islands. This neo-colonialist belief that places Europe and the United States on a pedestal permeates much of my communication today. I do not believe that my life is greater than if I had stayed at home and sometimes I regret making the decision to leave.

That feeling of being *less than* has never left me. I am still heavily defined by my country of origin, my social and cultural capital, and the colour of my skin. These statements, however, make me question the pervasiveness of these beliefs. How can we as Trinbagonians and West Indians hope to empower ourselves and free ourselves from this new mental and emotional colonization if we are always striving to rise above? Rise above what? What are we really trying to accomplish and is it even to our benefit? These questions swirl through my mind, especially as they relate to my worth, real or perceived. Do we have the power to define ourselves or are we doomed to be defined by the powers that once dominated our bodies and our lives? (How) can we as individuals reclaim that power? Will simple consciousness be enough to erase or minimalize our 'Third-World-ness' or are more actions necessary to end those ideas and perceptions of inferiority?

CONTEMPLATION

How we view ourselves, our environment even, is very much dependent on where we stand in relationship to imperialism in its colonial and neo-colonial stages; that if we are to do anything about our individual and collective being today, then we have to consciously look at what imperialism has been doing to us and to our view of ourselves in the universe. (Wa Thiong'o, 1986, p. 88)

These vignettes may appear vastly different on the surface but they share some common threads. Raised within a Eurocentric paradigm (Dutta & Basu, 2013), I struggled, and struggle still, to free myself from the ideas and representations that dominate much of the world in which I live. As I write this piece, I struggle with one of the same questions posed by Dutta and Basu: "What is the line between narcissism and the imperative to tell a story because it matters to the other stories being told, and to the politics of change?" (p. 156). When I began this piece I planned to look at different aspects of culture and portray vignettes that discussed race, gender, class, religion, and country of origin. Writing my stories took me on a different path, one in which my stories primarily reflected issues of class, socio-economic status, feelings of powerlessness, and perceptions of poverty. This project of decolonization was and is a challenging endeavour that necessitates "a multidimensional exploration of obstacles and opportunities" (Hedlund, 2012, p. 19). Returning to Richardson and St. Pierre's (2005) concept of writing as inquiry, I use this exploration and contemplation to reflect on and deconstruct my experiences as they relate to my life within this paradigm.

What does all this have to do with growing up in a former colony? How do any of these stories represent power and/or oppression? I approach this reflection knowing that it is important to understand the past in order to move forward toward the future. The future identity I am building through this process of decolonization is constructed through the discovery and rediscovery of my past (Hall, 2001). In attempting to recognize the contributors to and contributions of my own conditioning (Freire, 1998), I investigate this past and the way it has shaped my beliefs and practices, and those of others. In examining the power dynamics involved in these interactions and their influence on my thoughts, research, and teaching, "[C]oming to know the past [is] part of the critical pedagogy of decolonization" (Smith, 2012, p. 36), and is essential to my praxis.

Smith (2012) conceptualizes five conditional frameworks necessary for decolonization to begin: the development of a critical consciousness; a reconceptualization of the world and our place in it; intersections of ideas, social categories, and tendencies; disturbance in the status quo; and an understanding of the underlying power relations tied to imperialism. Using these five frameworks to deconstruct my stories, I have come to recognize the power of a colonized mind in approaching and understanding the influences of these histories on both self-perception and on the perception of others. It is easy to see too how these feelings can at times become their own truth. Those of us from former colonies are still the Other. "Like most 'others' our lives remain marginalized, our experiences undervalued, and our knowledge disregarded or contested within the mainstream" (Subreenduth, 2008, p. 46).

There is an element of violence in these stories, a violence that is both symbolic and quite subtle. I am dominated by ideals and ideas that are not my own but that have become so internalized that it is difficult to say where they end and my own decolonized identity begins. This violence touches multiple aspects of my daily life and has tremendous influence on my perspective of the world, especially now as I contemplate the lessons I wish to teach my unborn son. These questions and contemplations also permeate my professional practice. What hidden lessons do I perpetuate as I teach and as I research? I am far from being decolonized but can I as an individual still on this journey help others begin the same process? Although I am aware of Smith's (2012) five frameworks and use them in this project of self-study, is it enough? What is the next step and how can I take this knowledge and develop a new paradigm, one which frees my mind and makes an imprint on the world around me? At this stage, I have more questions than answers but my status as the Other has given me other ideas. While I still feel like I am leaning forward, I can, through critical autoethnography, continue to explore my perceptions and deconstruct my history toward both personal and professional growth, all while striving to free myself from the shackles of my mind.

From the outside looking in
From the inside looking out
Where does my journey begin?
And where will it lead?
I am just one of many.

NOTES

[1] Ban' yuh belly (Band your belly) is a Trinbagonian (see Note 3) expression that indicates the need to steel oneself for difficult times ahead. It refers to the practice of using a cloth band to support a pregnant belly when engaged in field work and other hard work.

[2] Commonly used by Trinbagonians (see Note 3) to refer to all United States citizens, regardless of whether they are from the northern or southern states.

[3] A term that refers jointly to both people from Trinidad and Tobago.

REFERENCES/BIBLIOGRAPHY

Dillard, C. (2012). *Learning to (re)member the things we've learned to forget: Endarkened feminisms, spirituality, and the sacred nature of research and teaching.* New York, NY: Peter Lang.

Dutta, M. J., & Basu, A. (2013). Negotiating our postcolonial selves. In S. H. Jones, T. E. Adams, & C. Ellis (Eds.), *Handbook of autoethnography* (pp. 143–161). Walnut Creek, CA: Left Coast.

Freire, P. (1998). *Pedagogy of freedom: Ethics, democracy, and civic courage.* Oxford, UK: Rowman & Littlefield.

Freire, P. (2000). *Pedagogy of the oppressed* (30th Anniversary ed.). New York, NY: Continuum.

Hall, S. (2001). Negotiating Caribbean identities. In G. Castle (Ed.), *Postcolonial discourses: An anthology* (pp. 281–292). Oxford, UK: Blackwell.

Hedlund, S. (2012). *The decolonizing responsibility of a "White" girl: An autoethnographic deconstruction of Indigenous (mis)representations* (Unpublished dissertation).

Humphreys, M. (2005). Getting personal: Reflexivity and autoethnographic vignettes. *Qualitative Inquiry, 11*(6), 840–860.

Oyewumi, O. (2005). Visualizing the body: Western theories and African subjects. In O. Oyewumi (Ed.), *African gender studies: A reader*. New York, NY: Palgrave Macmillan.

Richardson, L., & St. Pierre, E. A. (2005). Writing: A method of inquiry. In N. K. Denzin & Y. S. Lincoln (Eds.), *The Sage handbook of qualitative research* (3rd ed., pp. 959–978). Thousand Oaks, CA: Sage.

Smith, L. T. (2012). *Decolonizing methodologies: Research and indigenous peoples* (2nd ed.). London, UK: Zedbooks.

Subreenduth, S. (2008). Deconstructing the politics of a differently coloured transnational identity. *Race, Ethnicity, and Education, 11*(1), 41–55.

Walcott, D. (1999). *What the twilight says: Essays*. New York, NY: Farrar, Straus & Giroux.

Wa Thiong'o, N. (1986). *Decolonizing the mind: The politics of language in African literature*. Suffolk, UK: James Currey.

Wright, J. K. (2009). Autoethnography and therapy writing on the move. *Qualitative Inquiry, 15*(4), 623–640.

Dyanis Popova
Faculty of Teaching and Learning
School of Education
Virginia Tech
Blacksburg, Virginia, USA

M. M. ROSE-MCCULLY

14. CULTURE SHOCK

The New Normal

ABSTRACT

Using a series of vignettes spanning three years, the author examines how experiences in another culture affected her understanding of her role as a female in society. The vignettes show her grappling with insecurities over her place in a new culture, the juxtaposition between what she has always known and the new culture she is a part of, the process of embracing her new culture, and the dissonance between the two worlds upon her return to the United States. With two different views on the roles of women in society, the author struggles to reconcile the different sets of expectations she has for herself as she searches for the space where she belongs and the space where she wants to belong.

> We value autoethnography as an intimate research methodology for self-discovery and self-construction.
>
> (Toyosaki, 2009, p. 59)

LOST IN TRANSPORTATION

"¡Camoapa – Camoapa – Camoapa!" The *ayudante* yelled. As the bus helper, his job was to make sure people knew where they were going and to ensure their packages got there with them.

"Do you go through Boaco Viejo?" I asked in broken, unconfident Spanish. I had practiced the sentence over and over in my mind before speaking and yet, my tone of voice seemed to question my question. My chin almost touched my chest, my eyes stared at the feet of the man I was talking to, and my palms were wet. I tried wiping them against my dark blue jeans, but nothing helped. Between the late October heat, the threat of torrential downpour, and my nervousness, I could do nothing to keep them dry.

"Yes, of course! We leave in one minute. ¡Camoapa – Camoapa – Camoapa!" he continued, grabbing my bags and throwing them on top of the bus.

"No! Wait! Bags! Me! Here!" I tried to explain. It was too late. My bags were already thrown up top of the refurbished school bus. Three months of Spanish classes had not prepared me to think on the spot. "Camoapa isn't Boaco Viejo," I thought to myself. "I guess I don't really have a choice though. Some guy I didn't

G. A. Tilley-Lubbs & S. B. Calva (Eds.), Re-Telling Our Stories, 187–201.

know just threw my bags on top of the bus and I was told from the moment the plane landed, 'Don't let your bags out of your sight!'" Frustrated, I scrambled to get on the bus attempting to find a seat, hugging my backpack, protecting it from the dangers of being a white female traveling alone in the male-dominated, rural countryside of Boaco.

Everyone stared at me.

Awkwardly, I found a seat—the last available one on the bus—next to the window. Sweaty, nervous, overwhelmed, and exhausted, I pushed the window open allowing the hot, stagnant air to escape the confines of the overcrowded bus, letting in the hot, stagnant air from the overcrowded marketplace. For the first time since I had left the Peace Corps Office in Managua, my breathing was normal. I no longer held my breath waiting for an answer to a question, wondering if I was going to understand the answer or if the man I was talking to was going to understand me. I no longer hyperventilated every time I was about to speak, terrified that the words I was about to say would neither be in English nor in Spanish. I breathed deeply, feeling the oxygen fill my lungs that for hours now had been starving, unfulfilled by the shallow breathing reflecting my fear.

After a few normal breaths, I looked out over the marketplace. The sights and sounds were overwhelming.

"¡Gaseosa! ¡Agua helada! ¡Gaseosa! ¡Gaseosa! ¡Agua helada! ¡Diez cordobitas!" a woman hollered as she squeezed down the centre isle of the bus with her cooler of gaseosa [soda] and agua helada [cold water]. Observing her as she made her way from the front to the back of the bus was like examining a hard-boiled egg being sucked into a glass bottle. The lack of oxygen appeared to move her effortlessly through the path and her weight, mostly distributed in her stomach and back-side, seemed to relocate itself around her 300-pound frame based on how many people were in her way.

"¡Cebolla-cebolla-cebolla!" an older man yelled without breathing, offering his onions to all in the marketplace, "¡Cebolla-cebolla-cebolla! ¡Quince cordobitas la libra! ¡Cebolla-cebolla-cebolla!" He pushed his worn wooden cart carefully alongside the bus, balancing the hundreds of onions I presumed he had pulled from his field earlier in the morning. His sun-darkened skin showed signs of exhaustion, yet he did not struggle as he pushed his cart through the market and up the hill, out of the marketplace.

"¡Pan! ¡Pan tostado! ¡Pan con queso! ¡Pan! ¡Pan tostado! ¡Pan con queso!" From where I was sitting, I could smell the fresh bread the young girl was selling. I was almost tempted to buy a loaf, not because I was hungry, but because she was six. Her shirt had holes in the seams where it had been hand-washed in the river using large rocks as the washing board to help remove the layers of dirt and exhaust that I could already see being caked on from this dusty marketplace.

The stale air was ripe with what I later learned to recognize as the sickly sweet scent of tree-ripened mangos that were left on the tree one day too long. As promised, the minute came to an end and the bus lurched forward. I could feel it struggle up the same hill the onion vender had so easily traversed. We exited the marketplace and turned left to follow the bend in the road where the onion vender had turned right. As the *cobrador* pushed down the aisle collecting money or a bus ticket from each passenger, my stress level began to rise again.

"Where to?" he asked.

"Boaco Viejo." Phew! Those two words were all I needed to say. In that instant, my neck and shoulders instantly relaxed.

"Fifteen *cordobas*."

I handed him the money, waited for my change, and stared back out the window at the winding Boaco countryside. As the bus continued at a snail's pace on the 20-kilometer dirt road, stopping every minute to let passengers on or off the bus, I realized I had no idea where I was headed. My directions were, "Meet the school principal in front of the school in Boaco Viejo." What time is she expecting me? How will I get in touch with her? Where is the school? How long is the ride? My mind raced with questions that I could not answer. The only thing I really knew, because of the structure of Spanish grammar, was that the principal was female.

"Um ...excuse me?" I questioned trying to get the attention of the *cobrador* or of the *ayudante*. I couldn't remember who was who. In my state of panic and extreme nervousness, I had forgotten to remember who had which job. They, along with the driver, were all wearing the same turquoise polo shirt with an embroidered school bus where the front breast pocket normally would be. The bus was named "*Gemelos*" [twins]. Perhaps everyone that worked on the bus was a twin. Now, as I finally looked at them couldn't help but wonder why I couldn't tell them apart. They were definitely not *gemelos*. (I later came to learn that the busses themselves were the *gemelos*: there were two of these blue and white striped busses that carried the citizens of Boaco to Camoapa and back again four times a day.) The *ayudante*, the bus helper who threw my bags so easily up on top of the bus, was short, pale, and chubby. He showed none of the tell-tale signs of a man who worked outside all day throwing packages, boxes, and stacks of firewood on top of a bus. The *cobrador*, the bus's ticket and money collector, was tall, thin, and muscular with skin slightly darkened by the sun. If I blindly had to choose which of these two men did each job, I probably would have called it wrong.

The *cobrador* had given me the proper change for my bus fare, he had not asked me if I was a foreigner, and he had offered, using gestures instead of words, to place my backpack up in the luggage rack above my seat. He seemed nice enough, but he had been staring at me since I sat down on the bus. In that moment, I realized that some of the nervousness I was feeling was not nervousness at all. It was the uncomfortable feeling in the pit of my stomach that I had been feeling ever since I stepped off the plane three months ago, the feeling of being watched. Walking over to my seat, still staring at me in a way that made me push down the bile that was rising to my mouth, he stood in front of me.

"I am sorry. How long is it until we get to Boaco Viejo?"

"One hour," he replied.

"Could you please tell me when we get close to the school? I am supposed to meet the principal there and it is my first time going."

"We will be there in five minutes."

Wait! What?! I thought he said it would take an hour! Vocabulary—I knew I should have studied more. While I intended to ask what time we were going to arrive, I had actually asked how long the trip was. Unbeknownst to me, I had been blankly staring out the window for nearly an hour before finally gathering the courage needed to ask for help.

The bus stopped suddenly. The *ayudante* started taking my luggage off the top of the bus, casually throwing everything down to the *cobrador*. Carefully hugging my backpack, I shuffled to the front of the bus. The three steps I had to take to get off the bus terrified me. With each step, I wondered what this new town, this new country, this new life would bring.

Reflection

With my feet firmly planted in Boaco Viejo, I finally had a chance to reflect on my journey. How did I actually get there? Looking back at the years I spent in Boaco Viejo I wonder, how did I get anywhere?

From the moment I left the Peace Corps Office in Managua, my safety, schedule, and life were in the hands of men. While my direct Peace Corps supervisors and the Peace Corps Director of Nicaragua were all women, the head of security was a man. A few weeks earlier, he had made the decision that it would be safer for the (predominantly female) volunteers in the country to use only pre-approved taxi drivers when traveling within the boundaries of Managua. Each of the pre-approved taxi drivers was a man. Over the course of the three years, with all of the traveling I did within the country, I only saw two women driving taxis. In order to get a taxi, I had to ask the guard (a group of rotating Nicaraguan men lent to the Peace Corps Office by the United States Embassy) to call one up for me. Upon reaching the bus station, I had to get on a bus with a male driver, a male money collector, and a male baggage handler. There were published schedules, but the buses and taxis left when the men decided. If they did not feel like working one day, they didn't and neither did the buses. I was a 26-year-old female in the middle of an unknown town, blindly following the directions of men who, might or might not, know where I was going.

For the next three years, I relied on these men every day. I took the bus three times a week to teach in rural villages. I was extremely fortunate to always use the same bus to go to and from these schools. After the first few weeks, they stopped charging me every time and they would always stop for me no matter how full the bus was. This wasn't the case with the other buses that came driving through Boaco Viejo. Once or twice a week when I needed to go into Boaco to use the internet or go grocery shopping, I would take a different bus. These buses would often speed past me – not stopping – either because the bus was a minute or two behind schedule or because it was full. Once in Boaco, I would take a taxi to run errands. The taxi drivers, all men, could pick up a passenger at their own discretion and would charge "gringa" prices (white girl prices) until they realized that I spoke Spanish and that I refused to pay more than the actual price.

About once a month I would head into Managua which was probably my least favourite thing to do. The buses, while there was an official schedule, would run whenever they felt like it. And the tenacity of the non-pre-approved taxi drivers in Managua made my skin crawl and my stomach churn every time I went through the bus terminal. The pre-approved drivers also ran on their own schedules. They would agree on a time then frequently show up late or not at all. This complete reliance on men to get me from Point A to Point B was something that I had not experienced since childhood when my father was in charge of my transportation. "I saw myself as no more than a passive body being created by something other than [my]self" (Toyosaki, 2009, p. 63). I became a package—shuffled around by men with my personal needs and intentions left at the wayside as the men in this male-dominated society took control.

For the first few months, I allowed these men to lead me and I followed without question, much like I had done in my last two relationships. Eventually as both my confidence level and language skills improved, I regained ownership of myself becoming an active participant in the direction my life was headed. No longer just a package, I now was able to write my own shipping label with a known route and destination. I still had to rely on the men who ran the transportation system but, with time, my dependence on them boiled down to just a delivery system.

This bus trip was one of the first times that I realized how much my gender role was constructed by the culture in which I currently was situated. I suddenly found myself uncomfortably lost between two cultural norms for females. The instant loss of autonomy because of my gender knocked the wind out of me and eventually led me to wonder if I would ever belong in this new community.

THE *PIROPO*

Definition: a compliment, generally directed at a female.
Definition as I understood it through three years of "compliments": a statement, generally directed at a female, with the intention of letting her know that she is an object that exists solely for the men who are complimenting her.

The cement house was small by United States standards, but rather spacious for the four of us who lived in it—my Nicaraguan family, my host mother and her two sons, a 3-year-old and a 13-year-old, and me. Fortunately I had my own bedroom. Three of the four walls were made of cement blocks: two exterior walls that crudely met the tin roof and one wall that went up about seven feet before stopping three feet shy of the roof. The fourth wall was made of wood. It had been constructed just for me in an effort to give me some privacy. It too only came up about seven feet.

The house had an indoor bathroom furnished with a flushable toilet and a drain in the centre of the floor to allow the water from the shower to drain. With no running water, the shower consisted of a 5-gallon bucket of water with a small bowl in it. About once a week, when and if we had electricity, we would turn on the electric pump, retrieve water from the well, and fill the two bathroom buckets and the large water basin where we stored water used for bathing, washing clothes, and flushing the toilet.

Along with the lack of electricity, we had limited cell phone service. While most of the other volunteers were able to call home on a regular basis, I called home about once a month, if my phone was charged.

Although there was no window in my bedroom, the open wall structure permitted all noises to enter my small room. Nightly, the un-leashed neighbourhood dogs would fight, barking incessantly, causing my sleep to be continually disrupted. Even the roosters crowed all night long.

A few weeks into this new life, however, it wasn't lack of running water, electricity, or cell service or even the barking dogs and crowing roosters that kept me up all night long that bothered me. It was the men. The five or six hours of Peace Corps training that discussed the differences between men in the United States and men in Nicaragua was not sufficient. I was extremely unprepared for what the next few years had in store for me.

It had been nearly three years since I had last had a boyfriend. It was a choice I had made to force myself to find the "me" I had lost in the men I had dated. Nothing particularly bad had happened to end these relationships; I just woke up one day and realized that I wasn't ... me. Somewhere along the way, I became "my girlfriend." As I allowed my name to become "girlfriend," I let myself be defined by my role in the relationship—who I was in relation to them. I did what they did. I liked what they liked. I wanted what they wanted. I became so used to them making the choices for me, that I nearly forgot who I was, what I liked, and what I really wanted.

As a single, unattached woman, I went to work, came home, and sometimes even went out with friends—never with people I did not know and never with just men. I became so accustomed to the idea that men did not really exist in my world that I managed to ignore them altogether. Yet, one day, as I was walking down the street, I saw three high school boys sitting by the side of the road and something changed.

The sun was directly overhead. It was hot. It hadn't rained in weeks. The grass was turning brown, the ground had begun to crack, and the trees looked shrivelled, aching for the water they would not be getting for the next few months. In thirty minutes I would be home. My host mother would have lunch on the table waiting for me. I was pretty sure we had electricity this morning, so maybe there would be ice in it. If not, I was in for another lunch of rice, beans, plantains, and warm soda.

With every step, I nearly choked from the dust that also caked my sweaty legs. I carried my parasol, but it couldn't protect my skin from burning as I exited the school. As I walked along the dirt road toward my house, I greeted everyone. There were only sixteen houses between the school and mine, so I knew everyone's names. I taught most of their children or grandchildren as well. "*¡Adiós, Doña Ruiz! ¡Adiós, Don Felix! ¡Adiós, Rosita!*" I said as I passed by each house, naming every family member that I saw. "*Adiós, Profe Melissa,*" they would respond in unison.

As I walked around the last bend, I saw my house. It was still about ten minutes away, but Josías, my 3-year-old host brother, would be waiting for me at the green fence to play with him. Even though I was tired, sweaty, dirty, and probably stinky, that was exactly what I wanted. I noticed a group of boys that I had seen a few times hanging out at the high school. Since I taught elementary school, I did not know their names. They recognized me—after all, I was the only white girl in the town.

"*¡Tch! ¡Tch! ¡Oye! ¡Chelita hermosa! ¡Muah! ¡Muah!*"

I stopped. All of my blood rushed to my hands as they instinctively closed tightly into fists at my sides. I knew them. I didn't know their names, but they certainly knew who I was and my name—and yet they didn't care. Instead of calling me *Profe* or Melissa or even *gringa* (a derogatory slang word meaning "white girl"), they called to me like a dog. This *piropo*—this "compliment"—felt like a cheap cat call and made me feel like an object. For the first time in a long time I felt like an object occupying space, owned by the men who called out to me and expected me to respond. Many women would not get enraged at someone calling them "pretty," but this label of "pretty white girl" was not a compliment to me.

Reflection

Perhaps for the first time in my life, I felt the effects of being a white female. In the moment, I wanted so desperately to have dark hair, dark eyes, and dark skin so that I would not be the object that everyone stared at sitting on the bus or walking down the street in my community. I wanted to peel away my whiteness and blend in with the majority (Toyosaki, 2009).

I wondered if those boys said anything to the string of other females that followed closely behind me. After all, the females who followed behind me were Nicaraguan. Was I so caught up in the fact that they were saying something to me that I missed it? Was it normal to call out females like this? Would they do the same to any other new teacher in the community?

My experiences over the next few years would answer each of these questions: yes. Yes, I was so absorbed in my own personal thoughts and reactions that I did not hear them call out to the girls behind me. Yes, it was normal to call out females like this. Yes, they would do the same thing to any other new female teacher in the community—at least they would until they formed a relationship with her.

If I had been listening, I would have heard the "compliments" being thrown at the females who walked closely behind me: "*gordita Hermosa,*" "*flaquita Hermosa,*" "*negrita hermosa.*" Most females enjoy being called beautiful or pretty, but the

193

cynical, commanding tone of voice that these boys used made it feel more like a classification, with "fat girl," "skinny girl," and "black girl" preceding the word beautiful than a compliment.

Being classified as "white girl, pretty" based solely upon my looks made me feel like a piece of property, "empty, vulnerable, and naked" (Toyosaki, 2009, p. 61). I wanted to approach those boys and "reclaim my …identity even though I had not actively and consciously, on my own, claimed [it] before" (Toyosaki, 2009, p. 61). For decades, society as a whole in the United States has striven to avoid defining people by their physical appearance. But women, "women, in particular, are endlessly dissected to better serve media and consumer interests" (Khan, 2009, p. 1085).

> One day
> > every girl learns
> > she is female:
> > > hands grope
> > > eyes stare
> > > hips widen.
> Can we teach her
> > to love her body?
> > > A body housing centuries of oppression,
> > > decades of selflessness,
> > > years of abuse. (Mackie, 2009, p. 326)

Here in Boaco Viejo, these young boys classified women on a daily basis. Their classification was simply an observation. Being referred to as a "white girl" or "fat girl" was the way the boys distinguished one woman from the next, ensuring that each female knew that she was beautiful. While daily I "silently practiced, 'Hey, stop it'" (Toyosaki, 2009, p. 67), I couldn't convince myself to say it.

I felt like the only female in Boaco Viejo who was offended by these great compliments. If the Nicaraguan women were offended, they never shared that sentiment with me. My interpretation of their *piropos* was rooted in a society other than the one I currently lived in. Here, no one was offended by being called "fat girl, beautiful," "skinny girl, beautiful," or "black girl, beautiful." Over time, I began to wonder, is being called, "white girl, beautiful" really *that* bad? After all, despite my original interpretation of these *piropos*, these adjectives were used to let me know they were looking at me and their intention was not to offend, but to compliment.

THE BACHELORETTE PARTY

Over the next two years, these *piropos* happened with more and more frequency. I got to the point where I hardly even acknowledged the comments made by the boys and men on the streets where I lived. At times, when I did notice them, I almost felt beautiful. It was nice to know that someone was thinking of me. I had not dated for five years and had finally started thinking about what that next step was going to be once I returned home. It was at this point when I returned stateside for a week to attend my older sister's wedding.

As I put on my heels and argued with myself over what to wear, I thought, "I can't believe she is actually getting married on Saturday." My sister had been married once before, but this time it was different—she was actually sure.

"OK everyone! Let's see what we have in the bachelorette bag," the Maid of Honour squealed as she opened the largest Victoria's Secret bag I had ever seen. Slowly, she started to pull things out of the bag. "First. Things for the bride! Ooooooohhhh, we have a white feather boa. A Bride-to-Be sash. A giant ring. Oh my gosh! It lights up! You just have to turn it. There it is! It looks awesome!" We all giggled a little as we sipped our champagne. She continued, "I know there was at least one other thing in here. Where is it? Oh! I found it!" As her hand lifted out of the bag, my breathing became shallow and laughter quickly overtook me causing me to fall to the floor, grabbing at my sides as she pulled a pink martini glass out of the bag. While "looking for it," she had connected the battery in the stem, a penis with its head sitting in the centre of the glass, flashing blue, green, red, and white lights.

"Fill it with champagne!" was the only thing I could manage to say as I slowly regained composure.

With the glass now filled with champagne, the Maid of Honour continued, "Now stuff for everyone else. Everyone has to wear a light-up ring." She passed out the rings. While not my favourite thing to do, I put it on. "Now we have a black feather boa," she showed it to us.

"I'll take that!" said my sister's best friend from childhood. I was glad she decided to take it. Glitter and feathers are not my thing.

"We have the Maid-of-Honour button and sash set. I will wear these," she said as she slipped on the sash and pinned the button to her dress.

Nervously, I waited, hoping for something without glitter. I was the only one without something.

"And for you, we have ... THIS!" she exclaimed as she pulled a tiara out of the bag.

Pink. Glittery. Bitch. It was a pink glitter tiara. Instead of it having an intricate design, it spelled, "Bitch." "I should have chosen the black boa," I thought, kicking myself. There was no turning back now. I put it on and kept my mouth shut as we finished our glasses of champagne, left the cottage, and started the half mile walk to the bar. Decked out in the fine accoutrements that we had been given, we walked down the streets of Charleston, South Carolina.

As we walked (and walked and walked and walked), the bar that was only a half mile away seemed to still be a half mile away. At first, I didn't notice the men on the street calling out at us, but as the walk continued and my feet started to ache, I started paying attention.

"Don't do it!"

"I bet I'm bigger than he is!"

"Take ME out for one last test drive before you commit."

Seriously? Who says things like that?! I was used to hearing men throw around *piropos* in Boaco Viejo where I was living. After all, that was normal! Women were not considered equal to men, but here? Who did these white guys think they were? How, in a society where "equal opportunity" is a phrase that is used nearly daily, could these men think it was acceptable to speak to a woman in such a vulgar way? These overt sexual advances and vulgarities would never be tolerated in Boaco Viejo!

"What are you doing?" the three ladies questioned as I took the GPS (Global Positioning Satellite) away from the Maid of Honour.

"I'm cold. My feet hurt. We have been walking for an hour. I am going to get us to the bar." My patience was wearing thin.

"No need to go so fast," they quipped as I led them at a jog to the bar.

The only thing I wanted to do was get away from the random men who were cat-calling us as we walked down the Charleston streets. As we crossed the threshold into the bar, my head began to pulse. I quickly placed my hands over my ears as we passed the booming live music and shoved our way to the hostess stand in search of a table. We slid into the next available booth and started to look over the menu.

"Let's do shots!" the Bride-to-Be exclaimed.

"Should we order some food first?" I asked almost pleadingly. I looked at the motley crew. The Maid-of-Honour, at 34, the oldest of the bunch, had been married for a few years. She had a daughter and had been seriously thinking about leaving her husband. My sister's best friend from childhood was newly married. My sister had been a bridesmaid in her wedding only a few months earlier. My sister, the Bride-to-Be, was married at 21 and divorced by 22. She had been with her fiancé now for six and a half years. We all had different stories, different experiences; we were all at different stages in our relationships with the men in our lives: contemplating divorce, newly wed, at the threshold of wedding, and, in my case, single and unattached.

After staring at the menu for about fifteen minutes waiting for someone to take our order, I caught the eye of a waitress and signalled for her to come over. As I did, everyone at the table stopped and stared at me in horror.

"Tch! Tch!" The very noise that two years ago made me want to run and hide had now become such an integral part of my vocabulary that I made it without thinking twice.

Reflection

For two years I had lived and breathed in a community that was not my own. My role in the community as a culture sponge allowed me, over time, to feel less and less like an outsider. As Bochner and Ellis (1995) said so poignantly, "We not only live in the same world as our partner but also participate in each other's existence. To a certain extent we must not only understand each other's views of the world but also to make them our own" (p. 205). It was not enough to only exist in the community; I needed to be an active part of it.

In becoming an active part of my community, I inadvertently had put aside some of the cultural norms that were ingrained in me from childhood. I became accustomed to the calls of the Nicaraguan men in Boaco Viejo, yet found similar comments from white men on the streets of Charleston to be highly offensive.

While initially I considered myself an outsider with respect to the women and their opinion of the men in Boaco Viejo, my status as an outsider shifted as the women of the community permitted me to become an insider in their community and I began to see the *piropos* not as insults, but as compliments. As I learned and discovered more about my community and the men and women who inhabited it, my position within society shifted from being an outsider to being an insider (Turner, 2013).

As I became an insider in my new community and adapted to the role men played in society, I came home and felt like an outsider in my own. "A key problem with ideas of insiders and outsiders is that they essentialise categories, overlooking the significant differences within as well as between groups" (Tinker, 2008, p. 53). While I had become accustomed to two categories, men and women, I failed to look at the rest of the picture. For some reason I had no problem with men of other cultures making comments, but when people of my own culture did it, I thought there was something disrespectful about it.

I had created a dichotomy of two worlds: each one with different rules for the men that lived in them and each one with different rules for how I reacted to these men. In one world, I was a "white girl, beautiful," and in the other I was a beautiful girl, and I did not feel like either truly defined me.

I am a betweener!

I live life in-betweenness (Moreira, 2008, p. 672).

"CAN I HAVE YOUR NUMBER?"

It wasn't until after I finally returned to the United States and started teaching in an inner city high school that I realized just how accustomed I had become to the comments I had been hearing for three years from the Nicaraguan men in Boaco Viejo.

Ring, ring. Ring, ring.

"They always call during class. Keep working everyone. Please take over the class." I took the lead.

I had been interning at an inner city public high school for nearly two months and the classroom teacher was frequently interrupted to help out with any and all students who did not speak English as their first language. The teacher walked over to the phone and removed the scarf wrapped around her head. She had been losing her hair since her twenties and was now completely bald. The room was always cold and she used the scarf to keep some of her body heat in.

Ring, ring. Ring, ring.

"Yes," she answered the phone, "Yes, she is …. She does …." Looking up at me, "Can you translate?"

"Spanish?" I asked. The teacher nodded. "Sure," I responded.

"Yes, she is available …. Bring the student here …. She can talk to him in our office …. Make sure he has a pass …." She nearly hung up before asking, "What is the issue?" After a few minutes, she hung up the phone, looked at me, exhaled deeply, and said, "We will do it together."

Knock, knock, knock.

I immediately recognized the student. I had already spent two hours translating and talking with him in the school's guidance office earlier in the day.

"Come in," I said, opening the door.

"¿Y, ay? ¿Qué pasó?" I began, asking him what had happened.

The teacher stopped me. "We will talk about this in the office," she said leading the student into the closet that she called an office space. The three of us fit, but just barely. Two long tables lined the walls of the office and four chairs were carefully pushed under the tables. Pulling out a chair, the student sat down. Following suit, I pulled out a chair and sat down. The teacher remained standing.

"Tell me why you want to drop out," she directed the comment at the student.

He looked at me, "¿Qué dice?"

"You know what she said. You understand her. Why do you want to drop out of school?" I repeated the question—no faster, no slower.

"I work," he responded. His broken English reminded me of my own broken Spanish those first few months in Boaco Viejo.

"You have to be in school. You are 17. It is the law," the teacher said lying to the student. Legally he could have dropped out at sixteen.

He ignored her, looked at me, and, asked, "¿Cuántos años tienes?"

"Twenty-nine," I responded.

"¿Estás casada?" he continued. It was informal, but I let it pass since he was from Guatemala and they use the informal "you" differently there.

"No, I am not married."

"¿Tienes novio?"

"Yes, I have a boyfriend." This time, it was I who lied.

"Dame tu número."

"I will not give you my phone number."

"¿Por qué? Dame tu número."

"Why? I am your teacher. You may not have my phone number. Please stop asking."

"No importa. Dámelo."

"Yes, it does matter. No, you may not have my phone number."

"¿Por qué?"

"Why? Because it is inappropriate. You are a student. I am your teacher. You may not call me."

The teacher interrupted, "What does this have to do with dropping out of school?"

"Nothing," I replied, "he just wants my phone number."

"Why do you want to stop coming to school? You must keep coming to school," she said forcefully, looking at the student.

Again, he turned to me, "Entonces, tienes novio."

"Yes, I have a boyfriend."

"No importa. Seré tu otro novio. No tienes que decir nada a él. Dame tu número."

"It DOES matter and you will not be my other boyfriend. I will not give you my phone number."

The teacher opened the office door, leaving me alone with the student. Bothered, not by the fact that he had just spent ten minutes trying to get my phone number, but by the fact that he was 17, I looked at him. Most of the high school students in Boaco Viejo had had my phone number. I worked with them on various projects throughout the years I spent there and was constantly in communication with them.

The student sat there raising his eyebrows seductively. One single, solitary noise came out of my mouth as I laughed and shook my head. His "give it to me" lines and "give it to me" looks had not worked and I could see him searching for the words to ask for my phone number again. He felt entitled to my phone number, after all, he had the phone number of one of the classroom aides that I worked with (a 50-year-old Honduran woman with two high school students of her own) and I was a "gringa."

The teacher returned. "You have In-School Suspension for the rest of the day."

"But, Miss," he rebutted.

"No 'but Miss'. This is harassment. You are harassing her. She said once that you could not have her phone number. You may be able to act that way in YOUR country, but here in America*, we do not act this way. She said, 'No'!"

Reflection

The two worlds I had spent so much time constructing collided that day. The careful classification of what I expected from the men and women from Boaco Viejo, and more generally Central America, and from the men and women from the United States were no longer sufficient. While my conversation with this male Guatemalan student would have been considered annoying, but normal, in Boaco Viejo, the teacher in the United States saw it as completely unacceptable. I was shocked and confused when he was suspended. Nothing in the conversation was worse than some of the *piropos* and conversations I had with various men and high school boys in Boaco Viejo. Something about having the conversation in Spanish had made it seem completely acceptable. Deep down, I even found some of the conversation flattering. After all, who doesn't like it when someone asks for her phone number? But the real question is, would I have reacted the same if the conversation would have taken place with any other, non-Spanish speaking student? Simply answered, no.

Later that week, the student had a nearly identical conversation with a young, blonde, white, Spanish-speaking classroom aide. She had recently returned from a year in Honduras and had the same reaction to the student as I did. The situation did not seem to bother either the young blonde or me, but it did bother the teachers with whom we worked: the female classroom teacher I worked with and a male teacher in the same department with whom we shared a classroom. The male teacher decided to speak with the student the following week about the choices he had been making. The male teacher hoped to explain to the student why his actions were unacceptable and to present himself as a "good" role model for the student. The description of a "good" role model is defined by each culture and "[p]eople increasingly have more and more different role models around them, more options to choose from" (Garcia, 2011, p. 285). Unfortunately for this student, what he understood as normal and acceptable based on his experiences in his native country were not the same as the expectations given in the classroom.

The student had grown up in Guatemala where the role of men and women is strictly defined. Moreira (2008) discusses this distinction between the role of men and women in a Latino community in the United States. After breaking up a fight between two boys in a gym, Moreira sat one of them down to discuss why he got into the fight. The boy who initiated the fight had been calling him names, yet that is not what was bothering him.

> It's not the kid. It's my father. Mother died few years ago. It's my father, my sister, and me. When we get home from work, we're all tired. Buy my sister has to clean the house, cook dinner.... It's a lot of cooking. There has to be enough food for supper and lunch. Afterward, we eat and she prepares our lunch boxes, so we can have something to eat in the job. She washes the dishes, the clothes. She does everything. I felt sorry for her, so I help her when my father is out. One day he saw me helping her. He beat the shit out of me. While beating me, he said that he was raising no faggot. That I needed to be a man. Then we went to a bar and he told everybody what happened. That I was an embarrassment to him. He beat me a lot in the next days. (p. 675)

This distinction between the roles of men and women in certain Latino groups is something that I experienced first-hand for myself living in Boaco Viejo and something that I now had to reconcile as I re-entered my life here in the United States.

Closure

As I begin to re-negotiate my role as a female in the United States, I am left in a state of "in-betweenness." Just as I could not fully leave my cultural and behavioural expectations behind when I moved to Nicaragua, I am finding it equally as challenging to leave behind the new Nicaraguan cultural and behavioural norms that I have grown accustomed to as I re-enter life in the United States. The conflicting social and behavioural expectations for females in these two distinct communities has sparked an internal discourse in which I am navigating my perceived role as a female in society and the role I would like to have.

I frequently find myself justifying the actions of myself or others, validating these actions based on whichever cultural or behavioural expectation best fits the situation. I am constantly questioning why some women do not mind being completely dependent on the men in their lives and why women presenting other women with phallic objects is funny while yelling sexual comments in the street is considered vulgar. I remain uncomfortable with others turning me into an object, but feel flattered when they do.

The more I search for my place as a female in society, the fewer places I find that are willing to accept me, and even fewer are the places where I would like to be accepted.

REFERENCES/BIBLIOGRAPHY

Bochner, A. P., & Ellis, C. (1995). Telling and living: Narrative co-construction and the practices of interpersonal relationships. In W. Leeds-Hurwitz (Ed.), *Social approaches to communication* (pp. 201–213). New York, NY: Guilford.

Garcia Yeste, C., Ferrada, D., & Ruiz, L. (2011). Other women in research: Overcoming social inequalities and improving scientific knowledge through the inclusion of all voices. *Qualitative Inquiry, 17*(3), 284–294.

Khan, C. A. (2009). Go play in traffic: Skating, gender, and urban context. *Qualitative Inquiry, 15*(6), 1084–1102.

Mackie, C.T. (2009). Finding my… A story of female identity. *Qualitative Inquiry, 15*(2), 324–328.

Moreira, C. (2008). Fragments. *Qualitative Inquiry, 14*(6), 663–683.

Tinker, C., & Armstrong, N. (2008). From the outside looking in: How an awareness of difference can benefit the qualitative research process. *The Qualitative Report, 13*(1), 53–60.

Toyosaki, S., Pensoneau-Conway, S., Wendit, N. A., & Leathers, K. (2009). Community autoethnography: Compiling the personal and resituating whiteness. *Cultural Studies <=> Critical Methodologies, 9*(1), 56–83.

Turner, P. K., & Norwood, K. M. (2013). Body of research: Impetus, instrument, and impediment. *Qualitative Inquiry, 19*(9), 696–711.

M. M. Rose-McCully
Faculty of Teaching and Learning
School of Education
Virginia Tech
Blacksburg, Virginia, USA

MARÍA DE LA LUZ LUÉVANO-MARTÍNEZ

15. A REFLECTIVE JOURNEY THROUGH THE EXPERIENCE OF AN *AU PAIR*

From a Cultural Exchange Program to Domestic Labour

ABTRACT

The author writes about her experience as a Mexican au pair with a United States family. When she enrolled in the program she viewed it as cultural exchange, and as she lived through the experience, she realized It resembled more that of a formal domestic job. Her perception of her role changed through her daily interaction with the members of the host family. Following that line of thought as she wrote, she realized the difficulties of naming it either cultural exchange or a domestic job, and she accounted for the subtleties of the au pair relationship on a daily basis.

***

"I called the police so they'd go looking for you!" yelled Kim, my host mother. I pursed my lips to refrain from speaking. I couldn't believe what she was saying! A storm of confusion and unanswered questions shook my head.

"What happened?" I replied.

"Where did you and Susan go?" she asked.

During her scolding, the children (Susan and her siblings, Tom and Anne) picked up the pace and walked out of the house trying to avoid the reprimand. I understood that behind Kim's violent manner, which she wanted us to see as the uncertainty of not knowing what had kept us from arriving on time, concealed the fear of thinking that I could have kidnapped her daughter or done something wrong to her; eight months of knowing each other didn't seem enough to earn her trust.

For this family from New York, I was their first au pair. They'd had two nannies, one from the Dominican Republic and another from Spain, but no au pair or any reference to those dynamics. For the family, as well as for me, our coexistence would start defining itself from the start. Perhaps, they would refer to their previous experiences and I, to the information the agency had provided.

It was 2006 and I had been chosen by this upper class family to take care of their children. When I decided to enrol in the au pair program, I had just finished studying sociology and took the opportunity as a way to improve my English. Thus, I would have the chance to attend a language school in exchange for living with and taking care of the children of a family from the United States.

I was at the agency to leave the required documentation for enrolling in the program and I was very excited about the opportunity to go to the United States and learn more about their language and traditions. The agency, Cultural Care, in Aguascalientes, is based out of the house of the representative. It seemed thrown together and I thought it must be an informal agency, which made me feel distrustful, because it didn't look like an official establishment. "Is it a reliable agency?" I thought.

Who are our au pairs

Caring and committed

Au pairs are caring and committed, adventurous and educated young people, ages 18-26 years, from many different countries worldwide. They are eager to experience American culture while sharing their own unique backgrounds. While living in your home as a family member, they provide your family with up to 45 hours per week of personalized childcare. They have decided to venture out of the safety of their home and culture in order to grow and develop, to improve their English and to widen their horizons, both personally and professionally. Participating in the au pair program is a life-changing experience for these young people and they are excited to find a kind and supportive American host family to work and live with during that year.

Figure 1. Information on cultural care[1]

I remember the sound of my fingers drumming on the table, tap, tap, tap and the feel of the folder with my papers lying on my lap. The documentation included a photo album of me playing with my nephews, a $200.00 dollar receipt for a deposit that covered any administrative expenses, my passport and other essential documents I needed to formally enrol in the program. "Tap, tap, tap," went my fingers, drumming away the time before the representative assessed me. Meanwhile, doubts and questions about the legitimacy of the agency started to flood my head. Back then, local and national media commented on several agencies recruiting migrants when they were, in fact, devoted to human trafficking. They would lure and rip young women off, selling them the idea of going to another country to work as models, and once abroad were turned into prostitutes. I was truly anxious about it. Neither my family in Mexico nor I had ever heard about Cultural Exchange and their focus on offering educational programs in exchange for taking care of children. My father was the most sceptical about it. He didn't want me to participate in this type of exchange. However, in spite of all my hesitation, I insisted on participating and finally decided to take my papers to the agency. Even so, my father's doubts tormented me to such an extent that I asked myself if I should go on with the process. What if he was right? What if I was putting myself at risk due to my stubbornness about going abroad to study English? And why, if it was supposed to be a reliable agency, did it have its headquarters at a house in the city's outskirts? I literally felt like running away. However, I didn't, because I was frozen to that chair.

I took a deep breath, and inhaled and exhaled. "Calm down, Marilú, everything will be fine!" I tried to reassure myself, but uncertainty took hold of me. "Marilú, are you sure?" "Marilú, what are you doing here?" "Leave now that nobody's watching!" I told myself. The rational Marilú refused to believe the program was safe but, in the end, the other Marilú, the bold one, won! Yes, she won, and finally delivered that bunch of papers to the agency.

Once I enrolled in the program, the representative wouldn't stop smiling. It made me feel assured and she convinced me that the program was safe, as it was supported by the United States government, or perhaps I just went with my eagerness to study abroad and go through the experience in spite of my uncertainties. The representative didn't stop repeating that it would be the best year of my life, that as soon as I integrated into my "host family"-the title given to au pair hosting families-I would become a part of it. "Plain and simple," she added, I would become another member of the family.

The Interview

At 3 o'clock, I got an e-mail from the agency saying I would receive a call from Kim, my host mother, and the approximate time it would happen. I was prepared and tried to relax, but I was so excited I was shaking.

A family from New York, I thought. I couldn't believe it. At five o'clock, the phone rang. I was lying in bed and staring at the ceiling, waiting:

"What if they reject me? What will I do? I feel like time is short. If a family doesn't accept me in two months I won't be able to join the program," I said. I was almost 27 and you can't be older that 26 to join the Cultural Care program.

"Ring, ring, ring," the sound of the phone made me jump off the bed and run to answer the call. My heart skipped and jumped.

"Hola," I answered, as I wasn't sure it was her and I didn't want to sound silly if it was someone else I didn't want to hear me picking up the phone in English.

"Hello, this is Kim speaking, Can I talk to Marilú?" It was another language and she said she was Kim. It was she, indeed!

"Hi, yes, this is me, Marilú, how are you?" I answered, truly excited. You could hear the smile on my lips.

Conversation flowed pretty well. I must confess that my spoken English wasn't that good, but Kim understood what I said and I understood almost all her comments. We talked about my motivation for joining an exchange program. She asked me if I could swim, and sought my reaction to some hypothetical situations as, for example, a baby that wouldn't stop crying or one of the children having an accident. She also asked about the activities I enjoyed with my family and what I did with my free time, if I smoked, had a boyfriend, etc. I didn't ask a lot of questions, I was rather straightforward. I just remember asking about the time I would be attending school and why they needed an au pair. Kim answered that I would take care of Anne for a couple of hours during the morning and that I would cover the rest of my shift after Tom and Susan got back from school. After the conversation was over, I felt truly accomplished. As soon as I hung up the phone, I wrote to the agency saying I would join the family, because they had told me about the tasks they wanted me to perform and I didn't think they were too many.

In New York

The first place where all au pairs, male and female, go in the United States, is St. Johns University, Long Island. There, we were trained for a week. We learned first aid, road and highway regulations, and didactic strategies for working with children. My co-workers came from different countries: Switzerland, Germany, Honduras, Colombia, Argentina, Japan and Mexico, among others. In order to take class, we were separated depending on the age of the kids we would be taking care of, as that was the guideline for giving us the information we required. However, there were some bits of information that started to confuse me, since I'd started to feel as if they were training me to become a housemaid. Was it truly necessary to teach us how to use domestic appliances, such as the dishwasher or the vacuum cleaner? We all looked at each other while the teacher told us about all these things. We didn't understand why we were being given such information.

In spite of all the confusion, I felt truly happy; I was in the United States. The university campus was made up of several buildings and was surrounded by a lake and pines. That week of training consisted of having class from 8 am to 1 pm, and from 3 to 7 pm. We had lunch at the institution's dining hall from 1 to 3 pm and then we were free to socialize and make friends. We had a curfew for going to our rooms, which we shared with three other people from different countries, divided into male and female dormitories. It seemed awkward to most of us, since we had to sleep in a 3 by 4 meter area and share it with people we didn't know who didn't speak the same language. Even though English should have been a common tool to talk to each other, we were afraid to open up and chat. Sharing a bathroom was just as awkward. Even though our bathroom was separated from the guys', we still felt a bit uncomfortable having to get naked in front of the other girls. Since the showers had no partitions, it was intimidating to be seen by the other au pairs. In spite of it being our daily routine, many of us suffered through this situation. I personally decided to come up with a strategy. I realized I wouldn't be as exposed if I took my shower right before sunrise. However, I had to go to bed earlier that my classmates to take all my stuff to the shower without making the others uncomfortable. There were moments that we felt controlled with so many rules. Weren't we supposed to be in the land of the free?

With My New Family

Our last day in training basically consisted of exchanging phone numbers and e-mail addresses with all our classmates. We would finally go to our host families. We were all smiling and hugging each other, and some couldn't fight back the tears when saying goodbye. My hands were sweating and my heart was racing. One of my dreams was about to come true; my host family would pick me up at the university in a couple of hours. My new home was only twenty minutes away from campus.

To kill time, other au pairs and I took a seat on a long, hard wooden bench in front of the university's main building. We could see an SUV approaching from afar. My heart skipped a beat and I stood up. I think we all hoped that was our family. After parking in front of us, a woman got down, smiling from ear to ear.

Gina?" she asked.

When I heard a name that wasn't mine I felt as if in a beauty pageant where the panel calls out the chosen finalists to go to the next round and disqualifies the unwanted contestants. "Ugh!" I sighed loudly and sat again, this time on the school steps. I turned to see my classmates and felt disappointed for not being called out. Who would be next? Who would come to pick me up?

I could see another car far away. That would be the fourth family approaching and there were only four of us au pairs left. We all stood up on the porch, time seemed to slow down, none of us wanted to be last. The woman who got down from the van opened the trunk and, before asking for any of us, she got a bouquet of flowers. The four of us opened our eyes very wide. Each one of us desired to be the one for whom that bouquet of flowers was intended.

"Marilú," she said.

I can't believe it! I thought.

I could feel the tears of happiness in my eyes. I jumped off the steps, grabbed my bags and ran to hug them. It was my host mother and her younger daughter, Anne. Their eyes were wet and tearstained too. Kim extended one of her arms to hug me, while she held the flowers with the other. She kissed my cheek, which I didn't expect, and I kissed her cheek back. I took the flowers and thanked her, smiling.

I immediately moved to meet Anne and hugged her tight. She said my name right then:

"Ma-ri-lú!"

Anne was a one-year-old baby and she had just started to speak. Her effort and excitement when calling my name filled my heart with tenderness. I got into the car and we drove home.

On our way home, I started to feel like a member of the family, I felt truly welcomed after such a warm reception. The fear I'd felt started to evaporate, for they seemed like nice people. Thus, I left all worries behind and got distracted by the beautiful road. Pines seemed to embrace the highway, as if engulfing us. In spite of the copper colour of the trees, the view was truly breathtaking! All these sensations were being revealed to my senses. It was the middle of October, a time in which all the streets of Long Island grow a carpet of foliage in orange and brown. However, even though it was such a beautiful atmosphere, it awoke some nostalgia and homesickness within me.

My Position in the Program

I thought my first day at work would be easy, for I'd only have to take care of three children. I woke up very early in the morning and went to kitchen still in my pyjamas. There they were: Tom, Susan, and Anne, waiting in front of the TV. As soon as they saw me they smiled. Tom was very excited and took me to the freezer to show me where they put the bagels they all had for breakfast. Suddenly, Kim arrived and looked at me in confusion, then said:

"Marilú, you're in pyjamas!"

I didn't get the tone of her statement. For me, it was natural to be in pyjamas at 7 o'clock in the morning! At least it was at home in Mexico: waking up and having breakfast in pyjamas. I didn't think it was out of place, for Tom, Susan and Anne were in pyjamas as well, and wasn't I supposed to feel like a part of the family? I honestly didn't understand the point of her statement but, in order to avoid any kind of issue, the next day I showed up in jeans and a sweater. Afterwards, I understood that Kim expected me to dress in a certain manner before taking care of my daily chores, as any other domestic employee would.

In the beginning, it was pretty clear to me that my chores at the Robinsons would basically be focused on taking care of the children. I'd take care of Anne while Kim was at work. This meant I had to play with her, bathe her, feed her, tidy her room, and wash her clothes. With Tom and Susan I'd work as a playmate, besides feeding them and taking care of tidying their room and doing their laundry. The two first months went by according to the activities projected by Kim. Every morning, she would tell me about my activities for the day. We had a booklet the agency had provided in which Kim wrote down all the activities I performed each day. This tool would turn into some kind of logbook, as well as a control sheet for the agency, since they would need it in order to see if both sides had met their part of the deal. Within weeks,

Kim wasn't as rigorous with the booklet and stopped reporting all my activities during the day. After all, the coordinator never showed any interest in taking a look at it. That made us slowly forget about the logbook and, as we let go of some small obligations, we also let some other things go by.

I started to notice that some of my chores didn't fit into the descriptions the agency had given and what I had agreed to with Kim. Furthermore, it wasn't easy for me to live with somebody who was, to a certain extent, also committed to work. It implied living in an uncertain situation, for the limits between work and family had never been drawn; I worked and lived in the same place. This truly affected my capacity to distinguish between what I had and didn't have to do, and knowing my rights and obligations. On the other hand, the incongruity of the agency's stipulations about my cultural exchange made it a very different experience from my actual situation. The agency's representative in Aguascalientes had told me that it was more of a cultural experience than a job and that I'd have the chance to become a family member; that I would learn about their language and traditions. I wanted to believe that, for I refused to believe that, like many other immigrants, I had come to the United States to work as a housemaid. Being an au pair gave me some status; it meant that I was chosen by an upper class family to take care of their children and that I was in their country to participate in a cultural exchange, which gave me the migratory status of "exchange student" and not that of an employee or illegal immigrant. However, I was always confused about some things. Sometimes, I felt like another member of the family, but some other times the indifference, or even a cold shoulder, made me feel like no more than an employee. I was overloaded with chores and I had to work too many hours.

According to the agency, I wouldn't have to work more than 45 hours a week and only according to the agency's regulations. That way we would be able to control our working hours and our personal activities, which included attending school (Cultural Care, 2014). However, my schedule was overloaded with chores. It didn't matter if I had already covered my shift and my role defined itself day by day. Since we didn't report my activities anymore, I started to acquire new ones that weren't my responsibility. It became so natural that I had no real tracking of the activities I had to perform or any control over my working hours whatsoever. This started to interfere with my free time, including my attendance at English lessons. I started working two shifts a day; 5 hours in the morning and three or four hours in the afternoon. Furthermore, the fact that I wouldn't say no to some chores that I wasn't responsible for only led to me having to perform more activities. I thought I was doing the Robinsons a favour, just as I would for my family in Mexico. I truly felt committed to support them with whatever they asked from me without ever thinking they were taking advantage!

Not imposing limits from the beginning was but a mere reflection of a leaned behaviour at home in Mexico. I helped with the chores, for it was a silent agreement among us women. My sister, my mother, and I would devote our Saturday mornings to tiding up the house. I cleaned up the bathrooms, and swept and mopped the stairs and kitchen. I would usually finish before the others, as I didn't have as many chores. Thus, when they asked me if I could help them out with one of their chores I'd never say no, since I saw it as a gesture of support. I agreed to help my mom and sister when I finished before them, because I thought that if I ever needed it, they would do the same for me. As a result, I started to get used to saying yes and forgot about saying no, even when I was tired or had already performed all my chores.

The large number of chores at the Robinson's led me to question what would happen if I didn't put an end to it. However, I also thought it'd be an opportunity to earn some extra money. What else could I lose while being so far away from home and already immersed in the dynamics of a domestic worker? So, I talked to Kim and said I'd perform more chores if she agreed to pay me extra. That way I'd earn my weekly $120 dollars agreed to with the agency, plus $90 extra for doing all those household chores. It was a strategy I had thought of and, since I'd end up performing all those chores anyway, I thought I had better take advantage of the situation.

Thus, I had the opportunity to negotiate with my host mother. That way, instead of her hiring someone else to do the house chores, I'd do them in exchange for extra money. I also agreed not to tell anyone about our agreement or she would get in trouble with the agency for making me do things that weren't my responsibility. In addition, I felt ashamed of telling my friends and family in Mexico that I was working as a housemaid. I thought about the fact that in my country, such an occupation is deeply stigmatized and expected to be performed by women with few or only one or two years of elementary education. I didn't belong to that group. I had recently received my bachelor's degree. My aspirations still consisted of preparing myself for continuing study in a professional graduate program. My participation in the exchange program was aimed at improving my English in order to be able to pursue my master's degree in England. Consequently, saying that I was another one of those women who end up working as a housemaid didn't have anything to do with my personal aspirations and I didn't want to be seen as just another immigrant who went to the United States to look for a better job. So, as time passed by, I started to question myself. Were my goals being fulfilled in this exchange program? Was I truly making the most out of my English lessons? What was I doing to learn more about the country's culture? What was I doing there, so far from home, doing things I hadn't planned and that I only did back home, in Mexico?

Between my chores, taking care of the children, and my need to keep studying, everything started snowballing, bigger and heavier every time, and I had no idea where it would lead. I would frequently promise myself not to do any more chores. I was so tired; I dragged my feet through seemingly endless halls. Not even the colourful view of the garden cheered me up anymore. I didn't know what to do. Should I leave the program or endure this silently for a few more months? I complained silently and beat myself up for not immediately going back to Mexico!

The kids spent most of their time at school on Mondays, so I would seize the opportunity then to perform my chores. I had to hurry in order to wash, dry, and fold their clothes, then put them in the drawers. While the children's clothes were in the washing machine, I'd vacuum, mop, and dust seven rooms, plus the living and dining rooms, as well as clean four bathrooms and change the sheets on four beds. I'd do all this from 8 am to 1 pm, and had to be ready at 4 pm. So, sometimes I had to hurry, because I still had to tidy the kitchen and then, on top of it all, serve the children their meal after they got back from school. That was every Monday for the last six months and every Monday I would tell myself, "only 18 more Mondays and I'm off!" "Only 17 more and I'm done!" "16 more Mondays and I go back home!" However, as soon as I realized that Mondays still dragged into months, I would feel annoyed. It was too long.

When I cleaned the master bathroom's mirror, I couldn't escape my reflection. I found my eyes looked sad and tired. There was no light in them. It wasn't the experience I had been waiting for so long. My reflection haunted me. Why wasn't I satisfied with the tasks I had agreed to perform? Could that pressure on my chest be translated into frustration? My goodness! Why did I agree to work harder? Why don't I have the courage to tell them that I didn't want to perform any other tasks than the one we had agreed on?

The Days of Cultural Exchange

Since the beginning, I talked about my interest in setting up a weekly work schedule, so that I could attend my English lessons. Kim took me to a community college so I could ask for information and enrol in English lessons in case there was a convenient schedule. I chose the 6 to 8 pm schedule on Tuesdays and Thursdays. I attended regularly during the first few months, but as time went by, there were weeks in which I only attended one class due to my working hours. I started to think that staying in the country wasn't worth it. Why had I lost sight of my goals? Why hadn't I insisted on studying English? Why hadn't I been able to draw limits, in my favour, when it came down to overloading my work hours?

Kim knocked on my door. I was only fifteen minutes into my one hour break.

"Yes?" I replied.

"Hi, Marilú, I'd like to have a word with you," she answered.

I opened the door.

"Sure! What's up?" I answered back.

"Sorry to bother you, Marilú, but could you please take care of the children from 5 to 7 this afternoon?" she asked.

"Of course, Kim, no problem," I consented and closed the door while she went to her room upstairs.

Sometimes I couldn't believe the things she asked me. Did she forget about my academic life or did she just play dumb to take advantage of the situation? I had never said no and was afraid that they'd stop thinking I was a good person, so I always tried to have a good disposition and performed any task she asked from me. However, during my break, the only thing I did sometimes was sit in my room with the light out, for if the children saw the light on they knocked on my door so

I'd play with them, whether or not I was on a break. I had virtually no privacy and my time belonged to them almost completely. How could I separate chores related to the children when they were linked to the rest of the family? How could I complain about performing tasks that weren't my responsibility when these were the same I'd perform for my family in Mexico as a sign of support?

In the beginning, I didn't care about helping my host family with everything they asked throughout our day, but in time, I started to struggle with myself for not saying no since I wanted to think of myself as a part of the family. I felt the duty to support them unconditionally with everything related to taking care of the children and tiding the house. Nevertheless, if I took on the role of a housemaid, the ambiguity of jumping from one role to another didn't let me draw a line between them, once again, for fear of not being accepted. Suddenly, I had turned into the woman who performed all the house chores. A time came in which I felt so strained that my age, my studies, or even the agreement I had made with Kim about my working hours couldn't relieve me from my ever growing discomfort, which had also become more evident.

One Monday, Kim entered the laundry room with a basket full of dirty clothes and said:

"Marilú, please do this laundry with the children's. We shouldn't be wasteful and the machine isn't full."

"Of course, Kim, I got it!" I answered.

I stood there, like so many times before, talking to myself. It was one of my many strategies to release my anger and frustration, for most times I had no one to talk to about my problems. I started shoving the laundry into the washing machine, chewing on my anger.

"This can't be happening! It's way over the top! Doing the laundry means I also have to dry and fold the clothes too. It's too much," I thought, but kept it to myself, since I didn't want to be responsible for an unpleasant situation, even though I had the right to say no.

In spite of this kind of exploitation being so common and talked about among other au pairs, my peers and I never complained about it with any the coordinators. I concluded that, mostly among Latino au pairs, there was a tendency to keep silent about this type of mistreatment in order to flatter our host parents and feel more integrated. Furthermore, the notion and magnitude of family integration, conceived of the process in which au pairs adapt to the dynamics of host families (Luévano, 2012), was so significant that it transcended the performance of the task in itself. Thus, integration became a huge part of our activities. I think that is the reason why we accepted responsibilities that weren't ours. We were looking for acceptance and to be seen as another member of the family. I was like Martha, an au pair friend who once told us she always did more than what was expected; sometimes she did all the family's dishes, walked the dog or dusted the living room, even though these activities weren't her responsibility.

In my case, I finished my chores by dinner. In spite of it being beyond my working hours, I'd join them. Kim cooked while I'd set the table. Sometimes I asked the children to help me set the table so we all cooperated. Kim, Tom, Susan, Anne and I sat together every day. Peter, a busy family man, would seldom share the table with us during the week. Due to his busy job schedule he was hardly ever at home. The children left the table as soon as they finished, leaving only Kim and me at the table. We used that time alone to talk about our day, how we felt, or if anything out of the usual had happened. After our talks, which I always enjoyed very much and made the best out of by practicing my English, Kim cleared the table while I always offered to do the dishes, tidy the kitchen, or mop the floor. Even though it wasn't my responsibility, I did it out of thankfulness for them sharing their table and conversation with me. These occurrences made me feel like another member of the family, for they had taken into consideration that I was performing chores in which I shouldn't be involved outside my working hours. Moreover, I think that when we, au pairs, experienced these feelings of integration, we also felt the need, if only to a certain extent, to thank our employers. That fact made us feel truly committed to the family, causing us to do more and cooperate voluntarily with domestic labours, just as we would have done with our own families (Luevano, 2012).

Willingly performing activities that weren't our responsibility became some kind of moral currency (Hess & Puckhaber, 2004) we used as a resource to fit in and feel accepted by our host families and our labour was the means through which we reinforced family ties between both sides. This phenomenon constitutes a cycle of self-assignation, since we were willing to perform some chores –which we later assimilated as part of our roles– in exchange for acceptance and integration. Furthermore, the relationship between performing tasks we didn't have to and family integration grew strong (Luevano, 2012). I remember Maria, another friend from Mexico. One day, she argued with her host mother, because she asked her to clean the kitchen. Maria refused to do so saying that it wasn't her responsibility. Her host mother made her do it, arguing that it was a house chore that the last au pair did and thus, she'd have to do the same. Maria didn't know what to do. She was confused and talked to one of the representatives about it. The representative answered that, if she didn't want to wind up in an uncomfortable situation, she should cooperate with such tasks. After all, she was a part of the family. As a result, Maria had no other choice, but to perform such tasks.

At the End of the Exchange

During the exchange, I tried to position myself as a sociologist whose target was analysing such types of programs, the justification for their existence and, above all, why were there specific types of interactions among the au pairs, the agency, and the host families. I was intrigued by the U.S. Government providing us with student visas, when we spent more time performing domestic labour. I focused on the experience, instead of the general context. I tried to disassociate the social position of the families who hire such services as being a possible explanation, only leaving the agency and the au pairs through which to find an answer. When I couldn't find a convincing explanation, I became interested in problematizing this in my master's thesis, which began as soon the exchange came to an end. I talked to other au pairs about their experiences, for I was very interested in getting to know them. Those talks became a constant for us to learn which chores we had to perform or not, for we only had each other as a reference. However, each of us saw how the line blurred between the limits and our frustration. It was difficult to distinguish our actual activities from acquired responsibilities, for each one of us had made a different agreement with their host mother and our activities depended on each family's needs.

Another subject worth mentioning is gender, for all the negotiations made between the family and the au pair seem to be made by women. Most times, agreements are made between two women; meaning, between a mother and an au pair, between an au pair and representatives, and between representatives and host mothers. It is unusual for a male figure to be present during these negotiations, as the host father delegates all decisions on the matter to the mother. In my case, and for many other au pairs, it was pretty obvious that the host mother had been in charge of making the final call when hiring us, a fact that only reinforces sexual divisions at the workplace (Bikova, 2008; Salazar-Parreñas, 2001). In this phenomenon, it was quite evident that host mothers chose au pairs to entrust domestic labour to them. This could also be understood as the purchase of subordinated gender relief in the household for host mothers (Hondagneu Sotelo, 2011). They transferred their domestic responsibilities to the au pairs, replicating the female nature of domestic labours.

FROM INTERPELLATION TO REFLECTION

I returned to Mexico with lots of stories to tell. After being abroad for a year and a half, I wanted to expose everything the au pairs had to deal with when enrolling in such Cultural Exchange programs. Being familiar with their daily experience helped me confirm that many of us had bought the idea of that year being the best of our lives.

With all these experience-based notions about the Cultural Exchange program revolving in my head, I started my Master's wanting to research the global condition of these programs. How did these exchange programs work in other countries? Where did they recruit more au pairs and where were they interested in migrating? As a sociologist, I started to analyse these occurrences and made the most out of my knowledge in sociology, for I had first-hand information about being an au pair. I had my own testimony, that of other au pairs, and of the agency, as well. Having all these elements at my disposal, I brought up these programs as something more than just cultural exchange channels, for they satisfied a very specific demand. With such testimonies at hand, I started to question the subject of my thesis, a space in which I wanted to discuss the true role that many of us au pairs tried to reshape so we wouldn't feel like we had failed at making our dream come true. We knew we were migrant women, but we refused to accept our role as housemaids and that was why we held on to the idea of becoming a part of our host families. I wanted to portray the journey through which I had undergone so many life experiences and personal achievements, as well as the frustration I had felt at times due to my working conditions, my loneliness for being away from my family, and despondency for not feeling like another member of my host family.

With this impetus to start work as an academic researcher, I started to gather the testimony of thirteen au pairs I had met during the exchange in the United States. I thought their experiences were revealing and full of the data I needed for my research. Some had abandoned the program only a few months into the exchange and others had extended their program, like I did, for another six months, or even nine or twelve. Some had to take care of three, four or even five children. Other au pairs had to split their time, between living with the host mother for a week and living with the host father for another week, and so on. I focused on trying to establish if most of us had performed extra chores just to feel like another member of our host families. Based on this data and my personal experience in the matter, I designed a survey, with strategically chosen questions, that would provide more data and help me achieve the target of my research. Based on these questions, I created an analysis matrix that would contain all testimonies gathered during the interviews. Once I was done with the interviews it was time to analyse them.

I felt like a true researcher! Even so, in spite of being able to bring my own experience into the subject, I was asked to be as objective as I could. Thus, I had to leave my own experience aside and trace the issue as a researcher. With this methodological conditioning, I wrote exclusively about the other au pairs, while I tried very hard to separate my own experience, and what I already knew, from the subject study so that I wouldn't influence my findings. But, isn't any data analysis permeated by our own experience? And, if possible, how could I dissociate that analysis from the data processed by the researcher?

ON AUTOETHNOGRAPHIC INSIGHT

I finished my master's thesis with a sense of accomplishment; I felt I had done something important for my career. However, I still felt the need to tell my story as an au pair. In this quest for finding the media that allowed me to share my experience, I finally came across the forum in which I could rediscover my experience as an au pair and talk about it. I became part of an autoethnographic group of researchers with Silvia Bénard and Gresilda Tilley-Lubbs. There I could work on a written essay to elaborate on my journey as an au pair, on how I constructed and deconstructed the role of the recruiting agencies, the host families and the au pairs themselves. At the same time, working on my testimony from an autoethnographic point of view enabled me to visualize and understand the different methodological paradigms that took me, as a researcher, to fulfil my own investigative purposes.

I realized my experience belonged to autoethnography, for it was a scenario in which I could elaborate freely on my subject. Thinking that my paper could have physical presence (Colyar, 2013), I recalled my days as an au pair and took over my own testimony. I took the opportunity to write about a few –or perhaps many– au pairs and shared the situations of vulnerability we had undergone during our Cultural Exchange program.

I gained insight through the many sides from which I looked at the Cultural Exchange program. While writing my master's thesis I was convinced that these programs were involved with a formal labour market. However, when I got immersed in autoethnography, I triggered a reformulation process and understood that these exchange programs actually have a functional basis. They become a link in a chain of child support through which young women interested in learning about another culture could become a part of a host family, in this case, from the United States. Still, in practice, the ends can be distorted, as they adapt themselves to the needs of the agencies and the host families, but focus on fulfilling needs related to domestic labour.

Today, I understand that every time I talked about my experiences to the other au pairs, I saw my reflection in theirs that way, I had unconsciously started to redefine that which, in principle, I thought I would be and that which I had turned into. Through reflection, this redefinition helped me cope with many difficult situations and enabled me to finish the program with a different vision. I reformulated my position within the system and understood the utilitarian side of these exchange programs, and also discovered a key element for the good relationship between host families and au pairs: the information with which you understand, live, and feel everyday coexistence.

The desire to talk about my experience was what drove me to rewrite my story. I wanted to give some insight, if at least a minimum, to those youths interested in participating in those au pair cultural exchange programs. That is why I chose autoethnographic insight as that methodological path to tell one's story and be able to unveil personal answers and interpersonal dynamics (Finlay, 2002). Autoethnography gave me the opportunity to find myself in recounting my everyday life as an au pair. The experiences of other au pairs still sound in my head, like a reflection of the situation each one of us was living and only became visible due to that moment of externalization. Only a few of us made a deeper analysis and even fewer have had the opportunity to talk about it, such as I'm able to do it here.

I truly wish to support others with my testimony and to shed light on the experiences of those who had been or plan to be au pairs. I hope they find their reflection in my autoethnographic exercise and let it shed light on their experiences. If my testimony reaches at least one person, I'll consider this a success that was worth all the trouble.

NOTE

[1]   http://culturalcareaupair.com/our-au-pairs/who-are-our-au-pairs/

REFERENCES/BIBILOGRAPHY

Aguilar, M. (2014). ¿Atrapadas en un cuento de hadas?: Tras las representaciones de s mexicanas ante la demanda de trabajo doméstico y del cuidado en EUA. In S. Durin, M. E. De la O., & S. Bastos (Eds), *Trabajadoras en la sombra. Dimensiones del servicio doméstico latinoamericano* (pp. 535–562). México D. F., México: CIESAS – EGAP.

Bikova, M. (2008). *A family member or a family servant? Why Norwegian families hire au pairs: A quality study.* Bergen, Norway: University of Bergen.

Colyar, J. E. (2013). Reflections on writing and autoethnography. In S. Holman Jones, T. E. Adams, & C. Ellis (Eds.), *Handbook of autoethnography* (pp. 123–142). Walnut Creek, CA: Left Coast.

Cultural care. (2014, November 7). Retrieved from http://culturalcareaupair.com/what-is-au-pair-childcare/benefits/

Finlay, L. (2002). Negotiating the swamp: The opportunity and challenge of reflexivity in research practice. *Qualitative Research 2*(2), 209–230.

Hess, S., & Puckhaber, A. (2004). Big sister. Are better domestic servants? *Feminist Review/Labour Migrations: Women on the Move.* 65–78. doi:10.1057/palgrave.fr.9400177

Hondagneu-Sotelo, P. (2001). *Doméstica: Trabajadoras migrantes a cargo de la limpieza y el cuidado a la sombra de la abundancia.* México D. F., México: Porrúa.

Luévano-Martínez, M. (2012). *Los programas de intercambio cultural de Estados Unidos como trabajo doméstico formal.* México D. F., México: FLACSO-México.

Rambo, C. (2013). Twitch. In S. Holman Jones, T. E. Adams, & C. Ellis (Eds), *Handbook of autoethnography* (pp. 627–637). Walnut Creek, CA: Left Coast Press.

Salazar-Parreñas, R. (2001). *Servants of globalization: Women, migration, and domestic work.* Stanford, CT: Stanford University.

María de la Luz Luévano Martínez
Departamento de Sociología y Antropología
Universidad Autónoma de Aguascalientes
Aguascalientes, Aguascalientes, México

DYANIS POPOVA

16. WATCH WHAT YUH SAYIN'

The Power of Language

Trinidadians are a special people of dat there is no doubt,
Doh care what odders say or how dey run dey mouth.
But of all de special talents dat we Trinis possess,
Is de way we talk dat ranks us among de best.
At de street corners, in de shop or at work on any given day,
Is to hear us talk an' carry on in our own special way.
De colourful words, de antics, and de accent all combine,
To create a whole new language dat has stood de test of time.
De way we express ourselves and de way we converse,
Is truly an art of which every Trini can boast.

(Browne, 2001, p. 11)

ABSTRACT

The author explores the power inherent in the use of language in our daily lives. Connecting her ideas and experiences with her Trinbagonian culture, the author notes that language is not only an instrument of communication, but is also representative of class, community, and cultural norms. Switching among variations of U.S. and Trinbagonian English, she examines the meanings and intersectionalities of her experiences as she navigates the influence of this power differential on her life as an immigrant to the U.S.

INTRODUCTION

For a Trinidadian, language and dialect are a large part of how we express ourselves and how we identify each other. For many, it may just sound like just another form of English but for us it is so much more. There is unity in the way that we speak …we can identify a Trini *off jus'* one word. No matter where we go, just a hint of that recognizable lilt can make a place seem more familiar. It is often that same lilt that causes some people to ascribe certain characteristics to the speaker, characteristics whether intentionally or not, label one's intelligence, class, level of education, and much more.

G. A. Tilley-Lubbs & S. B. Calva (Eds.), Re-Telling Our Stories, 219–230.

It has also now become the language of Facebook. Trinis far and wide, even those who have not returned to the country for decades, use the local lilt and its accompanying expressions to express themselves to each other in writing. The use of dialect itself is often a topic of conversation. In sharing her late-night frustration with her daughter, my friend Sammi, who lives in Northern Germany and whose husband is German, laments:

> My 4 an half yr old is quarrelin wit me at haff-pass-ten in de night about drinkin COLA instead of MILK before she FIIIIInally falls asleep ...she guff-up like chuff-chuff fuh me! not me dis hour de night nah. she could quarrel widdee faddah when he reach home from work at midnight; & bet yuh BOTTOM DOLLAR she stayin awake like soucouyant til he reach home! (Excerpt from Facebook conversation, 2014)

This statement translates basically as:

> My 4 and a half year old is arguing with me at half-past-ten at night about drinking COLA instead of MILK before she FIIIIInally falls asleep ...she was seriously pouting! I simply cannot deal with that this late at night. She can argue with her father when he gets home from work at midnight; and I can guarantee that she will stay awake like a soucouyant[1] until he gets home!

For many of us, this typed dialect is reminiscent of a warm hug. It is a way in which we can keep our past connected to our present and future, and it is also a way for Trinis both at home and abroad to place emphasis on ideas and feelings. A new Facebook group dedicated to ex-pat Trinis abounds with posts asking people for their own translations from Standard English into Trini English as a way to make the members feel (re)connected to their language and their histories.

MOUT' OPEN 'TORY JUMP OUT

[Once you start saying a little, the entire story will be revealed][2]

Trinidad and Tobago, a twin island republic just seven miles off the coast of Venezuela, was a Spanish colony for almost 400 years (occupied by mostly French settlers), and a British colony for about 150 years after that. The island itself is very diverse ethnically and linguistically, including people from a mélange of country of origins: about 40% East Indian, 37.5% African and the rest Chinese, European, Syrian, Lebanese, Caribe, and Arawak ...and I could go on.

Through a shared history of slavery, indentureship, and inequality, the official language—English—is spoken in three main forms: what we call Trini dialect (spoken with peers and in informal situations), Trini Creole, and Tobagonian Creole (both *proper* adapted British/Standard English). The two latter forms are spoken in formal or professional situations, with those of previous generations, or of higher social status. Many Trinbagonians[3] spend most of their time in one linguistic realm or another …I was fortunate …I lived always in both. Language in Trinidad and Tobago has always represented class and community. As in many other cultures, it represents not only an instrument of communication but also transfers and transmits cultural norms (Wa Thiong'o, 1986). The way that you communicate in formal situations can tell others about your upbringing, education, and status. There is a language for your peers, and one for your elders and other members of the real world.

COCKROACH HAVE NO RIGHT IN FOWL PARTY

[One should not find oneself involved in anything where one is unwelcomed or out of place]

I attended a "prestige"[4] high school in the capital Port-of-Spain, where we were primed to be members of the middle class. I was a Bishop's[5] girl. My friends and I took pride in what Youssef (2005) describes as varilingualism: a type of code mixing among our different variations of English. We liked being able to fit in anywhere and everywhere. We could blend in with anybody. Members of my family often stressed the importance of being able to attend a fancy dinner with the Prime Minister as well as being able to share a conversation with someone who might be living in the street. In spite of this flexibility with speech, there was power in using the language of business, the proper language of the colonizers: the Queen's English.

I displayed this "Queen's English" during my first year in college while in some long forgotten classroom at a university in the United States. The first week of class I sat up and raised my hand confidently, asking "May I borrow a rubber?"[6] The laughter emanating from every corner of the room still echoes in my head. I remember the heat rising in my cheeks, and the tears that threatened to expose themselves regardless of how tightly I squeezed the muscles around my eyes. Tucking my tail in shame, I exited and never returned to that classroom or interacted with any of those people again. For the first time in my life, my speech made me feel less than those around me. It was almost a year before I interacted socially with other Americans[7] on campus. Whenever I opened my mouth, I could hear those echoes, which to this day still prompt moist eyes.

Yuh betta watch what yuh sayin'….

Fast forward same semester … Freshman English … and I got a B? I did not get B's, especially not in English. I can recall the big red loops bemoaning my spelling and my stomp to my professor's office, Oxford English dictionary in hand. I remember the rough yet shiny curls that swirled above her brow line and the left eyebrow that stayed raised throughout my explanations.

"What exactly do you see to be the problem here?" she began tersely.

I tried to calm both my nerves and my anger as I responded, "Well, you noted problems with my spelling, but according to the Oxford Dictionary my spelling is impeccable!"

She calmly stated, "You seem to like putting the letter u in far too many words."

She looked away from me then and proceeded to matter-of-factly return to grading papers from another class.

"That's the way it's spelled in British English. I am from the Caribbean and that's what we use there."

"Well you're not *there* now are you ma'am." She scoffed. "You are *here*. And this is America. You need to use *American* English."

In shock, I demanded, "You're not really going to destroy my grade for that are you? This is my first paper. A warning or note about your expectations would have been nice."

That eyebrow rose even higher.

"If you can't spell, you just can't spell."

She turned to look pointedly at the door, then returned her gaze to the stack of papers on the table before her. I stood in silence for a minute while coming to terms with the fact that my complaints were having no impact, and that the conversation was effectively over. It was the subsequent trek to a sympathetic Dean that righted what I perceived as injustice and a disregard for my grammatical excellence.

That semester, it was the Bishop's girl inside me who *knew* I was smart that helped me hold my head high. I was deflated. This blending in was just too hard. That one instance, my first semester at college, shaped the way I perceived education and my place in it. It also had considerable impact on the way I viewed myself and my place as the Other. This professor had all at once helped establish a chip in my self-confidence, and re-opened an ancestral wound of whose existence I had been unaware. That one instance strengthened my decision to avoid what I perceived as intolerant Americans. It was not just that first moment in the classroom with that isolated group. Was it all of them? I had thought that this was a land of diversity and understanding. I felt disillusioned and simply …I hurt. I hurt in a way I had not ever felt before. My worth had come into question. I struggled with self-perceptions and new directions, finding friends among the Others, the disenfranchised, the lonely, and the foreign. For the next few years, I surrounded myself with colours, flags, music, and languages from a thousand places. The International Student Centre became my home away from home and the place where I found all my friends. There could be no threat of blending in and losing myself when everyone I knew was so different.

The aforementioned experiences, my use of British vocabulary and spelling, reflected a deeper issue of my speech and the way it represented who I was and what I stood for. Here in the United States, my speech was interpreted differently than I had ever before experienced. More and more of these experiences pushed me into my chosen corner at the International Student Centre where the simple act of cross-cultural communication was more valuable than the specific words I chose to use. In many cases, students at the centre were just happy to be understood and to find themselves part of our hodgepodge community.

Around Americans, the language of Caribbean schooling, this proper English, was nothing but a weight around my neck in this new place. It isolated me from the miniscule black community on campus as sure as the colour of my skin removed me from the overwhelmingly white population. The slang and dialect I used with my friends in Trinidad was a foreign language here. The common dialect used within the black community on campus was equally foreign to me, and for many within that community it was also a projection of race and their relationship with it. Unbeknownst to me the colour of my skin was supposed to dictate my behaviour, speech, and choices in everything from food to music. The way that I spoke, the type of English I used, somehow related to how black I was and to my insufficient rejection of white culture. By the same token, the colour of my skin itself prevented me from blending in with the white community with whom my speech patterns seemed more compatible. I felt trapped, struggling to understand these new politics and expectations.

Overall when I moved to the United States, my Caribbean-ness was erased, and I was often simply viewed as another member of the African-American community. My identity, like that of many Caribbean immigrants, was tied to the land of my birth rather than the colour of my skin. The primacy of race (Freeman, 2002), as defined by the United States context, trumped all, and defined me in the eyes of many. My blackness both negated the multiple ethnic heritages of my grandparents and essentially rendered my unique cultural identity invisible to the general populace (Guy, 2001). Had I stayed in New York, where I had first arrived, I could have hidden within the city's Caribbean enclaves and remained more *Trini*. It is a choice that many, including my mother and aunt, have made in order to retain a sense of closeness to our home language and culture. I could have also gone to Washington D.C., Miami, Atlanta, or Houston, and achieved the same results. Although our language is officially English, these communities, like many ethnic neighbourhoods in New York, offer solace and kinship for those who have had to leave home behind. But here, in southwest Virginia, before the existence of social media, my foods, music, and pastimes were lost to me. I was alone.

This Caribbean blackness, however, definitely did not endear me to many of the African-Americans I encountered. I can still hear the echoes of my ex-husband's black friends in Washington D.C.:

"Have you ever been black?"

In their minds my speech, and even my hobbies, evoked whiteness. There was no justifying the fact that most people I knew spoke back home spoke that way and that I wasn't trying to prove that I was better or smarter than anyone. I can still see multiple pairs of blank eyes accompanied by awkward, barely hidden smirks after I finished speaking. I can still remember leaning in to my white ex, urging him to discreetly translate parts of their conversations as the slang was unfamiliar to me. My speech made me one of the Others, an outcast. Friends and even members of my own family who had assimilated to U.S. culture repeatedly echoed the sentiment:

"You know he's blacker than you could ever be, right?"

What did that mean? Was it a simple cultural observation or a disparagement? Should I be offended that my Slavic partner was considered more authentically black than I "could ever be?" Just because of the way that I talked?

Yuh betta watch what yuh sayin'....

This speech, in all its forms, in which I had once taken immense pride, had become a burden. It represented my arrival at a maze through which I had no idea how to navigate. I practiced and I practiced in an effort to become a little less distinctive (if only I knew then what I know now) and I have to say I made great strides. At that point in my life there was pride in the skill of my American mimicry. If they didn't know I was different, then they couldn't belittle me. Only with a few expressions or in a few specific situations did I lose myself to my Trini twang. Some things still continued to challenge me linguistically. To this day, my friends still giggle when I say weird *<where-d>* or beer *<beahr>*. Overall though, I must ask myself, was it my shame and my fear than cost me my dialect? Where had this shame come from and why was it now a part of my daily experience?

I refer to the cost or loss of my dialect because in my efforts to become less distinctive, there were years where I couldn't even evoke its tones from between my lips. I tried so long and so hard to hide myself in this obscure American-ness that in retrospect, I lost myself. My experiences during that first year in college reshaped not only how I perceived myself, but also how I portrayed those perceptions to the world around me. Without social media, I had no true connections to that language except through my parents. This was back when I still wrote long letters to friends back home and waited anxiously for weeks, hoping that they would not only get my note but that they could find time to reply. Back then, there was no use of dialect in our letters. That language, in both its formal and informal articulations, was dead to me and I was determined to make new friends and embrace this new life in which I found myself.

In the remainder of this piece, as I explore the meanings and intersectionalities of these experiences, I switch between variations of American and Trinbagonian speech to share some of my confusion, hopes, and expectations. At present, I am still navigating this labyrinth, but the difficult reflections that have emerged as a result of my explorations have challenged both my reflexivity and my writing. In what follows, representations of Trini speech are presented in italics to allow for some distinction from the standard Western academic utterances that have now become a second language to me.

DE DEEPER DE DARKNESS DE NEARER DE DAWN

[When things seem darkest, relief is nearby]

As I stood and read parts of this reflection during my presentation at a recent qualitative research conference, I struggled to find my voice. Similar to the way that I speak these days around my American partner in my Southwest Virginia home, I read by ear, mimicking smiling American television reporters with their appropriately melodic undertones. I have always excelled at linguistic mimicry. I found great pleasure as a young woman in the fact that I could imitate almost any accent or dialect just by hearing it a few times. My grandmother often regaled me with stories of my initial forays into this "skill" when I encountered tourists as a small child.

In my current linguistic incarnation, I toss…*an' ah turn, shiftin' real fas'*, wondering how my *allyuh* became y'all, how my *cuffs* became punches, how my *sal'fish buljol*[8] for breakfast became bacon, eggs, and toast, and more recently still, biscuits and gravy. What did I give up when I conceded my accent? What was/am I really trying to accomplish? I know that back then I was just a lonely nineteen-year-old trying to fit in, but now? Why do I continue? Is it even my choice anymore? It is almost like the slow, indiscernible loss of a first language. Acknowledging Norton's (1997) assertion that "identity constructs and is constructed by language" (p. 419), how do I now construct my social and cultural identities? I now encounter those who tell me I am no longer *Trini* enough, that my new accent has somehow weakened the authenticity of my voice.

"I still Trini. Dat will never change. I not adopting nobody accent."

As I sit here typing this reflection, this statement from a Facebook conversation among ex-pat Trinis echoes in my mind. It infers that adopting an accent is tantamount to no longer being Trini. My American accent, my abandonment of my mother tongue "looks like a dreadful betrayal and produces a guilty feeling" (Wa Thiong'o, 1986, p. 7). As such, I often struggle with the question: How authentic am I? Those close to me from previous generations have maintained the lilting melodies of a Trini *riddum*[9] in spite of their American experiences, but I have been distracted. Do my Facebook conversations even come close to regaining that aspect of my identity or am I just fooling myself? Indeed, how authentically Trini am I now and what does that even mean?

Yuh betta watch what yuh sayin'….

Brown (2010) describes authenticity as a conscious choice of how we practice the way we choose to live. She relates authenticity to "the daily practice of letting go of who we think we're supposed to be and embracing who we are" (p. 50), noting that this choice means:

[C]ultivating the courage to be imperfect, to set boundaries, and to allow ourselves to be vulnerable; exercising the compassion that comes from knowing that we are all made of strength and struggle; and nurturing the sense of belonging that can only happen when we believe that we are enough. (p. 50)

This leads me to ask: Who am I? Do I have the courage to be imperfect? Is my imperfection found in the perceptions of American others as I use my home dialect or through the perceptions of Trinidadian others as I use my American accent?

How can I come to terms with the power that exists within each and genuinely believe that regardless of the way(s) in which I speak, that I am truly enough?

I hear the voice of my maternal grandmother:

"Yuh have to talk properly!"

"Act like yuh have some broughtupsy!"

But forget proper!

So many words have become lost to me.

Words like *maga* and *chinkey* both mean small,
Whereas *lingay* just means skinny and tall.
I no longer *mamaguy* people with flattering words,
But now refer to this tactic as offering possibly disingenuous comments.
I no longer *lahay* or *skylark*, I loiter instead.
And no more *Mama yo!* Or *Ohgadoy!*—now I OMG!
I still miss *liming* with friends—it sounds more fun than just hanging out.
And I think often about the fact that I can't be *vikey-vi* in academia,
So I work hard to be purposeful.
But what I really miss from my island home the most is
de ol' time *dingolay* where the music consumes both my body and soul with
de riddums of lifetimes past.

A recent trip to the West Coast. Dinner in a smoky dimly lit room where the soft strains of jazz fill the air. A table for eight with one American, six Trinis living and working in various parts of the world, and one St. Lucian working in Trinidad.

St. Lucian to me: Whey you from?

Trini (Australia): She from Trinidad! Yuh doh' know she's Dennis' daughter?

St. Lucian: Well she doh soun' Trini. I cyah really tell.

Trini (Australia): Dah's because she went to Bishops! All a dem does talk like dat …proper proper! It just geh worse when she went to the States.

Through all this I sat, my face growing redder, feeling shame that I had yet again slipped back into the American accent to which I had become far too accustomed. I had been called out, singled out. Yet again.

Yuh betta watch what yuh sayin'….

As I write and I contemplate, maybe this is the reason I hold on to my Trinidad and Tobago citizenship so dearly. My passport may be my only remaining proof that I belong, that I have not sacrificed it all, and that there is some uniqueness left in me. Family and friends have encouraged me for years to file for U.S. citizenship but I have felt no drive, no desire to even consider applying. I have lived here for more than sixteen years but without that navy blue booklet, emblazed with our national coat of arms, am I no more than just another ex-patriot, another daughter who abandoned the life and lifestyle of her grandmothers and grandfathers to live in the land of plenty?

And what of my infant son? Am I left with nothing of my homeland to give him but stories of times long past? He will most likely share the lilting mild southern twang of his American father rather than mine and he will most likely grow up as "just" another American with a foreign born parent. With this too, he may face another set of challenges. Like me, his father has also struggled with preconceived notions of who he is and what he stands for based on that twang. He too worked as a teenager to soften his accent in order to lessen both assumptions of his hillbilly-ness and fear that others deem him a simpleton. This feeling of powerlessness and the privileges invoked by speech is not my burden alone to bear. Yet I still feel alone and challenged under its weight. I bring my son into this world of power, privilege, and the judgment of others. He will be a mixed kid with a potentially mixed accent in a mixed-up world.

Yuh betta watch what yuh sayin'....

Will my son have trouble understanding his Caribbean grandparents and great-grandparents? Will we have to stand in separate lines to enter the country I will always call home? Have I improved his chances or narrowed his options? Will this American son even further lessen the way that others perceive my authenticity? Does it even matter at all? As usual, I am left with more questions than answers.

MORE IN DE MORTAR DAN DE PESTLE: LANGUAGE AS POWER

[There is more to the story than meets the eye]

There is definitely power in both these "languages" I speak. This American dialect is not a cop out, but rather a mode of acculturation into a society that often equates foreign accents with a lack of education and intelligence. This adopted American accent means that though some may not be able to look past my colour, they cannot use my speech too as a means of limiting my opportunities and experiences. I have begun to *think* in this new accent and it wrenches my soul. In addition, switching in professional situations has become increasingly difficult as my shame triggers seem to be more active under these conditions. My initial mimicry has now become part of my mechanics. The conscious switch I once took for granted has become an unconscious action. My fight to be equal, to be not thought of as less than because of my accent has backfired. Now AM I less than ... what I once was?

In my efforts to reclaim *de Trini* I sometimes find myself over-compensating, over enunciating in ways I would not have at "home." I worry about going home. I worry that someone will call me out for leaving my culture behind. This wasn't a welcomed choice, but one borne of fear, fear that all the spewed hate I hear about foreigners will be ascribed to me. Maintaining my home dialect (just saying home still makes me smile) grants me full access to the land and people of my birth. It is a code that includes words, intonation, and gestures that make our identity unique.

Like that aforementioned hug, it is a familiar comfort to which I can turn when I am in doubt. It connects me to my past and provides succour on the path into my future.

This idea has become more apparent and more pertinent to me as I have become more active in the world of academic presentations. One particular annual conference has become a gathering point for Trinis from several continents in the field of education. This group of Caribbean academics includes my father, my step-mother, my god-father, and several friends, both old and new. We usually stay in the same hotel and often share meals with each other as we connect both personally and professionally.

Last year I presented one piece as a first author and listened as my father and god-father both made presentations of their own. This symposium involved others too, not just Trinidadians, or even people I knew. I was however, not only the youngest presenter, but the one who had not been home for the longest period of time. The vast conference room was large enough to have a noticeable echo and I watched as the scattered audience leaned forward in rapt and respectful attention. Dressed in my navy blue Express suit with the matching pointy-tipped shoes I had splurged to find online, I twiddled with the name badge that hung on a loose cord around my neck.

I sat among the audience as the others presented and for the first time, I truly listened to each presenter's intonation and voice. These were all tenured or tenure-track professors who were well respected in their fields ...and not one of them adopted or attempted to adopt an American accent. They each spoke formalized English, but each maintained the distinct lilt of their homeland. For the Trinis, there were no long letter a's here and though *dese t'ings* were clearly vocalized as a professional "these things," there was no mistaking the fact they were foreign, and for them that held no shame. I began then to question the motivations for my American accent and I remember for a moment feeling mournful, as if I had suffered some great loss. I had become alienated from a central aspect of my culture without even realizing it.

Hogan (2000) notes that in some cases involving persons from the Caribbean, this sense of alienation is so severe that the person:

> [I]nternalises the alien culture after extensive education, typically including a period in the metropolis. His/ her racial or ethnic origin prevents true acceptance in the foreign culture, and the internalization of the foreign culture makes him/her (in Achebe's phrase) 'no longer at ease' in the home culture as well. (p. 17)

I felt aimless and afloat at that moment. It was probably at that juncture that I started my efforts to reclaim my accent in professional situations and to invoke the pride and power that I perceived lay therein. I still struggle with this daily as I interact with my teachers, my students, and my peers. Reclaiming my accent during this journey that is in no way complete, this accent which so clearly helped me define my identity, has made me feel like I have found a sense of place and belonging again. I have found a personal island and am once again enjoying the sense of having solid ground beneath my feet.

WHERE HORSE TIE, IS DERE HE HAVE TO GRAZE

[Wherever you are and whatever your lot in life, you should make the best of it.]

So this is my daily struggle. As I speak to my family and my friends …my language still changes. I find that every day that passes without the salt breeze of my island kissing my skin and tousling my hair, even though I am reclaiming this accent, I am less and less able to switch at will. It is no longer as easy as it once was but I have now become conscious about how I verbalize my thoughts and ideas. Through the ideas of Dillard (2012), and as memories of home grow fainter and I become a tourist in my own country, my dialect helps me to (re)member my histories, to (re) present myself and my ancestors, and to (re)search not only myself but the world around me. I give reluctant credit to social media outlets that allow me to keep in touch with Trinidadian current events and network with others as we confront the same struggles, some more than others.

Through my research, I have become fascinated with Wa Thiong'o's (1986) use of the concept of a cultural bomb and how it applies to my life, my search for authenticity, and my struggle with my use of language. A cultural bomb is often the effect of a legacy of oppression that destroys a group's belief in "their names, in their languages, in their environment, in their heritage of struggle, in their unity, in their capacities, and ultimately in themselves" (Wa Thiong'o, p. 3). For me, as an individual struggling with identity through language, I am still unsure as to the true origins of my feelings of shame, but I am certain that I felt this bomb explode upon my arrival to the United States. This dialect, through which I have regained my sense of pride, is the result of centuries of struggle and connection. Though it may hold no political sway, it retains a power in my search for my personal identity and sense of belonging as part of a growing Trinbagonian diaspora.

Dillard (2012) notes that "memories are part and parcel of the meanings of identity, of the meaning of who we are, and how we are in this world" (p. 11). Will my memories be enough to hold on to an identity that threatens to leave me behind? Though I have begun my journey of reclamation and take great joy in using my Trini dialect at every possible opportunity, I still ask myself many questions as I continuously reflect along this passage. In a conference presentation in 2013, Dillard noted that those who do not define themselves WILL be defined by others. How will I be defined? How AM I defined by the aspects of my "language" I choose to use and (re)member?

NOTES

[1] A mythical creature who, through the practice of witchcraft, abandons her skin late at night, becomes a ball of fire, and travels to others' homes with the intent of sucking their blood.

[2] Each of the subsequent subtitles represents a Trinidadian expression, the definitions of which are taken from Mendes (1986).

[3] A common term used to combine residents of both islands into one representation.

⁴ High schools are usually described as either "prestige" or "government." The term prestige is used to identify schools that are historically religious schools, often separated by race or class.
⁵ A specific term referencing girls from Bishop's Anstey High School in the capital, Port-of-Spain. The expression connotes a strong-willed, determined, and often argumentative nature. Each "prestige" school has its own reference and connotations./
⁶ Eraser.
⁷ Used in this piece to refer colloquially to persons born in the United States, not generally to those born in the Americas.
⁸ A common dish in Trinidad and Tobago made with boiled and shredded salted cod and often a blend of diced onion, tomatoes, and bell peppers.
⁹ Rhythm.

REFERENCES/BIBLIOGRAPHY

Brown, B. (2010). *The gifts of imperfection: Let go of who you think you're supposed to be and embrace who you are.* Centre City, MN: Hazelden.

Browne, M. (2001). *Trini talk: Dialect poetry and stories* (2nd ed.). Trinidad: Miguel Browne.

Dillard, C. (2012). *Learning to (re)member the things we've learned to forget: Endarkened feminisms, spirituality, and the sacred nature of research and teaching.* New York, NY: Peter Lang.

Freeman, L. (2002). Does spatial assimilation work for black immigrants in the US? *Urban Studies, 39*(11), 1983–2003.

Guy, T. C. (2001). Black immigrants of the Caribbean: An invisible and forgotten community. *Adult Learning, 12/13*(4/1), 14–17.

Hogan, P. C. (2000). *Colonialism and cultural identity: Crises of tradition in the Anglophone literatures of India, Africa, and the Caribbean.* Albany, NY: State University of New York Press.

Mendes, J. (1986). *Cote ce, cote la: Trinidad and Tobago dictionary.* Trinidad: John Mendes.

Norton, B. (1997). Language, identity, and the ownership of English. *TESOL Quarterly, 31*(3), 409–429.

Wa Thiong'o, N. (1986). *Decolonizing the mind: The politics of language in African literature.* Suffolk, UK: James Currey.

Youssef, V. (2004). 'Is English we speaking': Trinbagonian in the twenty-first century. *English Today, 20*, 42–99.

Dyanis Popova
Faculty of Teaching and Learning
School of Education
Virginia Tech
Blacksburg, Virginia, USA

LISA WEVER

17. SOJOURN

ABSTRACT

Using poetry, the author reflects on her journey through years of cultural confusion. She writes about ultimately finding a sense of self based not on race or ethnicity, but on her sense of purpose and relationships with others.

LOOKING BACK

I am
Oldest daughter,
Tomboy, brown haired tangled.
Clumsy, fair skin bruised and skinned up.
Loved.
Running, chasing fireflies.
Hide and seek with flashlights.
Learning to ride fat cantankerous Cocoa, reliable Captain.
Dreading relentless chores; the barn, the house, the garden.
A bright flash,
A shooting star.
Where did it all go?

I am
Responsible, reliable.
Not the popular girl, yet not the misfit.
Loved.
High school; chorus, soccer, friends, sleepovers …then
BOYS, football games, drama.
Small town,
Small, narrow minds.
A growing sense of disquiet.
Questioning my adoption.
Who am I?
What am I really?

Finally.
Answers.

G. A. Tilley-Lubbs & S. B. Calva (Eds.), Re-Telling Our Stories, 231–242.

Not the answers I expected.

I am
Not an English/German girl,
Not really my stepfather's daughter.
I am a
Tuscarora/English girl.
Tuscarora?
A Native American tribe.

I am
The daughter of a man I never met.
Uneasy,
Confused.
What does it mean to be Tuscarora?
Does it change who I am?

Too much to think about.
No one to ask.
Only see "Indians" on TV.
Noble savages
In books.
All the lies my teachers told me.
Push it down.
Block it out.
Escape.

Flee to university.
Find a purpose.
Social worker ...go out into the world.
Help the masses.

I am
A young woman.
Full of silent sympathy,
Unintentional privilege.
Good intentions riddled with deficit notions.
On my own.
Diverse city;
Racism, social inequality.
Poverty, injustice,
Marginalization.
Am I part of this?

Denial.
I can't be part of this,

I am not really white.
I am not part of the establishment,
The system.

Plagued by questions.
Unrest,
Confusion,
Anger.
Still pushing it down,
Blocking it out.

Doubts, confusion, unrest, anger,
All roll aside.

I am
Smitten.

He is
Just black.
His Chickahominy Indian family denied.
Based on the 1924 Racial Integrity Act
You are either white or Negro.
No Indians allowed in Virginia.
European family denied as well.
The paper bag rule erasing heritage.
His grandmother's skin, as an infant, is darker than a paper bag.
Warrants "Negro" stamped on her birth certificate.
Total disregard of her white mother.
The "one drop rule"
One drop of African blood
You can claim no other.

We are
Parents
Of a precious, beautiful, brown baby girl.
Amazed by our fortune,
Amazed by the ignorance.
The thoughtless questions,
"What a beautiful baby....
Where did you get her?"

I am
Transfixed.
Breathing in the wonder.
First steps, first words.
Baby pools, sandboxes.

Sleepless nights.
Reading Margret Wise Brown's classic lullaby:
Goodnight Moon, a million times.
Tea parties, Lego villages,
Living the fairy-tale.

Too soon
My perfect job
Becomes unbearable.
So much poverty
Neglect and abuse.
Teenage boys in coffins,
Preteen moms on the street.
Hunger, despair.
Smug judges,
Unjust justice system.

I am
Exhausted.
I miss my child.
Rethink my purpose.
Back to university
Years of academia.
Insomnia
Exams
Journal articles
Student teaching.
No time for unease
Questions.
Ignoring the vague feeling of
Something missing.

New career.
Exciting, fulfilling.
Urban schools.
Warm demander
Loving my students.
Sense of purpose restored.
Time with my child,
My husband.

I am
The mom who makes 10 dozen cookies at 11pm,
Chairs the bake sale committee
Sews Halloween costumes at the last minute.

The teacher who takes her students to
Soccer games
Parent-Teacher Association events
Outings.
Wife
Mother
Teacher
Soccer coach
Potter
Gardener.

Loved.

Until
Deployment.
The military term for troop movement,
A family's term for anguish.

I am
Filled with loneliness
Terror.
Praying to a god I don't believe in.
Making deals I have no right to make
No intention of keeping.
Send him home safe,
Please, please god.
Send him home.
But my husband doesn't come home.
A shell of that man returns.
A hollow, morose shell.

Depression.
Silence.
The fabric unravels.
Changed man
Despondent man.
Disconsolate wife,
Wretched legal resolution.

I am
Failed wife.
Tenuous
Scared,
Alone.
Mom and dad to this precious child.
Hand to mouth existence.

HOVERING

I am
Lost
Floundering.

Until

Opportunity on the Mattaponi Indian reservation,
A tiny beautiful strip of land
"Given" back to its original inhabitants.
Teaching
Reading.
Learning from the elders,
Beadwork and pottery.

I am
Sandwiched between the Pamunkey
And the Mattaponi rivers.
Paddling my modern day canoe
To Wahunsenacawh's resting place.
White men called him Powhatan,
The leader of the Indian tribes.
Easy to bask in the tranquillity,
Forget the disquiet
The loneliness
The ache.

I am
Immersed in the culture.
Traveling to powwows,
Gatherings of Native Americans from many tribes.
Dancing
Sharing stories
Eating traditional food.
Mexico to Canada,
Making friends
Meeting family.

Unlearning the mistruths of the history books.
Witnessing the effects
On indigenous peoples of
The invasion
Brutality
Greed

Genocide
Boarding schools
Broken treaties
Manifest Destiny.
The white man's belief
That the entire North American continent was
Theirs for the taking.

Every despicable act imaginable
Perpetrated by people who look

Just like me.

Confusion,
Rage,
Shame.

I am
The physical incarnate of white privilege.
White privilege I don't want.
I don't deserve.
Every fibre of my being wanting to be
Tuscarora.

Don't want to be any part white.
Don't want to be part of the horror.

White Anglo-Saxon Protestant culture has me,
I don't want to have it.

Don't want to be a member of the wannabe tribe,
White people who want to be Native American
Because they think it's chic
Cool.
Oblivious to the marginalization
The horrors of the past
That bleed into the present.

Can I learn to be indigenous?

That sounds ridiculous.
Something white people would ask.

I am
Not really white.

I
Immerse myself in the ways.

Years of studying
Travel
Teaching on the reservation.
Passing on the traditions.
Local tribes:
Mattaponi and Pamunkey kids.

The disquiet is still here.
Can I unlearn 30 years of white culture?
Can't change my fair skin,
Can't erase the privilege.

Despair.
Acrimony.
Depression.
Insomnia.
Vitriolic rants to Native friends
Who don't understand my rage.

They question my anger.
"Why do you want to be Tuscarora?
Why can't you be happy being white?"

I lash out.
I am not really white.
There is a difference between me
And the appropriators,
White people who are pretendians,
Pretend Indians,
Those whose grandmothers were all "Cherokee princesses."
Native American tribal royalty.
There was no such a thing.

I am eligible for a tribal ID card
A piece of paper
Government issued
To prove my lineage.

I have the blood quantum
White man's way of counting the savages.
How much Native blood runs in my veins?
Half.
Half of my blood.
Every ounce of that blood
Fights the whiteness
Foisted on me by my mother's culture.

Can I unlearn 30 years of white culture?
Can't change my fair skin.
Can't erase the privilege.

Will I ever be accepted?
Will I ever be Tuscarora?
Should I keep trying?

Anger gradually fading to
Righteous indignation
That dies down to embers.
Embers of apathy.
Leave of absence from the reservation classes.
Not going to drum rehearsal,
Powwows.
Unanswered phone.
Isolation.
Silence.

Months pass.
My mom worries.
I don't visit,
Don't call.
Can't tell her about the struggle.
Don't want to hurt her.
Can't explain it.
Too tired to try.

Silence.

Paddles dipping in the water
Try to break the silence.
Ospreys and eagles fly over the river
Raucous fighting for lunch.
No appetite
For food
For this life.
Even the tranquil waters of the Mattaponi River
Can't pull me from this stupor.
I have to find an answer.

I am
Despondent
Until
An elder gently
Chides me for being selfish.

Selfish?
Me?
How am I selfish?
I just want to know who I am.
What I am.
I want to be part of my father's culture.
I want it to be MY culture.

Shame encroaches.
I did leave those children with no teacher.
Why would they want to learn from a white lady anyway?
No matter how hard I try
I'm not Tuscarora.

Her answer.
I did not want to acknowledge
The answer.
All comes down to
Nature vs. nurture.
Raised by a white family.
Granted white privilege.
Never facing discrimination.
Only learning customs
Ceremonies
Language.
Second hand
From a tribe that is not my own.
I won't ever truly be Tuscarora.

My father was not there to teach me,

And the cultural tie is in the matriarchal line.
In marrying my white mother he denied me
The right to call myself Tuscarora.
But even more than that,
You have to live the ways
Be immersed in the culture.
Live the discrimination,
The otherness.

I am
Quiet.
Empty.
Reflective.
Mourning the loss of my indigenous self.

The culture I never really had.
The elder's words a balm on my scars.
"It does not matter that you are white.
Who you are is about the lives you enrich,
The children that you teach,
The children that love you,
The wrongs you can eliminate."

I can respect the ways,
Teach the next generation.
Fight for indigenous rights.
Walk lightly on the earth.
Leave something important behind
Without being Tuscarora.

I raise my daughter in the ways.
She will not live with the doubt,
The confusion.
She knows who she is.
What she is.

I give my daughter a sense of self,
Of pride.
She is the fancy dancer.
Chickahominy and Tuscarora.
The best of the turtle and the wolf clans.
And somewhere in between,
I gain a sense of myself,
Who I am and
What my purpose is.

I am
Culturally, a white woman.
A white woman hell bent
On changing the system,
Making injustices visible,
Making marginalized peoples heard,
Educating our children.

SOARING, FULL CIRCLE

Moving back to the city,
My little girl going off to university.
Starting over.
Again.

He is
Brilliant.
Articulate.
Accomplished.
Single dad.
Three creative, handsome boys
And one beautiful little girl.

I become
Wife.
Mother of five
Scholar.
Teacher
Activist.

Loved.

Lisa Wever
Faculty of Teaching and Learning
School of Education
Virginia Tech
Blacksburg, Virginia, USA

MAE HEY

18. TWO BRAIDS

ABSTRACT

Boozhoo, Mae Nindizhinikaaz. The Great Lakes nindoonjii. Gaawiin mashi ningikenimaasiin n'doodem. (Hello, my name Mae. I come from the Great Lakes. I do not yet know my clan). This is a poem describing how I live at my intersection—a woman of Indigenous and European decent. It begins to explain the de-colonization of my mind so that I may re-inhabit the path I am supposed to follow.

***

I am packaged in two braids
Allowing me to be recognized
By myself and others.
It is the reflection I see in a window

Through which someone else acknowledges me.

But two braids are the product of traditions
And the expectations of Disney.
It is a decolonized stance
And a colonized over-simplification
But it is a choice I make every day.

Grandma was not a princess
Nor was grandfather a war chief.
It stings being told I speak like *Zhaaganaashi*[1]
And equally when I am called Pocahontas.
My riddled quantum longs to be *ogichidaakwe*.[2]

But probably *gijigijigaaneshiinh*[3]
Is my *we'enh*.[4]
Fragile in appearance, yet endures adversity
As a subtle reminder that winter will not last forever.
I grow where I am planted.

My two braids show allegiance
Like a flag I fly

G. A. Tilley-Lubbs & S. B. Calva (Eds.), Re-Telling Our Stories, 243–244.

That reduces the need for interrogation
Because that is uncomfortable
For everyone.

My two braids will remain.
They are timelines and companions.
They are comfort and ritual.
They are a whispered reminder of not having cancer
But I should not exploit their power as a shield.

NOTES

[1]   *Zhaganaashi*-white/English person in Anishinaabemowin.
[2]   *ogichidaakwe*-woman warrior.
[3]   *gijigijigaaneshiinh*-chickadee.
[4]   *we'enh*-one who guides you.

Mae Hey
Faculty of Teaching and Learning
School of Education
Virginia Tech
Blacksburg, Virginia, USA

GRESILDA A. TILLEY-LUBBS

19. RECONCILING TWO SELVES IN THE SAME BODY

ABSTRACT

While participating in an institute with other critical pedagogues, the author became aware of her two Selves: the US English-speaking Self and the Spanish-speaking Self. With startling clarity, she realized why people had been telling her that she exhibits totally different personalities based on the language she is speaking. More surprisingly, she realized that her epistemologies and ontologies were diametrically opposed depending on the dominant Self. Using the lens of autoethnography, she examines how power and privilege determine her actions and her words depending on whether she is thinking in English or in Spanish.

RECONCILING TWO SELVES IN THE SAME BODY

Barcelona, Spain
October 2013

Speaking Spanish
Something I often do
Both in work and friendships.

Speaking Spanish "fluently"—
Varying degrees
Depending on
Tiredness,
Comfort level
Recent contact with Spanish speakers.

Nothing I can depend on—ever.

A glass of Malbec
May loosen timidity and tongue
Unless tiredness wins…
To turn off my brain
AND loosen my tongue—
Not always a good thing.

My Mexican friend Luis and I
Following my husband Dan,

G. A. Tilley-Lubbs & S. B. Calva (Eds.), Re-Telling Our Stories, 245–258.

Our friends Shirley and Eelco
Down a narrow winding Barcelona street.
Speaking Spanish.
Exhaustion of the transatlantic flight
Nearly overcome.
Engrossed enough in our conversation
To feel comfortable
With Luis, a dear friend.
Meeting occasionally throughout the year
Staying in regular contact
On Skype for work projects.

Planning our annual critical pedagogy institute
Next year in Chihuahua.
Collaborating with the *Instituto de la Pedagogía Crítica,*
The IPEC
To integrate with colleagues, students, community.

Lagging behind the others.

Speaking in Spanish.

Passing closed shops –
Telephones, herbal medicines, produce.
Yellow-y lights shining from small restaurants
A dim glow
Warming the chilly October evening.

Shirley asks:
"Luis, where's that little restaurant
Where we ate the other night?"

Change of conversation
In topic and language.

Quickly covering blocks,
Chitchatting about restaurants,
Barcelona,
Life.

All in English.

In Spanish.

Luis turns to me,
"Hermana, you are a completely different person
Speaking Spanish.
In English

246

Your body language and facial expressions are different.
Your voice is even different.
You are two different people."

Stopping and staring at Luis.
How do I think and act differently
In Spanish?
Is it only language?
Or is it the comfort and intimacy
Of talking with dear friends like Luis,
Who calls me his *hermana,* his sister?

Speaking with strangers
Often tongue-tied—

In English and in Spanish.

Speaking with close Mexican friends
A certain freedom to be me.

Did Luis pick up on that?

Or is it more.

Reaching our destination
Sitting in a tiny restaurant
Eating Catalán food
Drinking sangría and red wine
Continuing our group conversation.

In English.

Luis' observations forgotten.
My two Selves blended.

For the moment.

Days spent with Luis and other Mexican friends:
Sandra, Rafa, Marina, and Sofía.

Daily visits to CREA,
The research institute at the University of Barcelona.
Working with the teacher education students.
Observing elementary and adult classrooms
Spending days thinking and living in Spanish
But as an outsider
Not like in Mexico.

Like a member of the Mexican group.

All observers and outsiders in a foreign country
Where we happened to share a language.

Every day in Spanish

At night in English.

Dan, Shirley, and Eelco.
Luis, Sandra, Rafa, Marina, Sofía.
Dinner.
More conversation.

In English.

In Spanish.

The computer switch in my brain
Toggling back and forth between

Spanish and

English

Just as happens with my work.
It is natural,
Normal.

Our Mexican friends from Chihuahua spoke little English.
Unlike Luis—
Mexican New Mexican,
Totally bilingual.

Evenings bilingual

Translations for English speakers,
Who understand limited Spanish.

Translations for Spanish speakers
Who understand limited English.

Switching.
Living in the in-between
Bilingual
Bicultural
Space.

Valletta, Malta
October 2013

Luis heads home to New Mexico.
The rest of us go to Malta

For the critical pedagogy annual meeting.

The afternoon of the second day.
We gather by the pool at the hotel
In small interest groups
My group works on community—
How we work in communities
How our community work informs our scholarship.

Mary speaks from her chair by the pool,
"Okay, what are we supposed to talk about?"

I attempt to establish a focus,
"Community work.
What do we do in the community?"

Antonia chimes in:
"We need to look at the inequities of capitalism.
Latinos in the US are trapped
By the inequities of capitalism."

I counter in a strident tone:
"The other group is tackling theoretical frameworks.
We are focusing on our work in the community."

We must stay on track.

Antonia insists:
"But you can't talk about the Latino community in the US
Without talking about capitalism."

My body stiffens in resistance.
We can't deviate from our agreed-upon topic.

The discussion continues for some time,
Antonia and I respond to each other.
Annoyed tones of voice
Often prevalent in academic discussions.

Someone disrupts the disruptive cycle.
"I'm going for a swim in the Mediterranean."
Gradually people stand up and drift away.

I tuck my annoyance aside
And go find Dan
To vent.

We continue meeting and discussing.
Meals and social times punctuate the days.

Saturday, the last day of the meeting.
We gather at Hotel El Castillo
A rooftop outdoor café provides
A beautiful view of the white city.

Drinking coffee
Wrapping up a week
Of emotions and thoughts and ideas.

Speaking in English

Accommodating the majority of people
All speaking some level of English –
An international group:
Canadians, Australians, English,
United States Americans, Dutch, Mexicans.

Sandra, Rafa, Marina, and Sofía now able to follow along a bit in English
With my intermittent interpretation.
Random comments float through the air,
Our thoughts already on the way to the airport.

Most folks say goodbye and leave.
Antonia now joins us
And begins speaking in Spanish.

"I hope in Mexico we spend time working in communities –
An opportunity to see the impact of capitalism on Mexican communities."
Antonia speaks of the same issues
As by the hotel pool.

I listen in Spanish

Everything makes perfect sense.
I nod in agreement.
Engrossed in her words,
Body tense with concentration,
Not with anger.

Luis' words come back to me.
Am I a different person in Spanish than in English?

Two ways of thinking and reacting.
My body stiffened before.
Now I relax into Antonia's words.
My English-speaking Self morphed into my Spanish-speaking Self.
A conversation focused on Marxism and capitalism
In the context of marginalized and vulnerable communities

Seems logical.

In Spanish I say:
"Antonia, I am so sorry.
Please forgive my rudeness the other day.
I realize my reactions
Resulted from my thinking like a gringa.
Now I am thinking in Spanish.
I think differently.
Everything you say makes perfect sense.
It made no sense to me in English."

Antonia stands up to hug me.

But after I leave her presence
I think in English,
Still unconvinced about Marxism
As integral to my community work....

Is it friendship?
Language?

If we had the same conversation
Again in English
How would I react?

Champaign-Urbana, Illinois
May 2014

I perform the narrative form of this poem
At the International Congress of Qualitative Inquiry.

First in Spanish
For the Day in Spanish and Portuguese.
I am reading the words
That originally constructed an identity
With Mexicans.

Reading and performing
I stop.
"I can't continue."
I realize I am co-opting identity.
I have so much power and privilege.
I can't claim identity with those
Who are so oppressed in my country.

The following day
In English

But with an explanation of what happened in Spanish.

More questions than answers.

Guanajuato, Mexico
June 2014

Another conference.

In Spanish.

Presenting a paper on critical autoethnography (Tilley-Lubbs, 2014).
Introducing myself.
Spanish literature major.
Spanish teacher at all levels.
Researcher in the Spanish-speaking community.

I finish.
César, a long-standing Mexican friend and colleague, says:
"You were a Spanish literature major.
Why don't you cite any of those authors in your work?
Stumbling.
"Critical autoethnography focuses on
Autoethnography
And critical pedagogy.
It's natural that I refer to
Carolyn Ellis, Art Bochner, Laurel Richardson.
Paulo Freire, Joe Kincheloe, Shirley Steinberg."

"Who were your favourite authors in Spanish literature?"

I dredge up memories from many years ago
At the University of Illinois.

Unamuno, Azorín,
The Generation of '98.
Fascinated by their dissection of the apathy
Experienced by Spaniards
Following the Spanish American War
And the loss of an empire.

García Lorca, Muñoz
Censored by the Franco government.
Voices silenced.
Exile.

Ana María Matute
Finding the beauty in life following
A devastating Civil War.

Neruda, Mistral
Poetry flooding my soul with more beauty
As the words form images of longing
In my mind.
In my intellect.

Jorge Luis Borges
Drawing me into the magical web
Of labyrinths and
Words that tumble over each other and
Create images that slip and slide into
The depths of my soul
As I sink into the mystical mysteries of Judaism.

César's eyes bore into mine.
"Can't you see how those are the authors
Who shaped your thinking?
Can't you see how they fit into your current work?
Everything you just said has its roots in that literature.
You need to cite those authors.
Let the researchers in the US know what we have to offer."

Stunned.
Speechless.

The kaleidoscope shifts.
The new picture answers so many questions.
The colours blend and morph.
The abstract becomes more defined
But still shaky.

I remember Frida Kahlo's painting,
Las dos Fridas
Capturing her conflict
With her European/Indigenous identity.

My two Selves are different.
Dealing with ethnicity in a sense,
But differently.

I am Appalachian
Rooted in the Appalachian Mountains
Heritage primarily English, Scottish, Irish, and Native American.
My great grandfather Cherokee.
The same genealogy shows
A far distant relative in the Spanish Armada

Crashing on the banks of Ireland in 1588
Unable to return home.
He stays in Ireland,
Anglicizes his name.
Téllez becomes Tilley.
The rest of the story is what would be expected.

Stories from many years ago.
I am neither Spanish nor Native American.
I grew up in the United States,
My home for all my life.
My skin white
English my first language.

Both the source of my power and privilege.
Different from those who grew up Native American
Or "Hispanic" in the United States.
My West Virginia heritage as a coal miner's daughter
My continual struggle with issues of self-esteem—
West Virginians regarded as hillbillies,
Uneducated country people. (Tilley-Lubbs, 2011)

But I never experienced
Discrimination
Loss of human rights
Experienced by many Native Americans and Hispanics
On a daily basis.

I am *gringa, gringa pura.*
Pure US citizen.

Despite the title of *mi hija cubana*
Bestowed on me by my dear Cuban friend Conchita
Who,
Declaring me to be more Cuban than her daughters,
Called me her Cuban daughter,
To whom I referred as *mi mamá cubana*

So how do I explain it?
The assumption/presumption
Of another identity when speaking Spanish?

How do I explain why I never had to learn Spanish?
Two years of high school French—
No more at my rural Illinois high school

Switching to Spanish—

But I already knew it.
Completed three years in two,
Then majored in Spanish at the University of Illinois.
A bachelor's degree,
A master's degree in Spanish literature.
A certificate of studies in Spanish
From the Universidad de Salamanca.

All second nature
Flowing out of my mouth as easily as English.
Never struggling with verb forms,
Not even the subjunctive.
Reading obsessively in Spanish,
Writing papers with nearly the same ease
As in English.

Scholars writing in their learned language
Have less access to language's emotional affect. (Pavelenko, 2005)

Not the case with me.

Or is it?

I believed English was my practical language.
Spanish my language for
Philosophy,
Poetry,
Deep thinking,
Meaningful discourse.

Nonetheless....

December 2014/January 2015

An argument with Silvia, another long-time friend and colleague.
Heated words.
Anger in her email.
My reply

In English

Whereas we normally correspond

In Spanish.

As I write, I reflect in an email to Silvia:

Why did I choose to write in English?
Was it because

I couldn't say what I thought in Spanish
Because I wasn't saying that everything was wonderful?
Probably what I would have done in Spanish.

I also feared being honest
And sounding harsh and hurtful.
Painfully aware
I am not speaking my native language.

Is Spanish my language for being a
"Good, nice person?"

Do I love Spanish as a way to be
Exotic and romantic?

Why does talking about some topics in English feel clunky?

Why does Spanish seem natural
For expressing the radical love (Freire, 1970)
Of critical pedagogy in my work?

Why does Spanish help me to move critical pedagogy
Beyond a theoretical perspective
To a lifestyle,
A way of thinking about the world?

In English, I am committed to critical pedagogy
As a theory,
But I live a very US American lifestyle....

Chihuahua, Mexico
October 2014

Another critical pedagogy meeting.
I raise these questions
Reading an excerpt from the original essay.

Rodney later approaches me.
"Why does it matter?
You are a bridge—
A bridge between
English-speaking and
Spanish-speaking worlds.
Embrace your role."

Dan asks the hard question:
"So what?
What does this all mean?"

256

I answer truthfully that I don't know.
I'm not listening to voices in my head,
Just expressing gut-level,
Fundamental
Down-in-my-soul feelings of identity
To resolve.
Or not.

Not that
"I'm finally accepted by someone without reservation."
Not "It's cool to be fluent in Spanish."
Not other similar self-affirmations.

I asked before
[A]m I co-opting identity
Or am I performing the reality of my life (Tilley-Lubbs, 2012)?
Working in the community
Performing outsider/insider (2012)
Interpreting
Socializing.

Being the grandmother of a Mexican American grandson
Performing insider/outsider.

The surrogate mother/grandmother of Mexican friends
Performing outsider/insider. (Tilley-Lubbs, 2012)

Friendship based on intellectual and heart connections.
Moving past exotic tourism of the other.

Coming to see community members
As individuals
Not all friends…
Some acquaintances.
Some disillusionment.

The title of this poem
Suggests that I wish to
Reconcile my two Selves within the same body,
But do I?
Is that possible?
Is it desirable?

Are there even two Selves?

Or have I simply blurred the borders
  Geographic,

Cultural,
Linguistic? (Tilley-Lubbs, 2012)

Creating a porous space
Undefinable
Indescribable.

Moving in the in-between.
Visible/invisible positionality.

I write as inquiry (Richardson, 2000),
But the answers still elude me.

I will continue seeking.
Writing to connect the personal
With the sociocultural (Ellis, 2004).
Uniting the Mystory (Pelias, 2013; Ulmer, 1989) with
The worlds that shaped me.

REFERENCES/BIBLIOGRAPHY

Ellis, C. (2004). *The ethnographic I: A methodological novel about autoethnography.* Walnut Creek, CA: AltaMira.

Freire, P. (1970). *Pedagogy of the oppressed* (M. Bergman Ramos, Trans.). New York, NY: Continuum Publishing.

Pavelenko, A. (2005). *Emotions and multilingualism.* New York, NY: Cambridge University.

Pelias, R. (2013). Writing autoethnography: The personal, poetic, and performative as compositional strategies. In S. H. Jones, T. E. Adams, & C. Ellis (Eds.), *Handbook of autoethnography* (pp. 384–405). Walnut Creek, CA: Left Coast.

Richardson, L. (2000). Writing: A method of inquiry. In N. K. Denzin & Y. S. Lincoln (Eds.), *Handbook of qualitative research* (2nd ed., pp. 923–949). Thousand Oaks, CA: Sage.

Tilley-Lubbs, G. A. (2011). The coal miner's daughter gets a Ph.D. *Qualitative Inquiry, 17*(9). doi:10.1177/1077800411420669

Tilley-Lubbs, G. A. (2013). The baptism/El bautizo. *Qualitative Research in Education, 2*(1), 27–37. doi:10:4471/qre.2013.14

Tilley-Lubbs, G. A. (2014). La autoetnografía crítica y el Self vulnerable como investigadora. *REMIE: Multidisciplinary Journal of Educational Research, 4*(3), 268–285.

Ulmer, G. (1989). *Teletheory: Grammatology in the age of video.* New York, NY: Routledge.

Gresilda A. Tilley-Lubbs
Faculty of Teaching and Learning
School of Education
Virginia Tech
Blacksburg, Virginia, USA

CPSIA information can be obtained
at www.ICGtesting.com
Printed in the USA
FFOW03n1437080517
35440FF

9 789463 005654